REINVENTING EVIDENCE IN
SOCIAL INQUIRY

REINVENTING EVIDENCE IN SOCIAL INQUIRY
Copyright © Richard Biernacki, 2012.

All rights reserved.

First published in 2012 by
PALGRAVE MACMILLAN®
in the United States—a division of St. Martin's Press LLC,
175 Fifth Avenue, New York, NY 10010.

Where this book is distributed in the UK, Europe and the rest of the world,
this is by Palgrave Macmillan, a division of Macmillan Publishers Limited,
registered in England, company number 785998, of Houndmills,
Basingstoke, Hampshire RG21 6XS.

Palgrave Macmillan is the global academic imprint of the above companies
and has companies and representatives throughout the world.

Palgrave® and Macmillan® are registered trademarks in the United States,
the United Kingdom, Europe and other countries.

ISBN: 978–1–137–00727–8 (paperback)
ISBN: 978–1–137–00726–1 (hardcover)

Library of Congress Cataloging-in-Publication Data

Biernacki, Richard, 1956–
    Reinventing evidence in social inquiry : decoding facts and variables / Richard
Biernacki.
        p. cm.—(Cultural sociology)
    ISBN 978–1–137–00727–8—
    ISBN 978–1–137–00726–1
    1. Social sciences—Methodology. 2. Content analysis (Communication)
3. Discourse analysis. I. Title.

H61.B4746 2012
300.72—dc23   2011051408

A catalogue record of the book is available from the British Library.

Design by Newgen Imaging Systems (P) Ltd., Chennai, India.

First edition: July 2012

10 9 8 7 6 5 4 3 2 1

Printed in the United States of America.

CONTENTS

FIGURES

Series Preface

CULTURAL SOCIOLOGY IS ALL ABOUT THE STUDY OF MEANING. Yet, the methodology for doing that empirically remains a point of contention. Philosophical arguments pitting "interpretation" against "science" go back centuries, doubting that the two can mix any more readily than oil and water. In recent years, however, many have claimed that new research methods have emerged that provide a breakthrough. With the formal coding of large numbers of texts, meanings can be tamed. When applied to qualitative data, such quantitative methods can allow generalizations to be made that avoid the relativism and subjectivism of earlier interpretive sociologies.

In challenging this new methodological school, Richard Biernacki does something that nobody has done before. In addition to engaging in theoretical argumentation, he goes back to examine the original data to which flagship scholars applied their coding techniques. After critically reconstructing this data, Biernacki suggests that the published research claims are troubling: all that is solid melts into air. What appeared to be a rigorous new approach generating robust, intersubjectively valid, law-like findings is shown to involve the same interpretative choices, selectivity, and hermeneutic caprice as conventional idiographic and humanistic interpretation. There is no magic bullet. Rather than viewing formal coding as the new gold standard, Biernacki suggests, we should see it more as the ritual evocation of habitually accepted scientific norms. Only by demystifying this alchemical belief system can we open the way to a more honest and productive study of social meanings.

Intellectually ambitious, theoretically rigorous, and certain to be controversial, *Reinventing Evidence in Social Inquiry* demonstrates that discussions of method are too important to be left to textbooks.

CHAPTER 1

INSIDE THE RITUALS OF SOCIAL SCIENCE

> Concern for the foundations of social science research should require continual examination and re-examination of its first principles.
> —Aaron Cicourel, *Method and Measurement in Sociology*

LET ME START WITH AN IMPROBABLE MESSAGE ABOUT "CODING" as a technique of observation and record-making that social scientists have adopted to convert documentary sources into tractable "data."[1] The gist from my revisiting of primary documents behind the scenes is that when the most alert researchers in the business of cultural analysis reach findings by "coding" nuanced texts, their blurring of science with humanist interpretation proves to be unfeasible. Above all, in attempting to convert cultural meanings into "data" by sampling and coding, they astonishingly efface the boundary between reporting and creating facts.[2]

THE STAKES OF THIS BOOK

No matter how much researchers try to occlude coding as a pedestrian given, it concentrates the potential absurdities of what Mary Poovey has enigmatically termed "the modern fact."[3] Coding, a word that may introduce an aura of scientism, is just the sorting of texts, or of subunits such as paragraphs, according to a classificatory framework. The categories used to label texts can be chosen as you please: by references to topics (race versus class, the divine versus the secular), by the genre to which texts belong (gothic versus epic or sermons versus editorials), or by illustrated patterns of reasoning (say, positivist versus utilitarian). The multiplex, potentially indeterminate passages cumulate "as if" they were discrete units with labels, "facts." How coders apperceive verbal implication while engaging in systematic observation is not obviously different from the challenge that witnesses in a lab face. Fact-makers of all kinds draw on ticklish construal as much as on raw perception. Researchers at the lab bench as well as at the library table are governed by rules of thumb for reading. They take each fact (each datum or coding output) as a solid particular. Yet they presume no datum on its own is typical of any general pattern in nature or in society. This modern dilemma of induction contrasts with the traditions of Aristotelians, for example.[4] In that other long-reigning philosophy, a chosen particular is valued for representing directly, without need of additive theory, shared, universal commonplaces. For the coding results established as "facts," researchers have to imagine, not discern, what kind of invisible message or generality these ciphers *stand for* once they are organized, be it via intricate charts (as in figure 1.1) or via synthesizing descriptions. Ironically, researchers who visualize a pattern in the "facts" often assert it symbolizes an incorrigible theory for which no data were required anyway.

From a sociologist such as Michèle Lamont who intriguingly codes transcripts to chart *How Professors Think* and then verbally unravels her tables; from a critic such as David Herman who encrypts and then decrypts the necessary components of narrative sense; to a literary historian such Christopher Grasso who classifies the political genres through which eighteenth-century pundits reasoned—many are those who conduct themselves around a self-imposed circle. They would *turn meaningful texts into unit facts for the sake of converting these units back into meanings.*[5] What are the epistemological functions of the curious process of decontextualizing for the sake of recontextualizing?[6] Cumulating the coding outputs purchases generality only if we know the codes rest on justifiable equivalencies of meaning, which is to return us to the original verbal settings that may vary incommensurably. At stake in this book is a misleading way of knowledge-making that migrated from the scientific apparatuses of Francis Bacon into sociocultural inquiry today. Protocols of

Li Hsiu-tang: Graph of Coded Story

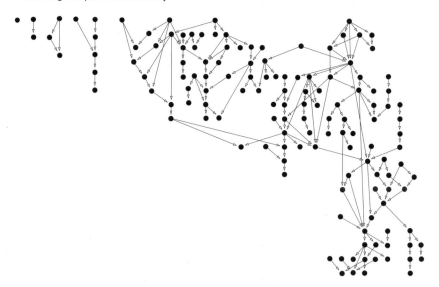

Figure 1.1   Narrative networks. "By treating events as nodes and relations between events as arcs, we transform narrative sequences of elements into networks."

Source: Peter Bearman, Robert Faris, and James Moody, "Blocking the Future: New Solutions for Old Problems in Historical Social Science," *Social Science History*, Vol. 23, 1999, pp. 511–12.

natural science authorize coders to isolate facts from their individually meaningful contexts and then to throw these bits into an independent diagram that challenges our imagination.

Very often, you may see, leading analysts of culture who qualitatively code the "meaning" of texts fail to recognize a distinction between the empirical and the mythical much more than do, say, Evans-Pritchard's classic Azande virtuosos in witchcraft and augury. The analogy is discomforting but complete. My thesis is that coding procedures in contemporary sociology, the beachhead for coding texts that is spreading into history and literature, follow the rites by which religious believers relabel portions of the universe in a sacred arena for deep play.[7] As in fundamentalist religious regimes, rejecting the enchantment of coding "facts" is nothing less than blasphemy.

The ultimate point of this book is to stand social "science" on its head as less rigorous than humanist approaches. The social "scientists" of culture, those claiming a kind of epistemological advantage via their coding apparatuses, are instead intuitive cultists without openly sharable procedure. Opposite much orthodoxy, humanist craft workers who footnote and who convey symptomatically the wondrous in their readings are truer to the ideals of so-called hard science conventionally understood.[8] As I endeavor to show, the nonsystematizing humanists still appreciate the obstacles to induction, the gift of an acute trial, the insurance of shared documentation, and the transformative power of anomalies.[9] My brief is *not* the cliché that humanist

" Just extrapolate from the empirical patterns of particulars"

Figure 1.2   Data interpretation as a Rorschach test. Cartoon by Nina Baker.

interpretation aims at insight different in kind. More subversively, I insist such interpretation better fulfills the consecrated standards to which social "scientists" ostensibly subscribe.[10] More than you might dream from Poovey's ordinary dilemmas of the "modern fact," it is mystifyingly opaque how coding facts are generated out of texts or how we generalize from such facts (figure 1.2).

THE GENESIS OF CODING

Where did experts first resort to the apparatus of coding when sacred texts long seemed to house allusive words, not itemizable "facts"? One of the original conjunctures, eighteenth-century Sweden, reveals much. The most widely distributed book in this locale, with over a million copies circulating, was the Lutheran Hymnal.[11] At the same moment, Swedish clerics condemned a popular supplement of 90 lyrics, *The Songs of Zion*, for transmitting theologically deviant messages. To be sure, this anonymous collection in 1743 had satisfied Sweden's royal censor, who read its passages conventionally. To prove that the supplement misconstrued the sufferings of the bleeding Christ for the forgiveness of the common person's sins, however, the learned Swedish official Kumblaeus counted its references to the redemption of humankind versus other themes related to the Trinity. He showed that the mentions of Christ as Savior in the supplemental "pop" hymnal were relatively "higher" in frequency than those in the Official Hymnal. The official version accented pious conduct without forgiveness. Dissenting literary scholars contested the reliability and validity of Kumblaeus's categorizing. They introduced context, not frequency, as the key to the *The Songs of Zion*'s meanings.[12] Something akin to the *Methodenstreit*, the recurring argument between positivists and contextualists in the human sciences, began sooner than most imagine!

The Swedish Lutheran Church used its text coding to build a case that choristers who sang the pop verses committed heresy even if the vocabulary on the page appeared innocuous.[13] The controversy put on view the circumstances necessary for coding and decrypting to be mobilized as a warrant: (a) no sacred institution could claim authority about what the texts intended *by mere reading*; (b) as a stand-in for sacred authority, interpreted meanings had to be constituted as new "facts" and their trends invented by induction; (c) the underlying system of meanings conveyed by the coding outputs was imagined to fill up a public domain; (d) the coding aimed to map and then refill this container of aggregated messages in the public sphere, treating the texts as packing material; (e) the coding was part of a panoptic ambition to survey messages and to govern them.[14] Nowadays coders in social "science" rarely claim pure objectivity, yet they posit a shared cultural landscape to be mapped from an epistemologically elevated point of view like that of an administrator.[15]

HOW MY QUESTIONING ORIGINATED

I stumbled onto the issues of coding through the self-questioning triggered by my own coding two decades ago. To supplement a cross-national comparison of factory practices, I plunged into classifying 916 worker complaints published in British union newspapers and 845 complaints in German ones near the close of the nineteenth century.[16] How similar were the foci of grievances among workers in well-matched factories? I came to feel that aggregating rhetorically complex complaints under a heading as "the same" ignored such dense qualifications that I was legislating meanings more than registering them.[17]

More recently, to reassess Max Weber's long-debated Protestant Ethic thesis, I attempted to estimate frequencies of themes of anxiety and interpersonal conflict in an assembly of diaries from Reformation Britain.[18] But a "diary" is not a natural kind, so my results varied appreciably by whether I included spiritual account books, prayer meditations, business diaries, or the other kinds of rich but exceptional journal writings that I unearthed from archives. From ministers to shopkeepers, diarists in this period composed without standardized "genres." Therefore one has to counterfactually estimate which of their genres (a few of which ruptured across entries in one and the same document) reasonably could have been expected to mention a theme before one can "count" with any significance how many actually *did* mention the theme.[19] The outputted "factual"-looking meaning depended on a difficult-to-justify counterfactual about who, given the purpose and format of the writing, likely could have and then did or did not mention a theme. It depended on postulating which causal systems beneath texts were analogous. By contrast, for comparing characteristics of, say, rabbits, you can define intelligibly comparable populations, what rabbits "are," without understanding much about how each came into being or how they typically function. With a text, you do not know what it "is" or to what significant group it belongs until *afterward*—when you understand most you can about its peculiar functioning in a larger cultural field.

The problem that derailed me, the nonexistence of natural kinds ready for meaningful contrasts, was only an acute version of the circle that coders in social "science" encounter, even when they confine themselves to superficially more unified modern genres such as, say, "film reviews in newspapers." Despite publication in the same journal, reviews and authors start out from radically varying critical purposes, therefore incomparable ("causal") processes of composition-formation over time. It is more illuminating as *Wissenschaft*, methodical inquiry, to highlight and retest personal case judgments about what is comparable than to keep these choices behind the scenes as arbitrary unknowns. The issue in dealing with texts, as with cultural institutions, is that a researcher cannot pretend two artifacts *are* structurally generic and susceptible to the same classificatory grid just because they look functionally similar from our way of life or happen to be found in analytically similar "locations."[20] It is more transparent, therefore more faithful to inquiry, to assume radical difference in a population than to rush toward aggregating modern "facts" out of corpuses whose members are artificially assumed to have homologous structures.

My deepening skepticism about coding reached river bottom when I attempted to replicate results from a family of sociological classics. These gems relied more centrally than I ever had on qualitatively isolating the key messages in texts. Returning to coded sources themselves disclosed an array of missteps that was so breathtaking it upended most of what I had assumed governs scholars' coding. It seemed I landed upon circularly self-fulfilling procedures for generating "findings," difficult to comprehend changes in raw numbers across early versus late write-ups, misattributions, and untraceable sample sources. In this state of play, it was time to suspend the established framing by posing the deceptively simple question of Erving Goffman: "What is it that's going on here?"[21]

SELECTIVE BLENDING OF RULES OF EVIDENCE

Part of the answer lies in the continuing aftershocks of what Clifford Geertz famously termed an intensified blurring of genres as humanistic and social scientific inquiry make closer contact.[22] It is perhaps distinctive to reductive cultural sociologists reliant on coding that they have actively promoted a kind of muddling on which Geertz early on had laid his finger. Immediately after Geertz diagnosed "Blurred Genres" in 1983, sociologists modified his sense for their own purpose. Already by 1987 Wendy Griswold featured Geertz on this blurring to propose that "the sociology of culture can both subject its cultural interpretations to the definitional precision and validation criteria typical of the social sciences and be as sensitive to the multivocal complexity of cultural data as art history or theology."[23]

Of course these grand ambitions were concentrated in the craft of "coding" texts that Griswold as a sociologist of literature favored. By approximately "measuring" the meanings of populations of texts, coding tries to appropriate the best from two universes: the contextual appreciation of the humanities and the sampling and variable analysis of "hard" sciences. In Griswold's rendering, sociologists pore over a written corpus (divided into documents or subelements) with criteria for registering themes or other missives. Once they record the relative presence of textual features, the observations can in principle be nose-counted. Further, the "codes" assigned by this disciplined reading can be correlated with each other or with variables from the sociohistorical environment. Interpretation seems fused this way with "definitional precision."

In describing this intermingling of outlooks inside coding, it seems best to avoid the talismanic phrase "content analysis," a catchword that some social scientists would constrict and others widen. As if to combine narrowing and widening, Bernard Berleson argued that quantification is "the most distinctive feature of content analysis." Yet Berleson insisted that assessments of coding frequencies that are expressed via adjectives such as "more" or "often" are, in his words, "just as 'quantitative'" as percentages.[24] Others would like to limit the expression "content analysis" to word counts that can in principle be computer-automated. But in sociology at large, the coders Gilbert Shapiro and John Markoff found, the answer to "What is content analysis?" is that it "has often been used without any restrictions with regard to method, including even the ordinary reading of text provided it is done by a properly licensed social scientist."[25] I did not speak that loosely when I once suggested content analysis was systematic reading for which a researcher could render accounts.[26]

The plain term "coding" is more apt because it indicates only that reasonable care was taken to categorize text methodically and that the data creation process is traceable and retrospectively explicable, if not mechanically justifiable or reproducible.[27] "There is a significant consensus that whoever refers to their work as 'coding' rather than as mere reading is making a claim to participate in a scientific enterprise as distinguished, for example, from a literary or journalistic enterprise," sociologists Gilbert Shapiro and John Markoff wrote in 1982. "There must be some symbols—numbers, words, letters, computer codes—representing categories of analytic interest that are invariably considered, to be assigned or not after due deliberation, from all passages of text selected for study."[28] Coding also creates a log equivalent in scholarly importance to the anthropologists' or environmental biologists' field notes.[29] As anthropologists have come to view fieldwork less as scientistic observation and more as close reading of "culture" by a philologist, they have come to expect that researchers will archive field notes for public access.[30] As they see it, the *greater* the import of "interpretation," the greater the need for archiving documentation.[31]

In some quarters of sociology now, the researchers' performative "doing" in coding exceeds mere constative "saying" to crown all data happenings as warranted. "[T]here can be no such thing as intercoder reliability," Harvey Molotch and Marilyn Lester wrote in a premier sociology journal about their coding results, "because each individual receives a unique observational world."[32] In this view, as in that of the ancient Sophists, so long as the coding is about something in your head, however inconsistently applied, it cannot be botched. It is merely perspectival.[33]

Coding shares little with what Geertz had foreseen as promising about the blurring of genres.[34] Unlike Griswold, Geertz famously tried to keep the orders of textual interpretation versus explanatory (perhaps causal) social "science" in separate universes. Appreciating how people go about "constructing a representation, expressing an attitude, or forming an intention" could not be reconciled with "isolating a cause, determining a variable, measuring a force, or defining a function."[35] The merging that Geertz projected forward was to consist in social scientists turning away from the technology of fact gathering toward multiple *humanist* idioms of text analysis. The blurring of metaphors for limning human conduct *inside* interpretive inquiry was all Geertz had entertained. As the more rigorous, self-aware masters of how fields of meaning emerge, humanists were equipped to arbitrate models for scholarship.[36] The present volume tries to validate Geertz's preference.

Geertz admonished everyone about the experimental laxity that genre blurring was likely to produce, a presentiment soon confirmed in sociology's cultural turn. "All this fiddling around with the proprieties of composition, inquiry, and explanation represents, of course, a radical alteration in the sociological imagination, propelling it in directions both difficult and unfamiliar," Geertz wrote prospectively. "And like all changes in fashion of the mind, it is about as likely to lead to obscurity and illusion as it is to precision and truth."[37]

I suggest that for us to grasp how this unlucky fusing has moved along, it is best to rethink radically in what sense sociologists who code texts for facts about meanings are up to anything cognitively serious. In what sense is coding intended to be verisimilar? As we will see, sociologists' peculiar blurring of genres inspires them to plunge unintentionally into shenanigans as well as sacraments. Everyone knows that both humor and profound insight arise when speakers cross two unrelated standpoints that we ordinarily segregate by "the proper rules" of conversation.[38] Revisiting the intersection of the scientistic and interpretive worldviews retrieves just this kind of dual experience.

CODING AND DISSOCIATION

We scarcely require Erving Goffman's stories about omnipresent epistemological bluffing in social intercourse to recall how a magician best implicates beholders more deeply in an off-kilter frame. The magician focuses the audience's attention upon overt-yet-minor issues—"nothing up my sleeves!"—while the machinery that produces the observed "facts" remains out of sight. Having the witnesses attend to tangential issues reinforces the assumption that all can be rectified inside the magician's larger framing of what is going on.[39] So it is with talk of validity and reliability within text coding.[40] If we debate strategies for adjusting a coding procedure this way or that, we miss the overall gist of the operation and entrench ourselves more deeply in its suppositions.

My thesis is that social science presents coding as if it had empirical substance, whereas apart from self-confirming ritual its findings lack any reality. Ritual may not comprise the *only* frame by which to answer Goffman's question, "What is it that's going on here?" Who can guess: by the close of this book, you may insert my words into the genre of ritual as well, or perhaps into the genre of the protective containment of a larger academic joke.[41] As Max Weber would have insisted, only at the end can you can decide whether a researcher offers a fruitful model or nothing more than "a conceptual game."[42]

Alternatively, I will have succeeded if it dawns on some that reading documents is fraught with too many choices to produce "facts." I remain highly suspicious of my tentative readings as well. "Whatever it is that generates sureness," Goffman intimated darkly, "is precisely what will be employed by those who want to mislead us."[43] Goffman left it to us to discern how the riddle of cognitive framing applies to sociological practice and to one's framing of one's own results. Geertz expressed a similar kind of caution more cheerfully: "Keeping the reasoning wary, thus useful, thus true, is, as we say, the name of the game."[44] The only intellectual building material is self-vigilance, not the reified ingredients "theory" or "method."

As if this were not already a critique in excess, the present volume goes on to suggest that the only way to keep the reasoning wary is to segregate quantitatively inspired "scientific" procedure from interpretations of texts and cultures. Case study cannot prove a general divorce is required, but such is the only reasoning available. The incompatibilities that I think mandate this divorce are evident: (a) quantitative or abstractive generalizing starts by defining a clear target population about which to reason or generalize; (b) the relevant variables are self-contained once the research design is formulated; (c) correlations are between abstract factors in an open mathematical space bracketed for the sake of the procedure from unpredicted attributions of meaning; (d) there is a standard causal environment partially separable from the outside, unmeasured environment that makes cases comparable and that undergirds interpretable results; (e) finally, elements of the examined universe, including therefore separable text elements, each comprise events or features with potentially independent and potentially universal causes. Each of these features of inquiry is invalid and *reversed* for more purely humanist text interpretation: (a) there is no set of meaningful mechanisms known in advance to comprise the relevant target population or object of study; (b) the appropriate verbal contexts for processing and interpreting the texts is illimitable and potentially extrinsic to the sample; (c) only textual interconnections, not mathematical correlations in abstract space, bear relevant meanings and operate as structuring forces; (d) there is no standard causal environment producing the variables of texts, for the isolable features of the texts are interworked in their own universe of meaning and are not analytically independent "events" with causes; (e) the occurrence of covariation in text elements follows semantic interworking and the unique interpretive purpose of the author and the elements are not separable or probabilistically related to each other per models of statistics; in sum the texts are not information, but linguistic formulas at a remove from meanings that emerge only from personal construal.

To be sure, some quantitative "scientists" of culture now agree that interpretation is almost prior to measurement: "mathematical models have come to an era of decreasing returns to effort," sociologist Harrison White concluded in what amounted to a retrospective of his career. "Another way to say the same thing is that interpretive approaches are central to achieving the next level of adequacy in social data."[45] But what do quantitatively based social "scientists" mean by "interpretive approaches" and how do they fuse them with data mongering? I hope to show in the conclusion that a patois will not work. If you reconstruct how sociologists mix quantitative and text-interpretive methods, combining what is intrinsically uncombinable, you discover leg-pulling of several kinds: from the quantitative perspective, massaging of the raw data to identify more clearly the meanings one "knows" are important or, again, standardized causal interpretations of unique semiotic processes; to zigzagging between quantitative and interpretive logic to generate whatever meanings the investigator supposes should be there.[46]

In his lively *Dictionary of Accepted Ideas*, Flaubert's entry for "compromise" reads: "Always recommend it, even when the alternatives are irreconcilable."[47] It is hoped that this book will be "divisive" in the positive sense of splitting two distinguished universes of intellectual practice apart, that of quantitatively inspired sampling and variable analysis analogous to some "hard" sciences versus philological close reading and synthesis in the spirit of the humanities.

THE MODEL OF RITUAL PROCESS

Social scientists who code texts do not just gather "facts" as particulars, as in the scientific frame, but they proceed to import these "facts" into the humanistic frame as real appearances of a shared cultural universe. By this unusual move from data to ultimate meanings, their performances take on the gestures of ritual for contemporary society in its full anthropological depth. Let me discuss the guts of the ritual frame, why it may reveal the mechanics of demonstration in whole regions of sociology, and what we gain from intensive case study of the narratives that compose esteemed research publications. Then I will account for my choice of three exemplars of acclaimed research for attempted replication. In effect I recreate their experimental doings by gathering and checking their text samples (best anyone can) against the published results. Seeing for yourself how a finding derives from the raw material is supposed to be the commendable test of hardy inquiry. Among archive-based historians and antediluvian philologists, a revisiting of the documents in colleagues' footnotes is recommended, so each and all understand concretely how techniques of reading transformed evidence from the ground up.[48] This is similar to reviewing a mathematical deduction or repeating a laboratory discovery to witness an adduced phenomenon. Paradoxically, the ancient disciplines of attentive reading and those of mathematical reasoning or lab recording are in this respect close affiliates to each other in emphasizing the transparency of data, the traceability of results, and the importance of vicarious-if-imperfect "replication."[49] In many regions of natural science, experimental results are irreproducible until the original investigators are consulted on how to proceed, resulting in a measure of open, back and forth "How did you do it?" questioning.[50] The American Historical Association's "Statement on Standards of Professional Conduct" likewise has mandated since 1987 that investigators "make available to others their sources, evidence, and data, including the documentation they develop through interviews."[51] And in sociology?

In sociology the blurred genre of reductive text coding enables an anomalous professional zone to emerge for which norms are up for grabs. Almost no one in social "science" undertakes replications of published coding anyway.[52] What is genuinely informative about producing text "data" by coding, the philosophically reflective practitioner Roberto Franzosi has suggested, are not the classified objects but what they disclose about the mental universe of those doing the classifying— and, I believe, the ways of knowing they prescribe for the ritual audience.[53] To preview what ritual performance accomplishes, the symbolism of carrying out the coding intervenes to decide what the codes symbolize.

Looking at social scientific research as an incarnation of ritual is not a belittling simile. It is a potent explanatory key. Durkheim has already paralleled sciences and rituals for us as motions of collective representation, without thinking any the less of either variant of symbolic world-making.[54] Ritual is not a default for labeling what is allegedly a misfire or "non-science." Even less is ritual another name for politico-historical discourse considered ideological.[55] Instead, ritual is a distinct mode of communication and performance that reconfirms timeless models by which people can regenerate their social relations or professional roles.[56] The ungoverned space opened up by the burring of genres lets sociologists inscenate deep social meanings with simple, repetitive models—known in sociology as "theory." The platform of sociology also offers scientific performers privileged resources for having their intentions nostalgically accepted as authentic (the "methodological canons" of coding method).[57] And the reliance on sampling diagrams and visual displays of text structures supplies investigators with a segmented ritual space to explore novel solutions to moral doubts or dilemmas ("implications of research"). Inspired by Thomas Kuhn and by others in his wake, most philosophers have rejected the ambitions of older intellectual programs for establishing across-the-board demarcation criteria that would ratify whether a knowledge-seeking practice follows scientific rationality.[58] We grant scientific logic too much if we suppose that "in its absence a disorderly mess would prevail."[59] I hope to suggest that in practice an alternative for generating shared "truth" has been ritual logic, an indispensable yet questionable part of human world-making.

We know full well that the guild members of the most excellent natural sciences break with the empty formalities of logic in how they train each other to assess the credibility of claims. For example, to enhance the relative credibility of a favored proposition, it is not uncommon for natural scientists to pragmatically rehypothesize their pet theorem as one of only two possible alternatives and then discredit the competitor. Or, in an equally questionable move, successful scientists assess one proposition as true if it seems like a real-world requisite for a consequent *and* that consequent has been deemed credible through extensive research.[60] Enduring research is often enough logically invalid while it elicits belief or trust by what Kuhn portrayed as a kind of "wow" factor in concrete demonstrations or predictions.[61] Therefore, do not read this book as a collection of indictments. My objects are unavoidable *patterns* of contradiction in the ever-expanding regions of "blurred" social science.[62]

The Ritual Circuit in Full

Ritual productions put their participants into a sequestered arena, whether the yard of the Balinese cockfight, the demarcated seminar room, or the armchair in which the cultural analyst, member of an imagined professional community, experiences a narration of discovery between two covers of a book.[63] This spatial and temporal bracketing from everyday life creates expectancy for witnessing new truths. It enables symbolic play to take off. You can rip everyday implements or emblems out of their original contexts and find new ways for them to work as "symbols" in the cleansed space of the performance. Yesterday's wine turns to Christ's blood at the Last Supper or Halloween cloaks into Shakespearean robes.[64] The coding of texts works much the same way, because the operation assumes one can convert regenerating meanings into an isolated token, a datum label. It dissolves an opus's multilayered architecture and resonances into a discrete, single-level cipher (or linear string of ciphers) that can be brought into previously unimaginable relations to each other. Thus, to call upon one of the most widely circulated findings announced in cultural sociology, Wendy Griswold disclosed in "The Fabrication of Meaning" that when she encrypted book reviews into discrete values of variables, the presence of her code for a book critic's apperception of "ambiguity" in a novel and her code for the critic attributing an arresting power to a novel tended to occur conjointly.[65] Ambiguity marked cultural power. But Griswold inserted the coding for "ambiguity" into a chart as indicating the thematic *content* that a reviewer explicitly mentioned the novelist as featuring inside the novel itself. Then she reinserted the same data for "ambiguity" into new relations in a second chart in which ambiguity characterized a reviewer's aesthetic *response* to a novel as a whole based on its departure from a reviewer's expectancies of genre.[66] We will see that the two renderings, mere presence of the subtheme versus the aesthetic response a novel elicits from the reader overall, often conflict with each other in the original readers' appreciations. Once Griswold dislodged a possible meaning from its home con*text* to make it an elemental "data" piece, she could convey it as an isolated token around the ritual arena to gloss it discrepantly.

A religious rationale for transcoding text elements for recombination in a ritual arena is to reach a more penetrating appreciation of reality. More phenomenally, the function of setting up formal symbols in a segregated arena of experiment is simpler. The function is to suspend the mundane ties of worldly context that weigh down creative hypothesizing. "Among the most important" functions of memos and diagrams, the sociologists Juliet Corbin and Anselm Strauss wrote, "are that they free you to work with ideas using a kind of free association, one idea stimulating another without constraints of either worrying about logic or staying too close to reality, at least for the moment."[67] An operation as simple as Griswold's map of new semantic ties ("correlations") between her conversions of the texts ("codes") suppresses the distinction between pattern *discovery* versus pattern *creation*. This elision is the basic cosmic doing of ritual overall. Ultimate truth and formal expression are not merely coordinated but indistinguishable in ritual. The root word "kosmos," which originally meant ornament, gave our language "cosmology" as well as "cosmetic."[68]

A ritual event flows through a sequence of three stages. As the influential anthropologist Arnold van Gennep proposed a century ago, the process opens with a phase of separation that detaches the audience from the flow of mundane events.[69] It suffices at a theater performance, of course, for the playhouse lights to dim and for the curtain to rise on what becomes a newly focused world of physical action on stage. A new state of concentrated expectancy is enough.[70] In ritual, however, the preparatory work in the phase of separation more explicitly addresses the audience's antecedent social statuses for the sake of breaking roles down into more fundamental or universally shared components. Victor Turner characterized this leveling of identities as a grinding down of the ritual participants "into a sort of homogeneous social matter."[71] Ritual orchestrators the world over accomplish this by stripping initiates of their ordinary clothing, flustering them with impossible riddles, or disorienting them by ordeals, as happens in tribesmen's huts or marine barracks. Reducing people to "prima materia" prepares them to move into a new conception of their position in society. Equivalently in a piece of sociology, it seems natural to start proceedings by theorizing agents as culturally disembedded and abstractly universal. The simplifying phase is orchestrated by hitting readers with a portentous theory that requires readers to dedifferentiate their statuses vis-à-vis counterparts. A classic example is Robert Merton's "Social Structure and Anomie." Merton has his respectable audience reconceive illegal deviance as the creative reuse of means to reach communally prescribed goals. His presentation not only levels the souls of innovators and criminals, but, by uniting us as equals, it transmutes malefactors into our next of kin.[72] In the demonstrations of coding in the present volume, the presentations reestablish moral clarity by scapegoating a sacrificial victim uncomfortably situated both inside and outside the community.[73]

Accompanying this narrative reduction, coding enacts a parallel separation from mundane circumstance by breaking texts down into purified ciphers for redisplay. In the ritual arena, this performance imitates an archetypal gesture for creating the world, characterized by Mircea Eliade as "the legitimization of human acts by an extra human model."[74] For instance, when sociologists encrypt inferential reasoning among narrative clauses in a story as if such linkages were ties between points in a network, they have invoked networks as the generative principle of meaningful composition—an academic equivalent for Eliade's notion of a "cosmogonic structure." Even the act of coding itself—creating meaning by bringing raw material into relation with schemata—can display the paradigm for sense-making in all the universe.

The second phase in ritual is the liminal rearrangement and interpretation of the coded encryptions mise-en-scène. Van Gennep in his presageful model granted this phase its autonomy as an extreme limit experience. Victor Turner, almost Van Gennep's apprentice in matters of theory, established this phase as the source of regenerative reflection on the human predicament.[75] In much professional sociology, this temporal and visual staging pivots on the interpretation of a simplified data diagram that bears features that ethnologists would describe as "multistable." Such a graphing is capable of being read from wildly different perspectives, we will see: as a space of interaction *and* of accidental co-occurence, or as both a temporal instant *and* a tracer of progression, for example. Or the diagram can take on multiple referents: the social, the psychological, or the fancied merger of both (back to figure 1.1). "We might think of the multistable image as a device for educing self-knowledge, a kind of mirror for the beholder, or a screen for self-projection like the Rorschach test," the theorist of icons W. J. T. Mitchell wrote of "multistabile" objects.[76] In anthropology the riotously evocative ritual object is classic for the so-called savage thought of threshold experiences.[77]

If the meaning of a diagrams of coding results is elusive or floating, there is no need to justify whether it conveys a discernible message at all.[78] In ritual it simply must, like cards turned face up by a teller of fortune.[79] More pertinently, as Ronald Breiger showed, for the tables of category frequencies that coding produces, sociologists are able to elaborate radically different models and stories that fit the data equally well.[80] Intricacy in the tables stimulates social scientists to imagine multiple levels of causality or to notice relatively peripheral jumps as signifiers.[81] Sociologists proliferate what they name "incommensurable families" of models for the same tables, as if newly perceptible interaction effects and "corner" associations are there to be multiplied at will, each inspiring a story about unseen "social forces" dancing conjointly.

In the third ritual stage, that of *reintegration* in Van Gennep's classic exposition, the insights generated from the liminal experiment are used to adjust everyday identities and social roles. In sociology, this extends to considering how a ritual's solemnizing offers a renewable model for clarifying sociologists' roles in the professional community or beyond. The riddle for analysis of social "science" as ritual is to determine how the free flow of the liminal phase culminates by reaffirming sacrosanct yardsticks and prescriptions that are worthy of perpetuation without end.

In sum, these three stages of ritual comprise a giant circle of encryption and then, in return, the deciphering of a self-made cryptograph. The looping starts when the analyst measures properties of textual units by breaking text into elementary pieces: themes, words, cites, or connections among them. Even qualitative coding requires that "units of meaning" be assigned to chunks of text "of varying size—words, phrases, sentences, or whole paragraphs, connected or unconnected to a specific setting."[82] This decomposition of the verbal leads to a nonverbal portraiture, with columns of statistics or diagrams that implicitly sponsor spatial substitutes for textual intelligence (figure 1.1). Since verbal meaning has no degrees of similarity to such geometric charts, the diagrams of coding results are perfectly analogous to idolatrous practices in religion.[83] This redepicting can use lattices, clusters, any iconic "look." John Mohr in his excellent synopsis of the interpretation of "meaning structures" described this reliance on the "iconic" appearance of diagrams of the aggregated codes. "Once we see 'visible patterns," he said as a methodological insider, cultural systems "become more easily understandable."[84] Guides to coding emphasize the importance of "graphical output procedures" so that "the data can be analyzed visually as well as empirically."[85]

The displays are so stripped down and geometrically stylized that they cannot help but stimulate illimitable analogies (figure 1.2). For instance, John Evans in *Playing God?* identifies which authors in a debate are cited together in the same publications, no matter what the argumentative voice (you can look ahead to figure 3.1 in chapter three). "[T]he question was which top-cited authors were *most similar* to each other *based on the texts that cited them.*"[86] "Similar" is the open-ended trigger for Lévi-Strauss's "savage" mind to turn on. As Nelson Goodman has remarked, since any two objects are alike in an unlimited number of ways, applying the adjective "similar" to them is empowering yet pointless unless one knows *in what respects* the two are to be matched: "'is similar' to functions as little more than a blank to be filled," Goodman explained.[87] As I understand it, Evans circularly equates "similar to" with belonging to the same statistical cluster [G 210]. This spatial proximity in the diagram of cites can be glossed as intellectual connection (not necessarily affinity) by infinitely diverse measures, setting into play the spins on physical symbols that Victor Turner hailed as the mark of liminal creativity. Critics have long complained that quantitative measurement in social "science" can beg the question of what is being measured, leading to counts without well-articulated *concepts.*[88] Thanks to the free interweaving of language with graphic tokens in ritual, pictorial analogy substitutes for conceptual refinement. *How* authors who happen to be "co-cited" are meaningfully "related" to each other in a diagram can be answered in the liminal phase of presentations such as Evans's *Playing God.*

Improvisation in interpreting diagrams is the motor of innovation. "Of course, as anyone who has employed these methods will readily testify, there is nothing simple or determinant about the interpretive work that one must perform after having completed a structural analysis," John Mohr wrote as an exponent. *"Any visual representation of a meaning structure is still largely a Rorschach test upon which one must seek to project an interpretation."*[89] Any technique for decomposing texts into "elementary units" and for subsequently tabulating patterns among their features is likely to yield an arresting chart of relations.[90] Which mappings are most revelatory and which projected interpretations of those mappings explanatory? As figure 1.2 brings to mind, no Rorschach guess is inaccurate.[91] John Mohr as a practitioner proposes an arch heuristic for construing diagrams of "meaning structures." Sociologists should limn the facts through knowledge of "what type of practical utility such a cultural system plays" in an "institutional system"—perhaps another Rorschach mirror of the institutionalized career paths of academics.[92]

In sociology the meanings the cryptographic exercise is permitted to reveal as the "right" ones summon an extratextual expectation about the social functions of the texts in the diagram of coding results, functions apt to reduce culture to a tool of forces working *outside* the diagram. The observable status of those forces is little different than that of bewitching ghosts, as in E. E. Evans-Pritchard's enduring study of oracles and magic among the Azande.[93] The Azande's circular logic parallels how "social" or "institutional" explanation of diagrammed coding outputs impresses viewers. Having jettisoned potentially recalcitrant text detail about the making of meanings, the stripped-down representation of elements lacks the wherewithal for speaking *against* a projected interpretation. The anthropologist Richard Shweder, remarking upon the tie between factual observation and inevitable confirmation inside the Azande's culture of oracles, found that it aligned perfectly with the functioning of Western formalized science: both modes of encoded knowledge cogitate, he noticed, through "reliability checks (double consultations), interfering background variables (counterwitchcraft), and measurement error (pollution)."[94]

Cannot we check the interpretation of diagrammed coding by triangulating diverse types of outside evidence for corroboration? In sociology this is the fabled marriage of hard "data" deciphered with qualitative islands of insight.[95] However, few among us imagine that when the Azande draw on surrounding information to validate their theory, the Azande increase the plausibility of their oracular encoding of the scene of a dead chicken. Similarly with sociologists' coding of texts, the graphs that result rarely have their privileged status as messengers of social forces disqualified by independent or unformalized evidence.[96] Consider an example we will encounter at greater length in chapter four: suppose we interpret the incidence of mentions of a theme that we posit from history should have been culturally central— a theme such as, say, "colonialism" for educated elites discussing literature from the British commonwealth in the mid-twentieth century. Whether explicit mentions of "colonialism" in texts are frequent *or* sparse, the Rorschach projection decides that colonialism was central, either because this underlying social concern *unleashed* a flood of words or, in reverse, because the social indelicacies of colonialism *suppressed* the expected loquacious fluency.[97] Either way, through verbosity *or* silence, the extraneously presumed social function of the text, that of digesting problematic colonial legacies, is necessarily confirmed.[98] Time and again in scientific inquiry based on coding, the outside contextual evidence said to enrich interpretation of the aggregate results does nothing more than circularly reinforce a hypothesized causative system whose relevance goes unquestioned.[99] Canonical guidebooks foresee a mutually supportive relation between contextual background knowledge and coding results. As more than one how-to manual for coding has promised for the betterment of social "science," between the cocontributing evidence of qualitative context and of graphically displayed coding output, "[t]he relationship is a *circular* one; each provides new insights on which the other can feed."[100]

FRACTURED DENOTATION AND ITS ALTERNATIVE

Separating coding tokens from their contexts lets investigators confound two operations: cataloging an item by placing it in a classificatory system versus understanding the semantic distinctions the item activates in the text from which it came. To illustrate, most everyone who has lost airline baggage has had firsthand experience with this result of coding. As the linguist John Lucy has explained, when you approach the baggage counter to file a claim, whatever your native sense of how you ought to describe your luggage, you are handed the same international laminated chart of types of bags (the system of categories) and you place your object in the system. Take this bland denotational task as a usefully neutral example of "qualitative" coding of the luggage unit. Every respondent can fit a sample of bags into the classificatory grid by landing upon what they consider a predominant feature (shape, size, fastenings, musical instrument container or not). Perhaps each coder behaves "the same." However the aggregate categorizations of lost bags turns out end of month, the results disembed luggage from most everything that contributes to its significance, that is, its semantics apart from pointing to a box to which the bag can be assigned. With which semantic systems are baggage distinctions structurally integrated (the taxonomy of Gucci and of Samsonite versus that of airport security?).[101] To extend the analogy, how and for what purposes do people use luggage or its language to communicate social identities in different contexts? By what kind of grammar do people put luggage into relations with other concerns?[102] Of course, to interpret the pattern of coding results from the laminated charts, you can go back to a culture's luggage practices for context, but using this outside (presumed) sense to interpret absurd data does not help identify the toxicity of the whole exercise. More generally, attesting that the coding could be made reliable or that the categories realistically tap into properties and meanings that *are* there (call it "validity") begs the question of whether the intervention of coding in the first place obscures or discloses focal meanings and their functioning. This luggage exercise concretizes how the denotative accuracy of discrete codes and their ability to condense a collection of analytically separated units have little to do with analysis of pragmatics, the unfolding of meaningfully organized practices. The same contagious mistake occurs whether coding comprises computer-automated word counts *or* the kind of coding on which I focus here, qualitative sorting.

What might systematic, retraceable inquiry into the meanings of primary texts require of us if it certainly does not entail this practice called "coding?" Let me preview a countertradition, although I would never crown it as a "method." In this alternative, evidence has the potential to challenge our preconceptions of what texts signify and of how they were put together. Not that we will always be attuned to hear the evidence talk back, but such a potential is requisite for texts to bring something of their own in relation to our interpretive model. The four conditions in this contrary tradition are: that we not grant epistemological legitimacy to the interpretive model with which we start; that there is no pigeon-holing of textual evidence to collapse it into our own system, as in coding; correlatively, meaning is bound to concrete, unsystematizable prototypes; and, finally, that we read the texts as they are embedded in a culture different from the one by which we create our ideal models as investigators. These are the four conditions summarizing the sociologist Max Weber's ideal-type applications. Nowadays sociologists ventriloquize Weber, an inaugural figure of cultural analysis across the disciplines, to smarten up the presentation of a contemporary notion. But as we will discover in this book's conclusion, Weber's ideal type agenda, programmatic as it will always remain, guards against over-rationalizing methods that confuse investigators' analytic categories with those naturally "in" the evidence.

As many know, an "ideal type" in Weber's research program is an extreme distillation of traits in iconic form that can be contrasted against a family of historical cases. Workable examples include Weber's portrait of Richard Baxter as a prototype of ascetic Protestantism.[103] Or, to recall how an ideal type is similar to a purified genre in literary study, there is the sociologist Will Wright's simplified picture of *The Far Country* as an archetype of a "Western Cowboy movie."[104] Most famously, to concretize the ideal type of a high-surveillance society, Michel Foucault called upon Jeremy Bentham's 1787 plan for a "panoptic" prison.[105] As the dual character of each of these examples suggests, an ideal type emerges from both showing and describing: it is "shown" concretely in a slice of evidence and the relations among its features are verbally adumbrated. The purpose is to dramatically accentuate the makeup of an historical artifact so that a freshly sensitized researcher has a point of contrast for appreciating resemblance and divergence among other cases. The ideal type provides an optic but each case's textual details (as in Weber's portraits of Lutheranism or Pietism) do the work of explaining.[106] To code the evidence into variables and to seek the correlations among them was for Weber a misleading reification[107]: it leads us to confuse our imaginative aids with real entities, mistaking the theories we project upon correlations for quasi-laws.[108]

Weber summoned a distinguished German critical tradition whose purpose was to puncture exactly the kind of circular madness that constitutes social "science" as ritual and to replace it with more disciplined if less technical inquiry into cultural meanings. Weber recognizes (like a postmodernist) that our self-made models of knowledge, not "facts," are the only source of meaning. Rather than emphasizing the models' integration as a closed system, however, he accentuates their openness to overhaul by anomalous evidence. Method is the attempt to fix by some singular, privileged logic our conduct for eternity, freezing life inside a contingently powerful regime.[109]

HOW DID CODING OF TEXTS BECOME DOMINANT?

Before the Internet boosted the accessibility of written evidence, social theory moved documentary texts into the forefront of cultural sociology's evidentiary concerns. For a concept such as culture to become recoverable as a worldly object, it had to be imagined as "residing" in a location where the sociologist could establish its practical visibility. So long as sociologists had identified culture's workings with individual agents' subjective dispositions and thoughts "inside the head," surveys or interviews to elicit opinions appeared to offer sociologists privileged access to the conventions that make up a culture.[110] The move toward greater reliance on archival and published records had to be prepared therefore by basic changes in sociologists', anthropologists', and historians' postulates about culture.

Cultural theorists in the course of the 1970s began to designate publicly shared symbols or repertoires and not minds as the repositories and makers of whatever is communicable, therefore thinkable.[111] Geertz prepared the way with compelling case examples that "human thinking is primarily an overt act conducted in terms of the objective materials of the common culture."[112] Foucault supported this switch by theorizing culture as the thing-like deposits of discourse that agents activate to form their actions.[113] In particular, for sociologists to locate this furniture of culture and to uncover it systematically, they examined bodies of texts as storehouses of operative assumptions and ready-to-hand modes of expression. Researchers might never determine what individuals hazily were thinking, but they learned about objects more tangible, the vehicles *with which* individuals thought, the explanatory "mechanisms" of action and its construal. Few today think we have more immediate access to cultural happenings than through the material evidence they generate, in particular the texts that we make up about ourselves and others.[114]

From the 1980s onward, the number of articles or dissertations using content or text analysis across the social sciences seems to have boomed.[115] (Certainly I refute myself in citing indices that *code coding*.) The "core of contemporary large N qualitative analysis of texts," sociologist John Evans recently concluded, "is coding."[116] Coding devoured auteur film reviews, pornography, and protest speeches, suggestions of the illimitable variety of material upon which it fed.[117] Nowadays *The New York Times* discusses the advantages of using songs or blogs on the web to gauge social attitudes and individuals' feelings as opposed to survey interviews that are prone to elicit situationally artificial or "reactive" answers from respondents.[118]

If texts are repositories of publicly accessible meanings, how should investigators move systematically from the sui generis compositions in texts to map them as storehouses of "culture"? Sociologists have rarely entertained this prior analytic question for inductive technique: how to project from a group of object-texts a map of the communicants' tools for conveying meanings?[119] At least the sociologist Kathleen Carley accentuated this step in an unnerving conclusion to her 1994 review of text-analytic coding:

> It should be noted that research in this area is hampered not only by lack of methodological tools, but also by the lack of a clearly defined theoretical foundation. The types of theoretical issues that need to be addressed include: the relationship between mental models and language, the relationship between words and meaning, the role of emotions in text, the role of syntax in textual analysis, *and the nature of social knowledge or shared meaning.*[120]

Carley sought clear directives for stipulating the translation of text into recorded codes and then for inducing from these codes the structuration of meaning systems or cultures. By taking seriously the premise that the business of science is to systematize its use of the evidence, Carley reestablished just how difficult it is to infer cultural structures from raw texts.[121]

By contrast to contemporary bypassing of the problem, advocates of text coding as a science in the 1950s saw inference from lexical content to collective meanings as forbidding and possibly infeasible. Honest positivists found themselves compelled to speculate philosophically on the rules by which signs convey significance. "How much 'meaning' is there in any given word, slogan, sentence?" asked three early custodians of coding, Lasswell, Lerner, and de Sola Pool, in their 1952 handbook *The Comparative Study of Symbols*.[122] To answer, these researchers hypothesized that at a given moment for any "specific" social group, the relation between word and meaning, as well as between meaning and action, had to be determinant and "stable." Positivists concluded that correlations among "those who profess the viewpoint in question" could make sense only *after* a "theoretical analysis" of a whole cultural configuration at a temporal juncture.[123] As Lasswell surprisingly admitted, the message delivered by a word depends on contrasts to paradigmatically similar words that are *not used*, but that are invoked "in absentia, which have a psychological reality."[124] Even lexical counts of content present in a text had to postulate counterfactually what *could have been* there to access the production of sense.[125] All this questioning was foregrounded in the initial postwar era, when text coding remained largely an enticing, prospective method. This sensitivity was suppressed to realize coding as standard practice.

Coders' main response to this challenge of going from individual texts to collective meanings systematically has been to treat the issue as if it concerned exiguous measurement error, even when the original texts were difficult or foreign. This avoidance of the problem raised in the 1950s and recuperated by Carley may have violated horse sense, but it was necessary for lift off. Everyone (researcher, reader, dean) insulates what transpires in coding as an unapproachable black box.[126] Investigators vouch for their "data" but do not necessarily release information about the sample sources, let alone the goings-on by which they translated texts into outputted variables. It might be naive to demand absolutely explicit indicators for the multidimensional concepts that intrigue cultural investigators. When sociologists report coding results without mention of indicators, even for the most delicate themes, the authoritative warrant becomes the sociologist's personal experience of the text. Perhaps we should trust the coder "who was there" just as we trust the ethnographer on site to render indigenous expressions into scientific language.[127] Bernard Traimond identified this encoding process in ethnography: "The native speaks, the savant reconstitutes 'its reality' by the criteria proper to it."[128]

In actuality this parallel between coding and fieldwork breaks down in every way. The texts are nonreactive and constant. The coder is supposed to adhere to the rule of thumb that similar text elements should be coded similarly, "like treated as like," whereas every other domain of life, from courtrooms to admissions offices, suggests this may be infeasible for the adjudications that matter.[129] However explicit the coding instructions appear as formal signs, the bothersome Harold Garfinkel has inveighed, implementing them is all about makeshift imputation of what they might sensibly entail.[130] In the matter of coding procedure, veteran coder Roberto Franzosi wrote, "few of us dare disclosing the inner secrets of our alchemies."[131]

Despite this insulation, the systematizing aura of text coding lets most social "scientists" maintain that it is quasi-scientific data gathering rather than impressionistic adduction. The key credential is a promise that coders do not merely "read" texts.[132] As the entry for coding from *A Dictionary of Sociology* puts it: "Coding is also an important aspect of measurement, for in the act of coding we are making a measurement."[133] In research reporting, coding procedures are described in the kind of first-person narrative voice one assumes in recounting an operation at a lab, and coding results are shaped in the style of scientific discourse. Or, as sociologist John Evans presented his text explications, "the data show…"[134]

The stakes of the coding business reach beyond academe into literate civilization. In the Internet age, material for classification gathers inside repositories of demonic scale.[135] Coding easily becomes Promethean in its drive. A foretaste is the efforts to build comprehensive global archives of dreams, initiated, for example, at "DreamBank.net." If we can code thousands of dreams at this site, G. William Domhoff has declared in all seriousness, "these late-night movies in the brain can be incorporated into ambitious theories seeking to explain all aspects of the human mind."[136] Just as ambitiously, Michael Stubbs notes that the creation of text corpora of hundreds of millions of analyzable sentences may bridge the chasm between two poles of language that have long been considered analytically irreconcilable. Saussure's concept of *langue*, the ideal structure underlying expression, was the real object for study while at the other pole, concrete instances of usage, Saussure's *parole*, remained merely anecdotal. In effect Stubbs proposes that putting online most all parole may enable coders of sentence structures *empirically* to collapse one analytic pole into the other: "Large corpora provide a way out of the Saussurian paradox, since millions of running words can be searched for patterns which cannot be observed by the naked eye (compare devices such as telescopes, microscopes, and X rays)."[137] Whether any cultural structure can be adduced by induction from surface patterns will strike some as doubtful.[138] But the vision is clear enough: when the encoded texts are all-encompassing, they will not illustrate an ideal model of cultural structure; they will *become* that thing-like structure itself.[139]

The mapping of texts as containers of items has entered the pop mainstream. Word and theme frequencies in political speeches are graphed in the press as if they comprised news stories.[140] This format of fact-gathering may have a prescriptive effect, encouraging people to consume these addresses as parcels of themes in actuality.[141] No surprise. To a complaint that his cubist portrait of Gertrude Stein did not much capture her, Picasso is rumored to have answered, "No matter, someday it will." In our time, after the press dissected and rearranged President Obama's "2,400-word Inaugural Address" by word and theme counts, the rhetorician Stanley Fish naturalized this statistical manufacture as a populist tool for locating the individual speaker's verbal energy.[142]

The logic of parsing, coding, and reinterpreting texts as "data," like many tools, is turning invisibly from a hypothetical convention into the pivot of a worldview.[143] The littérateur Franco Moretti, a director of Stanford University's Literary Lab, recently pitched network diagrams generated by coding (identical to the method to be dissected in chapter two) as a science of all human culture.[144] In the *New Left Review* he wrote:

> A network is made of vertices and edges: a plot, of characters and actions; characters will be the vertices of the network, interactions the edges, and this is what the *Hamlet* network looks like...You see the possibility here: different uses of language emerging in different network regions. Style, integrated within plot as *function* of plot...A model for the relationship between what we do, and how we think about it: this is what a plot-style continuum could provide...an enormous amount of empirical data must be first put together. Will we, as a discipline, be capable of sharing raw materials, evidence—*facts*—with each other? It remains to be seen. For science, Stephen Jay Gould once wrote, *fruitful doing matters more than clever thinking.*[145]

We have been forewarned.[146]

Three Studies for Replication

Each of the three primary demonstrations dissected in the present volume affirms a universal outlook on the sources of human identity, rationality, or literary meaning. Each engages in an extreme caliber of exploratory "deep play" in which one can experience sociology's equivalent of the sacred—or at least I did, initially. The first exemplar of coding research, Peter Bearman's and Katherine Stovel's "Becoming a Nazi," did not just bring into view the delicate structure of a Nazi autobiography.[147] When it mapped an invisible story signature, I saw it offering a novel way of fitting individual experience into the explanation of macro-historical events such as the rise of the Nazi party. The second study, John Evans's *Playing God? Human Genetic Engineering and the Rationalization of Public Bioethical Debate*, struck me as accomplishing the superlative and making it look easy.[148] The unresolved problem of Weber's *Protestant Ethic* and of entire regions of sociology is how to document which of Weber's abstract types of rational action, "value" or "instrumental," operates in a setting.[149] I had always supposed this an infeasible task because agents' ultimate ends, and thus the final context for framing their action, were independent of the immediate setting and unobservable as subjective attitudes.[150] In his study of the rationalization of bioethical reflection, Evans operationally sidestepped this problem of identifying subjective meaning, because he coded tangible features of texts that guided agents' reasoning.[151] As I understand it, he converted rationality into observable types of text composition and then viewed text composition as social action, a deft response to the challenge of operationalizing Weber's types of rationality. The third study featured here for intensive replication, Wendy Griswold's canonical article "The Fabrication of Meaning," seemed to squeeze hard "data" out of texts to resolve the humanist's vague but omnipresent question, how *do* people in fact go about imputing meaning to a text?[152]

These three exemplary works also share crucial similarities in how they positioned their methods in an ambiguous middle ground. None of the researchers resorted to reductive word or phrase searches, such as a computer executes. Instead, these sophisticated sociologists rejected cruder reduction and contrasted it to the more sensitive coding they sought to execute. For instance, Bearman and Stovel criticize conventional variable analyses of text contents for "crosstabulations of disembodied attributes." They concluded "Real lives are lost in the process, and real process is lost in the movement away from narrative by this abstraction."[153] These coauthors seek to examine "the process of identity formation" while avoiding "exogenous imputation" of agents' purposes.[154] Evans distanced himself from brute empiricism when he said he coded each text "descriptively and interpretively."[155] Griswold wrote that "the reviews were not coded for a set of predetermined attributes established either by my own perceptions of what the novels involved or by socioliterary theories."[156] Each of these sociologists therefore conducted interpretive coding yet, conversely, each downgraded purely humanistic approaches that produce findings that are not adequately verifiable or precise enough for generalization. In my view, each of these researchers epistemologically privileges their *blurring* of "hard" science and "soft" interpretation.[157] How is the proposed marriage of systematic observation with sensitivity to unique case context carried out in the mind of the investigator through coding?[158]

We may never find out, because none of the investigators was able to make available the record sheets, instructions, specific codings, or other materials that would link the source texts to the published classifications. Professors Bearman and Griswold undertook to locate their coding records, and they were patient in communicating about their efforts. For the stereotypical hard sciences as well as for the philological humanities, transparency of data in a research community is championed by journals and by granting agencies.[159] In the cross-genre of qualitative coding, this norm has become largely inoperable.

WHY PREFER INTENSIVE CASE REVISITING?

To effect a Gestalt-switch in how coding research is viewed, thick description of a handful of exemplars is required.[160] Critiques of pieces of research from inside the frame of normal science leave the impression that coding and inferences from it are rectifiable. My purpose is to ask more radically of the three main demonstrations whether they have a foothold in "scientific" reasoning at all. Place the artifact-case on the table, reenact its construction, disassemble it, ask how it might be put together differently, pesteringly intervene to see if its modeling represents worldly phenomena at all—those are my actions, and they demand scrupulous detail. Only with thick description can we dispel the faith that there "must" remain some residuum of conventional scientific content. A total dissection extracts constitutive contradictions all the way down and the principles by which domains of social research complacently prosper as sacralizing rites.[161]

Ethnographic revisiting of the case publications is necessary to show as well how social "science" publications take shape as performances. The natural sciences assumed their modern guises through the literary narratives that converted individual sightings into a shared experience of "facts." Historians such as Steven Shapin have dissected how publications' rhetoric and engravings were honed in the seventeenth century for transporting readers into a special zone for "virtual witnessing" of experiments.[162] In sociology presentations, the display of cluster diagrams, network ties, and gridded tables as witnessable objects is even more important for *producing* a sense of knowledge, not just for *presenting* its lineaments.[163] Quantitatively inspired sociology often fabricates its accounts by a mixed semiosis, combining a visual array of "data" with a narrative about a quest that primes the reader for entry into the shared ritual arena of "discovery."[164] The diagrams accomplish what words cannot on their own. As heirs of a discipline that carries unresolved theoretical tensions, sociologists can go only so far in verbally articulating how essentially different orders of phenomena—material institutions versus figural expressions, "social" forces versus interworked semiotic systems—interlock with each other.[165] Instead, diagrams of influence, affinity, or "socially" marked variation in the "data" meet this challenge just by displaying each of the sui generis causal domains—cultural meanings, social exchange, demography, urban geographies, and so forth—as *copresent* in the same graphic space of seeing and knowing.[166]

In the three exemplars of coding, we will see, this production of knowledge through performance on the page goes beyond Shapin's "virtual witnessing" to create new reports of several kinds: substitutes for real sources, reports that primary documents explicitly refer to specific topics these documents do not seem to mention overtly, or individual-level codes applied upon individual documents whose results perplexingly seem not to be itemizable or describable via individual-level codes.[167] The pervasive generation of simulacral facts shows they are globally intrinsic to a method.[168]

Reframing reductive sociology's circuit of coding and deciphering as a ritual process unearths surprising parallels to the course of natural science and philosophy. The basic notions of theory and truth in Western empirical inquiry derive from the ritual process of sending an individual observer into a sacred arena of witnessing that is removed from the prosaic. In ancient Greece, *theoria* named a pilgrimage one undertook by leaving everyday social relations in the polis to observe festivals, sacrifices, or oracular pronouncements in foreign locales where previously unseen interconnections in the world were disclosed.[169] The witness, the *theoros*, functioned as a messenger who returned home with news of these divine forces.[170] This process had three spatio-temporal steps—detachment from the human world with which one was familiar, witnessing in a neutral, sequestered arena abroad, and reintegration of this knowledge back home—obvious correspondences to van Gennep's three stages of ritual. Since the pilgrim detached himself from earthly affairs of his polis to achieve divine spectating, ritual was also a perfect model by which Plato eventually could explicate his concept of philosophical vision. Thus did we come to inherit our notion of "theory" standing outside contingent, prosaic affairs.[171] The Greeks' *theoria* conforms to the social "scientific" circuit of detaching data from context, witnessing encrypted patterns in a ritual arena, and then journeying back to enrich social life with a purified vision. This genesis matters, because it helps explain why, in my view, modern-day theory, fact, and other constituents of epistemology are secondary, abstract, and static elaborations ("rationalizations," if you will). They overlay more concrete and primary symbolic manipulations—makings, doings, happenings—in the ritual arena. With this principle in mind, my revisiting and replication of demonstrations, each in its own chapter, follows the ritual stages that erect a platform and carry out acts of theater.

Lab experiments in late seventeenth-century England, a founding site of the natural laboratory science with which we are familiar, also take on the look of a three-step ritual sequence if we may elaborate on the historian Steven Shapin's accounts of them.[172] In keeping with the ritual moment of separation, the legendary pioneer of natural science Robert Boyle conducted lab manipulations, like religious services, on Sundays or after prayer, or at least separate from the mundane flow of social life. Physical demonstrations such as his took place in gentlemen's homes, locales marked as neutral, trustworthy spaces for witnessing. On crossing the threshold into the site of experiment, Shapin suggested, the participants were to cultivate a heightened sense of awareness and of gentlemanly equality, similar in my view to Turner's and van Gennep's principle that novitiates sequester themselves to open themselves to transformative experience that can be transmitted to the outside. Afterward the implications of the lab results were "discoursed upon" at a transitional decompression site—a public coffee house, for instance—betokening I think the conclusive ritual phase of reintegration.

Why this possible convergence between knowledge-making enterprises, such as natural scientific experiment and the coding circuit in sociology, in resembling a ritual process? For reasons innumerable. In both kinds of orchestration, I speculate, one purpose of explanation is to replace the linear time of observed unique events with objectively "lawful" repetition or, as the classic analyst of myth Mircea Eliade announced, with the indefinite reoccurrence of underlying, extrahuman forms.[173] In both, the patterns that participants observe can be elevated to the status of consistently *meaningful* regularities only if the orchestrators shield the phenomenon from the interferences (profane "contamination") of everyday life.[174] This total insulation is accomplished by securing the boundaries of a lab site or, by analytic analogy, decontextualizing the diagram of "data" that is suspended in the blank space of a page. The sequestering of a purified arena in the liminal phase of a ritual meets this epistemological requirement. The ritual format is necessary to sponsor a divine coming to life of the ceteris paribus, "all else equal," clause. In contemporary philosophy of science, screening out interference is requisite for actualizing a packaged causal system or quasi-lawful explanations.[175] Analogously, in reductive cultural sociology as "data" production, to postulate a simple underlying mechanism that would generate the variation in coding outputs from ecologically incomparable texts demands that we fancifully expunge from view the multiple and idiosyncratic communicative projects inside of which each text feature was originally configured to function. Finally, of course, scientific dissent sometimes mutates into religious warfare: inquisitive speech puts one's life in the hands of aggrieved authorities.

In both ritual and in the objectification of lab experiments as "facts," verbal reportage depends on visual gesture, whether corporeal or in the graven images of charts and diagrams.[176] The parallels between lab experiments and coding as rituals are extensive because both enterprises look for tracking clues or tracers, but they paradoxically erect their own artificially isolating mise-en-scène in which these tracers are in turn read as *natural* indicators of forces that lie beyond. The manipulations and diagrams make what is conceptual, invisible, hypothetical, and therefore at bottom nonspatial suddenly intelligible by visual sensation.[177] That is how symbol-stretching in the liminal moment may transmute our conventions of reality.[178]

Unlike most historical writing, social "science" texts are explicitly performative, composed of utterances about the investigator's own doings, namely, the operations by which a paradigmatic model for knowing is found, put to work, and used to disclose new "data."[179] Blurred social science in the key of ritual usually unfolds the self-action of the researcher who starts or ends more like a hero-subject in his or her own narrative of discovery than does the historian in a history. The positing by the social scientist converts what goes on in a piece of research into a collectively sharable action.[180] And unlike most writings in history, social science reliant on text coding authorizes the perpetual repetition of its coding categories, the fundamental maneuver by which religions create a sense of eternity for their participants. This effect has become all the more vital upon the decline of Marxist prognostication. Fewer sociologists conjure the sacred by prophecies that overcome our personal deaths as individuals. Instead sociologists exercise their religious function as specialists who enact the transcendental categories for making possible the social meaning of words and actions.[181]

Of course digesting a piece of social "science" is "performed silently, in the lair of the skull."[182] Nonetheless, each communicant reading the latest book for the advance of a discipline understands this ceremony is replicated by thousands of others and that the impressions received will be treated with solemnity at professional gatherings, in keeping with Benedict Anderson's model in *Imagined Communities*. Subscribers consuming news for the "advance" of a discipline sustains the impression of a professional community moving through "clocked historical time." The individual witnessing culminates in the reality-sustaining power of a collective performance.

Social "scientists" have a logical need for ritual to paper over an epistemological chasm. In the era of the "modern fact," Mary Poovey has suggested, we are stuck with data in natural sciences, which, as a collection of particulars, we scarcely assume reveal an immanent order in the world. Social "scientific" coders leap from their particular "facts" to the general meaning not logically, not inductively, not inferentially, but *performatively*. They treat the coding outputs as units in the phase of separation and switch over in the liminal phase to recognize them as units *only in so far as they can rearrange them* as evidence for an integrative theory—marvelously reaffirming the dual faces of Poovey's "modern fact."[183]

Across how many kinds of knowledge-making practices may we profitably stretch the concept of a ritual event? Should we judge that much natural science and not just its poor next-of-kin, social "science," takes shape as ritual due to the staging of what is then taken as natural tracking? We have already noticed some potentially distinctive features of the variant of blurred social science. It relies on multistabile rather than univocal visual graphs. It manufactures statistical noise and uncertainty out of originally clear signals in the individual texts rather than, as in natural science, manufacturing clear signals out of originally fuzzy lab observations.[184] Above all, natural sciences flourish through heteroclite, destabilizing observations whose *recognition* as anomalous but implicative can stretch or overturn established classifications. This exciting recognition of conceptual mismatching is elided in social scientific coding, which insists on assigning everything a place. But the search for mismatches between paradigm and data in natural scientific experiment parallels, you will notice, Weber's supposedly unscientific, contrastive "ideal type" agenda, in which he crowned the gap between ideal type and evidence as the source point of discovery. This will offer a starting point for me to display the unsuspected parallels between humanistic ideal type research and practices of some natural sciences.

To exemplify the genre of ritual social "science," moreover, I will usually adhere to the narrow understanding of ritual as stagecraft organized to crystallize identities in social life. Anthropologists originally located this process in rites of passage, but many investigators apply van Gennep's model of ritual sequencing to interpret political dramas of "affliction" and redress."[185] These are the theatrical enactments by which tensions or violations in social roles in a community are symbolically heightened and then reassuringly reworked.[186] In contrast to what goes on stereotypically in natural science, this refiguring of social relations is a core purpose of sociology, certainly when that academic plaything is sculpted for professional buzz.[187] Since text analysis via coding tries to condense the commerce of life into tractable symbols, my hunch is that few academic undertakings are poised with more resonant equipment for the divinatory action of ritual.

CHAPTER 2

"THE ENTIRE STORY"

We use the technique of identifying nodes and arcs to code the entire story...
—Peter Bearman and Katherine Stovel, "Becoming a Nazi"

FIRST IRONY OF THE "MODERN FACT"

If the "facts" of social science are effectuated by a coding system, need these facts have specifiable referents? I open with this issue and with this case study because they show that esteemed practitioners of social "science" are ready to substitute raw sources one for the other, if the method for exhibiting the contents remains unchanged. This odd swapping takes place even when the "source" material carries the ethical seriousness of an inquiry into 1930s German anti-Semitism and the causes of the Holocaust. The real referents of the coding outputs are peripheral to research.

THE OPENING CASE

Peter Bearman and Katherine Stovel in their study "Becoming a Nazi" ventured upon one of the twentieth-century's documentary treasures, the Hoover Institution archive of nearly 600 autobiographies of Nazis. The genesis of the stories is as extraordinary as their contents. In 1934 Theodore Abel convinced Nazi authorities to sponsor a Germany-wide tournament to see who among the party members could write the most detailed and trustworthy life stories explaining how they had joined the movement. Few in 1934 could guess how Hitler would fulfill his prophecies. Only members who had been affiliated with the Nazis by the end of 1932, prior to Hitler's unexpected appointment as chancellor, were eligible to enter the contest. This filtered out opportunists who had trailed the party wagon. It is easy to agree with the verdict of Thomas Childress: "[T]hese essays offer the single most valuable source we have (or ever will have) for evaluating individual grassroots opinion within the National Socialist movement."[1]

No trace material could have attracted more exacting methodological expertise. If there be such a thing as cutting-edge research, this is it.[2] The senior author of "Becoming a Nazi," Columbia University professor Peter Bearman, directs the celebrated Institute for Social and Economic Research. The study appears so compellingly "scientific," its findings have been adopted as a paragon of how improved techniques of measurement can drive "cumulative" advance in sociology or exemplify replicable data creation.[3] Its method for coding of narratives diffused internationally.[4] Yet the supposedly "empirical" object of inquiry on which it rests, a Nazi narrative, becomes practically invisible since it is substitutable without limit and its shape is entirely construed rather than espied.

The documents seem tangible enough. The submissions—scrawled, typed, or elegantly penned—lie on every manner of raw scrap or fine stationary.[5] Some authors parsed their weltanschauung into numbered lineaments.[6] The literary templates on which respondents drew included the New Testament, in keeping with the feeling that Nazism comprised a religious mission.[7] The parchments are so immediately suffusive, why bypass their eloquence via fancy-built "data"?

To lend their formalization of Nazi conversion the touch of real individuality, Bearman and Stovel focused their coding on a single autobiography, that of Herr D., who was born near Trier several years before the outbreak of World War I.[8] They broke his voluble German run-ons into narrative clauses. Then these methodologists recognized as story connectors between these units an inference that "clause A" quasi-causally leads to or generates the meaning of "clause B" [76].[9] Figure 2.1

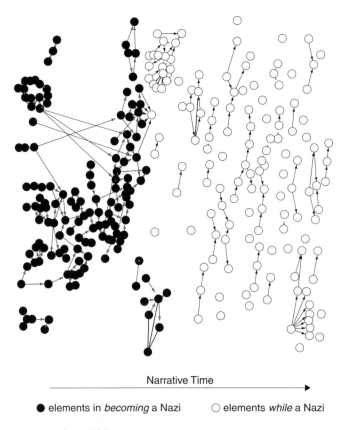

Narrative Time

● elements in *becoming* a Nazi   ○ elements *while* a Nazi

Figure 2.1   Structure of Nazi life history.

Source: Peter Bearman and Katherine Stovel, "Becoming a Nazi: A Model for Narrative Networks," *Poetics* 27 (2000): 78.

reproduces the visual output from Herr D.'s life.[10] The narrative arcs between statements yield a map similar to sociologists' maps of social networks. As Bearman and Stovel explain, such X-rays disclose stories' anatomies: their "structural properties, thereby revealing their morphological foundation, and making possible meaningful comparisons, even across narrative contents (or structural contexts) that are vastly different in scope and significance" [88]. We can quantify outward from any node the density of connections to prior feeder statements and then its effects upon recipient statements down the line.

To what end would researchers collapse every narrative motif into digital notation? Scientists usually start with inexplicable appearances to pry out what is intelligible underneath. But there is no opacity in Herr D.'s story that "Becoming a Nazi" resolves. If the rationale for reduction is fresh perspective, standards for similitude become moot.[11]

From the appearance of figure 2.1 Bearman and Stovel conclude that Germans assumed a Nazi identity by progressively shearing off competing kinds of social relations in favor of a simple trump identity, that of the party member. This type of master identity is absolute, they explain, because it dictates conduct independent of situationally specific relations to others. Graphically, this monolithic dedication to the party expresses itself in sparse linkages between life events, per the right-hand side of figure 2.1. In effect, Bearman and Stovel converge on what Hannah Arendt once proposed in her philosophical account of totalitarianism. As Arendt classically established it, a Nazi adherent was a "completely isolated human being who, without any other social ties to family, friends, comrades, or even mere acquaintances, derives his sense of having a place in the world only from his belonging to a movement, his membership in the party."[12] Bearman and Stovel apply equally extreme words:

> when the author is a Nazi—the self disappears. Nothing is left to operate the story, except for a mechanical agency...The [Nazified] authors of the stories we consider can continue to report the facts, but nothing beyond the facts. This is not because there is not a story to tell: they explicitly select facts to tell a story, but it is a banal story of action without actors. [89]

The disappearance of narrative linkages when one has become a Nazi signifies the loss of a self as a directive agent.

REPLACING THE REAL EVIDENCE

By standards of archival research, this coding enterprise, soberly outfitted with coefficients and fractions, becomes a ludic artifice if you return to the primary document. All the network data were extracted from a single Nazi story, but it was not an actual autobiography from Abel's collection. Help from Peter Bearman together with detective hunting established that the researchers coded instead from "The Story of a Middle-Class Youth," a condensation published in an appendix to Abel's book in 1938.[13] Although the intact story was at hand for Bearman and Stovel, and although they had secured English translations of complete stories from the Abel collection,[14] they coded instead from an adaptation that indicated with ellipses where connecting segments had been deleted.[15]

Substituting a selective encapsulation appears to violate the researchers' justification for their investigation. Their warrant for using autobiographies was that these materials represent the original writers' personal arranging of story elements for coherence. "Life stories," the researchers wrote, "provide an 'endogenous' account of how authors got from 'there' to where they are" [76]. That is the underwriting for Bearman and Stovel to claim that the threads discovered by coding trace the meaningful organizing of experience: "Our strategy," they affirmed, "makes use of *actors'* narrative accounts of their *own* becoming experiences."[16] The hidden structure of the story is supposed to reveal the hidden structure of the author's self, so Bearman and Stovel promise again that the connections they quantify were those *"made by the author* in putting the story together" [76; emphasis in original]. It may be difficult for those outside the ritual arena to digest the claim that "the entire story" [77] was coded when only a spliced proxy was treated.

What Bearman and Stovel processed were the connections that the outsider Theodore Abel wanted to present in support of his sociological theory. As an editor, Abel was prone to deleting the musings on personal life decisions or self-reflection on family relations and social relations—the very stuff that Bearman and Stovel report as strangely missing and as indicating an absence of selfhood when Herr D. acquires a Nazi identity. The abridgment excises about a third of the words from the original. By comparing the real to the ersatz source, box 2.1 illustrates why the whittled-down story yields misleading results.

BOX 2.1   DISCONNECTED DOTS

Example of fragmentation

Coded version: "Now every day brought something new, the acts of the new Reich's regime [1933]. One of the first laws related to the encouragement of agricultural activities. I no longer had to return home, for the miracle had happened."

Missing dots: What is "the miracle" and why does its occurrence mean Herr D. no longer has to return home?

The real dots: Only in the unabridged original does Herr D. explain that the family vineyard in December 1932 was near to foreclosure. On that suspenseful note, Herr D. paused this family story to report on Hitler's abrupt assumption of power. Then Herr D. returns to the suspended chain of family efforts to avert foreclosure—except, in Abel's abridgment, the reader does not suspect "miracle" refers to keeping the homestead. In the real story, describing a miracle unites two subsequences Herr D. had skillfully braided for tension. This connecting function disappears from the abridgement. Abel mistranslates "suspension of the forced auctioning off of farming establishments" ["die vorläufige Aufhebung der Zwangsversteigerungen landwirtschaftlicher Betriebe"] as merely "encouragement of agricultural activities" [D 15].

Examples of pervasive mistranslation

Abel abridgment: "Then [in 1932] the wearing of the uniform of the S.A. was forbidden" [271]. The original conveys the opposite: "Along with the ban on the

S.A., so also the ban on its uniforms was *lifted*" [D 11]. ["Mit dem SA-Verbot würde auch das Uniformverbot aufgehoben."]

Abel abridgment: "Many times I tried to join [the Nazi party]" [268]. What the original says: no such sentence or traceable fragments [D 8].

Abel abridgment: On the visit to Verdun: "There should be fewer cemeteries to remind people of the terrible fights" [268]. The sentence is concocted, since the original sentence contains no "should be fewer" and no "remind people" [D 7].

Abel abridgment: "I made up my mind I would have to choose between politics and family" [270]. This translation skews measurement of "social elision." In the original there is no punctual either/or dilemma. Instead, détente between family and politics is stressed: "I understood with time to distinguish exactly between family and politics" [D 10].

It is bewildering that Bearman and Stovel report "facts" about what is missing in Herr D.'s account when the relevant content was excised prior to their examination:

"In the *being* story, cognitions *never* bridge events or event sequences. This lack of organized connectivity yields a story that is marked by the absence of narrativity. The absence of narrativity results from the absence of a theory of the self." [85; emphasis on "never" added]

"[I]n in the being narrative…cognitions are relatively isolated from local events, and are *never* reflected back into the realm of action (i.e. into nodes coded as local event elements)." [85; emphasis in original]

"Being a Nazi induces the absence of self-reflexivity." [85]

Since this characterization of Herr D. pertains to a segment only nine pages in length for 1930–1934, let us check it against the source.[17]

Two years into "being" a Nazi, Herr D. journeyed with his sister toward a German firm in Italy. As told in the authentic version:

Here [in Innsbruck] a stroke of fate awaited us, here everything became something other than what we had foreseen. It was not our fault, for a sister notified us that my mother had experienced a severe auto accident and lay in danger of dying at a hospital in Trier. The telegram reached us Saturday. I told my sister that we ought not reach a decision in a mad rush, for at the very least my own future was at stake. We should, exactly as in military affairs, sleep on it one night. On the next day, Sunday, we made an excursion with the most beautiful weather to Iselberg Mountain. Here on the high lookout of the freedom fighter Andreas Hofer, we reached the following resolution after long reflection. We would turn around, for otherwise, as fate always ordains it, if we continued onward, our mother would die. If we returned, she might well regain her health. In the first case we would make reproaches against ourselves for the rest of our lives, but in the latter case we would spare ourselves, and perhaps even a more pleasant future lay in that direction. If we traveled onward and mother recovered, we would receive the reproaches personally from her; if we turned back home, however, it could also turn out that before we entered our home, she would already have been buried. We specifically had our wits about us. In the latter case we would relieve ourselves above all of this great reproach. It was our love for our mother that led us to turn around. I mention this, including the whole journey into the unknown, because it gave me more in relation to National Socialism than I could ever have received back in my hometown. [D 13]

Herr D.'s acute deliberation dramatically returned him to the womb of the German folk community. It is challenging to imagine a more self-reflective exercise of agency guiding all subsequent events. The explicit cognitions make untenable Bearman and Stovel's reports that while "being" a Nazi, "cognitions never bridge events" and that "cognitions are relatively isolated from local events, and are *never* reflected back into the realm of action."

How did the apparent inaccuracy originate? In the abridgement, the same incident is pared yet present: "We decided to stay in Munich overnight. We went to Iselberg, and there we made up our minds to go home. Love for our mother drew us." Here Abel's condensation of the story well into the period of Nazi membership, right side of figure 2.1, features clauses such as "we made up our minds" that moved action ("to go home"). The quantitative report that such linking "never" occurs is baffling. The autobiographer in the real document dramatizes self-reflection and self-initiated action in many other ways, as in box 2.2.

In the blurred genre of text coding, a text is indexed neither with humanist values as a sharable literary opus nor with scientific values as an information bank.

BOX 2.2   HERR D.'S AGENCY AS A NAZI

Introspection leads to travel: "In addition there were almost forceful reasons to benefit from a change of atmosphere, so that once and for good I would resolve things for myself [schneller mit mir fertig würde]. Such family issues one should not discuss, but I can say that these circumstances made it very easy to depart from my homeland for an indefinite period. It was on September 2 that I departed" [D 12].

Independent decision reaffirmed: "My sister accompanied me, as on so many journeys, this one too. From Frankfurt am Main to Nürnberg the line of travel took us to Munich. Here already we received a lot of letters. In almost every message they [the family] wanted to persuade us to turn around to home. That we did not" [D 13].

Independent thinking contrary to the party line: "The results of this election [the ebbing of Nazi votes in 1932] did not demoralize us. When I came back from Bernkastel with my brother late on election Sunday, where we listened to the semi-official election returns coming in, there I secretly fetched my backpack and put it in order with the necessary travel gear for myself, for I believed, now the hour had arrived, in which we should have to battle our way to state power with violence. I did not reveal this, my secret thought, even to my brother" [D 14].[18]

Lacking the imperatives of either perspective, norms for citing traceable sources may be suspended. Although a verbatim quotation from Herr D. appears in "Becoming a Nazi," this does not prompt a note as to which document is used [76]. As I would frame it, only when the coding apparatus itself replaces the sources to vouch for reality could social "science" rest on unattributed passages from an unmentioned abridgment corresponding to an unnamed archival file. Since the causes of this omission are systemic to the zone of qualitative coding, the opacity is normal rather than heedless.[19]

As a delicate anatomical whole, the scientific graphing hinges entirely on passages arbitrarily discarded. As Bearman and Stovel present it, "the most important nodes are those that bridge sub-sequences" [88]. To remove pieces from the board is like removing dominoes from a cause-effect chain. Narrative ties that the autobiographer may have labored to configure fail to appear at all. As in box 2.1, recovering these pieces suggests to me that the lack of webbing in the period of "being" a Nazi results artificially from chopping.

Even in the key of ritual, the matter of how perpetrators of the Holocaust emerged out of the twentieth century demands some earnest verisimilitude. Bearman and Stovel reject the political scientist Peter Merkl's variable-analysis of the Abel collection because it was distanced from "real lives" and "real process" in favor of a "tasteless cut and paste job" [72]. They write that "[o]ur specific substantive goal is to explore some of the pathways through which ordinary men and women became Nazis before the seizure of power" [70]. They warrant the objectivity of their result: "The position and role of elements reveal motive endogenously," that is, from inside the autobiographer's own world [75]. They enhance the reality effect by citing multiple archival sources: "In this instance, and in other NSDAP narratives, we observe the same general process: the Nazi self emerges from the elision of social relations through contact with other Nazis" [89]. Bearman and Stovel promise their diagramming captures the gist of numerous stories in their collection [69, 71, 89]: "The same pattern is present in almost all other becoming stories. One woman feels more and more like a Nazi as she progressively loses her eldest son, husband, and youngest son," they write. "With each loss she is drawn closer to the movement" [86]. These extensive historical conclusions mean "Becoming a Nazi" functions as more than a thought experiment. What is it that is going on here?

If findings rest on only the substitute document, why ornament them with such detail as "[t]he narrative of becoming has a density of 0.0174 (n of nodes = 139) while the being narrative has a density of 0.0093 (n of nodes = 142)"? Why fuss over mathematical procedures for winnowing data down to the core units whose removal would break the story apart [81] when the core has already been removed by substituting the airbrushed for the real text? Ritual, Victor Turner has written, "inverts, perhaps lies to itself, and puts everything so to speak into the subjunctive mood as well as the reflexive voice... the subjunctive mood of a verb is used to express supposition, desire, hypothesis, or possibility, rather than stating actual facts..."[20] The anthropologist Turner signaled that ritual is not intentionally false, only that it liberates practitioners from worry about being held to account in the mundane world. As Franco Moretti remarked in the concluding sentence of his book on coding novels, "opening new conceptual possibilities seemed more important than justifying them in every detail."[21] The coding circuit lets researchers try out in symbols what is on their minds—"experiment" both as playful trial and as lab science.

"Becoming a Nazi" presses us through the three stages of a rite of passage formulated by Van Gennep: it separates us from secular life, then moves us onward into liminal play, and finally reincorporates us into society with purified repertoires for redeeming ourselves and others.[22] Its noteworthy features—use of theory to estrange us from quotidian social life, playful inferences from iconic correspondences between the symbols, imposition back onto reality of truths derived from graphic symbolism—make sense by their function in ritual ordering. Our age proliferates cultural artifacts that cross biography with fiction, televised death with theater, or daily news with a Daily Show.[23] In the era of crossed genres, reductive sociologists digest even the Nazi calamity via such experiment as "science."

THE PHASE OF SEPARATION

Two techniques in conjunction erect the ritual platform for "Becoming a Nazi." First, a purifying social theory disorients us for narrow reinterpretation of data; then black-box coding procedures convert text into requisite unit "facts."

The network theory with which Bearman and Stovel initiate the proceedings has us view individuals as points defined only by their social relations to other points, accomplishing what Victor Turner called "the reduction of initiands to a sort of common human *prima materia*."[24] We are empty but for our connections: "The identity formation process is typically the product of the accretion of relationships" [75]. If I comprehend, the primary divide between kinds of network positions is between persons who manage diverse types of relations to others flexibly versus those who have rigid, confined relations to others. Diverse "role complements" sustain a multiplex identity, whereas homogeneous "role complements" sustain a master identity, like that of the Nazis, who by this theory are pulled away from family relations.

By modeling Nazi Party membership as adoption of a master identity, network theory makes Nazis similar to people closer at hand: "Similar dynamic becoming processes are also likely to operate in other contexts in which individuals adopt revolutionary identities that prescribe this worldly action in pursuit of movement goals, as well as for more mundane conversion narratives and the narratives of adherents of Alcoholics Anonymous" [73]. Bearman and Stovel write:

> Alcoholics (those who have gone through AA, and so consider themselves alcoholics) are alcoholics in all their social relations (Cain, 1987). Flagellants beat themselves whether anyone is watching or not as an enactment of the millennium. The action-set of Puritans is the same whether the relation acted on is a "father" relation or an "acquaintance" relation. [75][25]

These disjointed-yet-eternal recurrences let the reader imagine an ahistorical realm "beyond or outside the time which measures secular processes," as characterizes ritual expectancy and communication.[26]

The odd insulating effect of this homogenizing theory is recaptured if we ask who outside the ritual arena believes Nazis were handicapped in modulating the roles they assumed toward different kinds of people? Even at the "total institution" of Auschwitz, the evidence is overwhelming that zealous camp administrators functioned in the main by compartmentalizing, not by homogenizing, the social roles of revolutionary Nazi, lover, physician, father, scientific researcher, and so forth.[27] No one can forget the words of the Nazi hunter Simon Wiesenthal: mass murderers, Wiesenthal famously said, "were the same people who lovingly kissed their children goodbye in the morning and then a few hours later were gassing or shooting Jews."[28] As leader of the S.S., Heinrich Himmler toiled to perfect the architecture of murder. Yet Himmler's daughter Gudrun fondly held on to memories of her father's playfulness in Tip-Kick and of his carefree fishing outings with her siblings during the bloodiest years of the Holocaust. As she recalled it, "he always had time for us" and "was always there when a problem cropped up," suggesting Himmler adapted to specific needs of his children.[29] Zealous Nazis retained flexible "action-sets" as ever.

Social science carried out in a ritual arena delivers revelations apart from contingent events, however, so major "findings" are determined tautologously. If I understand Bearman and Stovel, they deduce what gives someone the master identity of a Nazi before any "facts" emerge from their experiment:

> By a master identity we mean an identity that gives rise to actions which is insensitive to context. Everyday identities give rise to action that expresses, and is constructed through, its relational basis...Since the master identity is insensitive to others, it cannot be built from relationally with others...The specific problem we confront is modeling the process of becoming when it operates through the elision of social relations, as is *necessarily* the case with master identity formation. [75; my emphasis]

Adopting a master identity is "necessarily" a story of "the elision of social relations," which posits at the outset all that is to be demonstrated, as with QED in geometry proofs. A careless abridgment of Herr D.'s words satisfies circular discovery equally as well as his real words. The tautology also explains why massive evidence from historians about the multiplex social ties of Nazis before 1933 could be disregarded. In 1976 political sociologist Juan Linz set the tone when he emphasized research on Nazi recruitment was shifting away from "isolated mass men" to "the gaining of control by devoted activists of a complex *pre-existing set of networks*."[30] In the decades since Linz's encapsulation, evidence has mounted that early Nazi joiners were not drifters but opinion leaders entwined in community organizations.[31] For example, the political scientist Peter Merkl concluded from the Abel autobiographies that for youth in Herr D.'s cohort, participation in civil associations prior to joining the Nazi party was "astounding."[32] About two-thirds of younger Nazis in the collection belonged to athletic, patriotic, labor, employer, religious, or paramilitary associations. This embeddedness can scarcely be reconciled with Bearman and Stovel's portrait from the same documents of proto-Nazis "drifting in a world stripped of social relations," out of which "the new Nazi self emerges" [85]. Bearman and Stovel were perfectly familiar with Merkl's research, which they footnoted to accent the novelty of their method. In a sequestered arena, ritual washes away sedimented scholarship for fresh insight.

So far we have considered how the network perspective alienates the reader from mundane contexts and formally empties out a dehistoricized space that is ideal for graphically "reenvisioning" the process of becoming a Nazi. Let us examine how the act of coding creates a substitute depiction of the substitute document. There are two questions: Is the black box of coding retrospectively intelligible when we compare the outputted morphology of the narrative links with the source text? Second, proceeding from the coding results, do we have a robust procedure for understanding what pathways extracted from life stories mean?

THE BLACK BOX OF CODING

For a ritual arena's patterns to be taken as revelation, they have to be given by grace, not by a questionable process that leads you seamlessly back to the quotidian. This performative logic mandates that the procedure generating the diagram of results, figure 2.1, goes undiscussed. According to Bearman and Stovel, their coding "works without imputation of motive, and without recourse to abstractions that propose independent and largely non-measurable effects of 'culture,' 'symbolic constructions,' or 'cultural agencies'" [74]. Instead, they measure "the *observable* narrative structure of life stories" by connections between clauses [69; my emphasis]. Let me try to disclose how the task of coding that Bearman and Stovel undertake is unprecedented in the literature; how most linguists and cognitive scientists do not think that complex narrative structures are "observable" at all; how Nazi autobiographies pose additional coding challenges since they operate in a culture foreign to ours; and how the complex voice of an autobiography of spiritual conversion complicates the enterprise. The "data" are interpretive guesses all the way down, with no bottoming out in ascertainable givens.

AN UNPRECEDENTED UNDERTAKING

In my experience, cognitive scientists have attempted coding like that of Bearman and Stovel for only brief, childlike reports.[33] The linguist they cite as their guide, William Labov, never construed narrative linkages, only the temporal ordering of clauses.[34] Bearman and Stovel offer impromptu metaphors for what they mean by a cognitive link, without clear indicators: "Arcs between elements are coded as present if one element 'leads to' another" [76]. These ties comprise "imputations, cognitive linking" [89]. They "are the connections, or imputations, made by the author in putting the story together" [76]. Only "the author's explicit connections between elements" are counted as links [76]. Or, rephrased, they are "causal relations between elements" [88]. Bearman and Stovel produce figure 2.2 to illustrate their procedure, and best of luck to anyone trying to recover the coding.

UNOBSERVABLE MEANING

An author rarely signals a "thus" between clauses to make linkage "explicit," Bearman and Stovel's indicator for coding the presence of a tie.[35] Sociologist Harvey Sacks showed in a memorable way that whether we see a connection between sentences depends utterly on cultural expertise. Sacks laboriously unpacked how we make sense

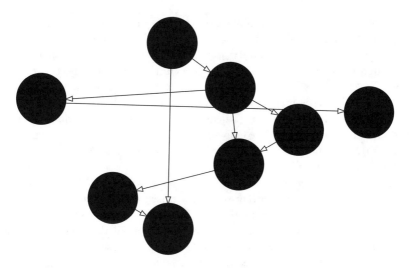

Figure 2.2   Graphic representation of the following narrative sequence: "When I was 16 years old my mother bought me some brown trousers. If she had known the significance of the color, she would never have bought them for me. I told her that they pleased me, and she also bought some for my brother...now I felt as though I were half a Nazi."

Source: "Becoming a Nazi," p. 77. Time runs from top down.

of "The baby cried. The mommy picked it up." Only placing mommy's action in our shared script for "mommies" makes it seem like the two sentences are describing a cry that provokes a response, a "brought-about" pairing.[36] We see "it" as a baby, the mommy not just picking up the baby like a grocery bag but intending to soothe the baby, the mommy as mother of that particular baby, and more. "Explicit"?

To literary minds, novels styled with loosely sequential sentences captivate us by demanding that we fill in the gaps, our own "meaning performance."[37] Dramatic omission and suggestive possibility in narratives stimulate our engagement as readers but render consistent coding nearly impossible.[38] If the author as an adult steps back into the perspective of childhood to speculate about connections between narrated events, do we score hypotheticals as a "causal relation between elements"? [D 2]. If not, we deny narrative coherence Herr D. labored to consider; if yes, we turn his questions into statements. Herr D. emphasized, "In this way, and in similar ways, I often thought, without in reality exactly knowing that I was thinking at all" [D 2]. If he inserts a formal "since" or "because" or "next" between two incongruous sentences about his childhood, is there a "leads to" relation ipso facto by grammar [D 6, 8]? If yes, we accept wording like a computer; if no, we discount Herr D.'s markers with our own perception. This kind of pervasive dissonance between the told versus the telling dissuades the cognitive scientists who reveal their coding protocols from tackling first-person reminiscence.[39]

ALIEN CULTURE

Treacherous issues for coding become intractable when we move to an alien historical context. In Herr D.'s text, we have to impose our own calls to decide if in the foreign Nazi universe Herr D. thinks two sentences show a "leads-to" relation that might not be suggested by schemas in our own culture.[40] In Hitler's worldview, art and insignia were such motivators that Hitler saw it as his job to personally design the uniforms and parade standards. In such a culture, Herr D.'s adjacent sentences about the government lifting a ban on Nazi uniforms and about more energetically working for the Nazis may express cause-effect—or not. If we put ourselves into the Nazi mindset, we may create a denser web of "leads to" relations among the events, especially after 1933. The following sequential affirmations can be united by linkages [D 16]: Hitler, who makes words come true, promises to give the German people liberty and bread and (thus?), next sentence, there is a decline in unemployment, and (therefore?) everywhere people are more goal-oriented and optimistic, and in so doing people are (thus?) inspired to live in a folk community, which (therefore?) inspires the working class to honorary deeds, leading (?) to hopefulness and improvements back in Herr D.'s home. From inside the Hitlerite model of causality, in which words and mass feelings are decisive motors, clauses about speeches and excitement are interchaining directive events. Is it not classic for outside sociologists to lose sight of "cause-effect" ties between occurrences that the natives see? Conversely, when can we *not* insert "thus" between sentences?[41]

AUTOBIOGRAPHIES AS JOURNEYS

Autobiographies about spiritual conversion pose unique challenges for coding the "presence" of links between clauses. The narrators describe the primary drivers of action as inner resolutions that sponsor multifarious actions besides more overt triggers.[42] As Herr D. describes this kind of umbrella cause,

> I raised my hand in an oath of fealty to Germany and to Adolf Hitler. Now I believed myself to be a Nazi, since I had after all sworn. Not all of this fit together completely, but in any case I wanted to be one now. I had to keep my promise, by further aspiring to strive to put myself inwardly at the disposal of the ideal. It is certainly no sense of superiority, it is much more the fulfillment of an inner demand for clarity. [D 8]

He describes his succeeding actions as attempts to deepen his insight into the Nazi ideal, reasserting their connections to his original epiphany. He continues to recast events as signs for whether he is "on the right journey" [D 10]. Now if we read Herr D.'s actions as logical results of these character-transforming moments of reflection, the loose morphology in the "being" period becomes densely interlocking. For he repeats themes of comradeship and authenticity to show how the changes in character interlock in toto. Alternatively, if the analyst refuses to see the accounts of inward dispositional change toward a Nazi identity as "causes" of Nazi action, then the methodology denies by fiat the organizing premise of an autobiography that is composed as spiritual realization.

Bearman and Stovel underscored that they pried open "observable narrative structure" [69], whereas it can scarcely be said to exist. In its place we find behind-the-scenes guesses whose reliability depends incalculably on radiating construals of culture.[43] If the results presented in "Becoming a Nazi" were to be taken for empirical research, would not Bearman and Stovel present their procedures in detail to show they can standardize measurement of "morphology" across cultural contexts as claimed [88]? Instead, the phase of separation requires an obscuring of coding technique to insulate the outputs against pedestrian questioning. What is a narrative link? The only warrant for validity is that created circularly by privileging ritual action independent of reference.

In each demonstration study dissected in this book, the coding circuit requires the researcher to dance between interpretive and scientific frames, forgetting what he or she knows in one frame to selectively reintroduce it in another. First the researcher grapples with texts to reduce their contextual complexity to outputted "facts." Then the investigator forgets this interpretive work for the sake of rearranging the atomic "facts" as mobile pieces. This canceling of a thicket of meaning enables Bearman and Stovel to treat figure 2.1 as a "morphological foundation" rather than as a paradoxical rendering. Further along, to justify glossing the stripped-down morphology, the researcher turns back to remember selectively some particulars of the context. Only a ritual theory of distinct phases, each with its own tunnel logic, can explain how the performance as a whole keeps running.

ARE NETWORKS STORY-LIKE?

Imagine that the data in figure 2.1 were derived from a computer that had supernaturally "map quested" the routes for getting from one clause to another in Herr D.'s story. Would an indisputable graph lead us to the corresponding verbal concept, that of a narrative world? Hardly, as narrative theorist David Herman summed up.[44] A map is only a navigational tool between vacant locations empty of plot. Stories develop contrary-to-fact expectations, what-if dilemmas, and metaphorical foreshadowing. A story swells to a thematic climax rather than to a blank node. This-brings-about-that linkages may erect standard units for comparison, yet verbally such chains are banal. The linguist to whom Bearman and Stovel attribute their coding format, William Labov, argued that the sort of quasi-causal chains Bearman and Stovel take as full-fledged self-expression are so primitive they characterize only children's competency.[45] To impose "standard network measures" on narratives, it seems Bearman and Stovel override their own guide's stress on disconnected evaluation as the criterion for mature narrative.

Converted to "being" a Nazi, Herr D. accents declarations that intensify the personal significance of upholding Nazi ideals despite obstacles. "Also here I had learned on my great journey: remain sincere and do not lead loose the way toward one's folk comrades"; "All things considered, these were downright interesting days in Saarbrücken, provided one was able just later to get used to the method of struggle"; "After this first time, when I realized how easy it was to conduct oneself in the sense of a Nazi, there it came for the first time into full awareness, that one understands this ideal only if one has felt it at the bottom of one's heart." These meta-comments are self-reflective and orient action, but do not seem to feed into temporally definite chains of clauses.

A puzzle in "What is going on here?" is why Bearman and Stovel persisted with network measures of narrative coherence when these contradicted both Labov and the patent narrative skill of Herr D. in the primary evidence. A life story often ends with a "coda," which psychologist Jerome Bruner's characterizes as "a retrospective evaluation of what it all might mean, a feature that also returns the hearer or reader from the 'there and then' of the narrative to the here and now of the telling."[46] Herr D.'s coda is about how volunteer activity in 1933–1934 helped him recognize "the noble meaning of our ideal" [16]. Notice the literary format of an extended coda registers as "disorganization" in figure 2.1, because the reflecting cannot prompt further action.

THE LIMINAL PHASE

In full-throated liminal play, the researcher uses the equipment on stage to subvert conventional sense for deeper insight. As in Victor Turner's characterization, the researcher disposes over "symbol-vehicles," the detached codes, that can be scrambled to reveal counterintuitive meanings.[47] In this phase of "anything goes," it can look as if "Becoming a Nazi" simulates facts that have no origin.

Ponder how Bearman and Stovel claim that Herr D. associates his love of order with straight rows:

> For example, in our illustrative story, one of the author's first thoughts is that nature is beautiful. This is represented in Fig. 2 as the sequence of nodes 316, which culminates in node 23, the recognition that nature is beautiful. This love of nature becomes associated in his [Herr D.'s] narrative with order—with straight rows of graves in cemeteries—order that is distinguished from the chaos of the republican period. [87]

"Straight rows of graves in cemeteries"? An invention, as far as one can tell. No mention in either the full original or in the Abel abridgment is to be found of "straight rows," headstones, or of "order" at a cemetery, period. The only description of a burial yard occurs in a run-on Herr D. delivers about visiting the warfield of Verdun:

> Even if in the landscape today very little of the grave fields from the frightful [World War I] battles of matériel is to be seen anymore, nonetheless the remnants of the Douaumont and Vaux forts loomed up against heaven as gigantic witnesses to this great happening and especially of the Bone House of Douaumont [*Ossuaire de Douaumont*] in whose memorial chapel I imagined myself able to hear the bequests of the unknown soldiers of our fatherland, who rest here now in foreign soil. [D 7]

No columns of graves here. The rationale for a memorial chapel at the Ossuaire was the tragic inability to reassemble body remnants into corpses for burial. When Herr D. recounts the long-lasting emotional effect from "war graves of thousands of German men" at Verdun, he features its guidance "on the way to a folk community," without reference to rows or order in that journey [D 7].

Whereas Bearman and Stovel stake the value of their method on empirical immediacy, their construal of "straight rows of graves in cemeteries" resembles avant-garde jouissance. Support for their parallel discovery that "love of nature becomes associated in his narrative with order" is equally evanescent. When they refer to a sequence that "culminates in the recognition that nature is beautiful," I think this is it:

> Here [in Barmen] I became able to see in a double sense. First taken purely literally. After several eye surgeries over the course of two years (each time I was treated in the clinic for about four to six weeks between longer time intervals) I regained my full visual acuity. How pretty nature was, now that I could properly gaze at it [Wie schön war die Natur, da ich sie nun so recht bestaunen konnte]. [D 2]

The "recognition that nature is beautiful" concerns nothing more than a ten-year-old enjoying restored eyesight. Nowhere can I find nature connected to order, and Bearman and Stovel present neither page numbers for mentions of "order" nor text examples of "order" for coding. With the blurring of genres in social "science," neither the humanistic care for citation nor scientific transparency for "data" operate.

Deep play in "Becoming a Nazi" is iconographic: the sheering of complex narrative ties visually in figure 2.1 supposedly represents the breakdown of Herr D.'s management of complex social ties upon joining the movement [89]. Should this analogy between breakdowns be taken soberly? If Herr D.'s self at the time of writing in 1934 is incoherent, how could that weakness *not* be projected onto the opening of his autobiography? If the data are cross-sectional from one sitting, so to speak, how did Herr D. mobilize strong narrative selfhood at one instant of writing and lose it the next?[48] Only by cordoning off a ritual arena in figure 2.1 can we imagine a closed causal environment in which variation in narrative form through time expresses changes in social being. Nothing more than insulating atomic facts in their own diagrammatic space rules out interference from circumstances more immediate to the narrative's writing. In reality, the shapes of Nazi autobiographies vary across archival collections according to how the writers interpreted their prompts.[49] When the messy process of creating signs as contingent intermediaries is of no matter, and when they become the essence of social being, one has entered the only realm where symbolic play merges with metaphysical truth: ritual. Previewing, we find in the liminal phase of "Becoming a Nazi" that

> —major themes in the story are mathematically scanned for relative network centrality, but this objective measurement turns the story on its head, legislating that what is declaratively prominent will fail to register as narratively connective;
> —messages are tallied from the frequencies and locations of contents, reversing the more essential communication by marked absence and by repeated metaphors;
> —the major finding that Herr D. progressively separates from social relations such as family is based on counting departures without counting reunions;
> —permuting the "data" yields counts that are interpreted as high or low, but there are no baseline comparisons to ascertain whether the measures have scalar import at all; and
> —the scientific worldview takes the occurrence of types of clauses as representing types of social relations, but the interpretive perspective shows the occurrence of the clauses are driven by story themes independent of actual social relations.

STATISTICS AS A PLAY OF WIT

To refill each empty node with meaning, Bearman and Stovel return to the autobiography to categorize each node as containing themes such as "order" or "anti-Semitism." Then they calculate the aggregate "power centrality" of each theme based on how strategically its mentions are positioned in the network. The statistic registers not just linkages from an element, but how tightly those linkages feed into controlling intersections [86]. Anti-Semitism, Bearman and Stovel find, is "characterized by low centrality" in Herr D.'s autobiography and in "most" of the others in the Abel collection [88]. Anti-Semitism is not a bridge theme and mathematically "rarely drives the narrative" [88].

The intricate calculation that anti-Semitism is "always in the background" [88] looks absurd if you examine Herr D.'s words:

> When I was all of eight years, the youngest of my two brothers died. He died in Bonn, by demonstrable evidence the result of a groundlessly undertaken operation by a Jewish head surgeon. Since I deeply loved my deceased brother, there rose in me as an eight-year old a rage against the head surgeon, and this still not entirely graspable hatred intensified itself with my age to a revulsion against all that was Jewish. [D 1]

> One of the acquaintances of my uncle, a baptized [converted] Jew, always brought me candy when he came. The name of the Jew has escaped me, but I certainly remember exactly that I never touched his sweets. Such events of my early youth, of which I can recount only a few due to the brevity of the [essay] content, brought up questions for me, most of which I could not answer on my own due to my age. There was an urge in me to clarify all the questions, even the simplest. [D 3]

> Once I carried the Swastiska into school. At first it did not bother the teacher at all, instead only two Jewish boys the same age as me. With them I got into the first tussle in my life. The two Jewish boys came against me, I defended myself with all my strength and was able finally to regard myself as the victor, for I had bent into more of a hook the nose of one of them and when this one saw blood, he retreated. Now I was justly proud to carry my insignia, except that it was for only a short time, since the teacher forbade me from carrying the Swastiska, because of the two Jews naturally. Thus were the Jews nevertheless victors in the end. [D 5]

Jews are pivotal in the autobiography, because precocious revulsion against them binds Herr D.'s childhood to his adult wisdom. Excluding Jews from the forthcoming community provides the thematic continuity to Herr D.'s life. It is so fundamental as not to trigger the isolable, minor deeds that show up in statistics about the story.[50]

Of course there is an impossibility built into measuring explicit references to an ethnic group that by Nazi ideology should be removed from the scene: If a prospective Nazi decides as a child he wants to keep Jews out of his life, *by that fact* Jews are less likely to figure in subsequent personal relationships and direct experience. Vehemently removing Jews from your life would likely lead to their network marginality, all the better to function as an implicit focal contrast to Nazi values.[51] It is ominous that Herr D. dramatizes Jews near the front of his story as foreshadowing, and then Jews disappear.

If "Jews and relations with Jews, also tend to have low centrality" [79] by mechanical counting, this number looks chimerical in the humanist verbal universe. Herr D. submitted his autobiography to party administrators, so it pivots on the means by which he supported Nazi electoral success and takeover. Since a Nazi did not battle Jews in the streets to accomplish the seizure of power (but did battle leftists) and since a Nazi did not try to convert Jews to the Nazi cause (but did try to convert other Germans), it is predictable, as the historian Richard Bessel reasoned, that anti-Semitism would play only a subordinate role in pushing forward personal events in Nazi narratives.[52] The centrality statistic would likely run orthogonal to the brutal yet disconnected declarations that one joined the Nazis out of hatred for Jews.[53] The Abel autobiographies do not always allude to Jews overtly, but when they do, they often highlight Jewish responsibility for macro-historical disasters: defeat in the Great War, corruption of morals, or economic exploitation. Incidental use of the word "Jewish" to designate corruption best affirms as commonsense the odious status of Jews.[54] Narrating the permeating significance of Jews for Germany as a whole, the issue behind issues, pushes them out of the foreground of Nazi personal life [84].[55]

Consider the *Ur-Text* of Nazi autobiographies, Hitler's *Mein Kampf*, as a baseline for network estimates of anti-Semitism.[56] In *Mein Kampf*'s initial 50 pages about youth and adulthood, scarcely a mention of Jews occurs. Hitler voluminously penned details of encounters with Social Democratic Unionists and the social bases of trade union politics. Then with an evaluative gloss, he crystallized preceding events with the affirmation that at bottom such topics are manifestations of the Jewish Question.[57] This dramatic condensation of the "meaning" of the opening 50 pages would not be tightly interwoven by quantitative counting of temporal "leads to" junctures. Whether anti-Semitism is complexly "networked" in a web of individual incidents or not has little to do with its virulence.[58] If Bearman and Stovel's work stood in the genre of empirical social science, would not they have shown that their measuring device adduces sensible variation? When the validity of measures is unquestionable, a ritual in which the form of the data is more important than any empirical referents is under way.

A SENSIBLE METRIC FOR "POWER CENTRALITY"?

Of course the "power centrality" statistic is entirely relative, pitting a theme against the others chosen for measurement. The statistic registers nothing except the semantic distinctions the researcher imposes by selecting the categories of coding. The weak "power centrality" of anti-Semitism in the narrative is in comparison to "chaos" and its opposite, "order," as well as "elision" and its opposite, "exposure to Nazis." (By elision the authors signify the denial or breaking of social relations.) Since the foci of these other categories seems relatively vague—"order" for goodness sake—there is scant ground for treating such a hodgepodge of categories as variables in a computation of their relative import for Herr D. Granted that each can assume the same role in calculation as a nominally defined "variable," this mathematical status does not render them sensibly comparable units. Only the confusion of the interpretive and scientific perspectives in the measurement process could generate the illusion that the statistic of power centrality "discovers" meanings in the text rather than "fabricates" meanings through a self-fulfilling apparatus.

In the autobiography it seems obvious that each of these five categories of "element content" [83] taps into semantic fields with incomparable levels of coherence and kinds of presence, and thus with incomparable ways of functioning in a narrative universe. "Order" is a remote connotation, "Jew" as it is counted more arguably a denotation. A broadly defined connotation such as "order" should in the course of things jump out more frequently and centrally than a narrow denotation. A narrative clause that is coded as connoting "order" carries multiple qualities, so the meta-content "order" can piggyback onto innumerable bridging clauses without an independent sense. For example, being impressed with the soldierly enthusiasm of the marching Nazi squads can draw Herr D. closer to the Nazi movement, but would we want to transfer the causal drive these men and their optimism contribute to the story over into the category of "order" instead? When is one coding validly for "order" or for "chaos"? For all we know, had Bearman and Stovel calculated the role of anti-Semitism in comparison to variables defined more concretely, anti-Semitism might pop out as "high" in power centrality.

NOSE-COUNTING VERSUS VERBAL SYSTEMS

Out of many potential meanings any category holds, a text realizes a limited range, depending on how it brings contrasts into play. What matters is how concepts function by contrast within a whole, not how we may count the atomized pieces and geometrically derived locations. In the Abel collection, the adherents to folk-ethnic (*völkisch*) ideology, the Nazi fertilizer, exhibited diverse contrasts between Jews versus Germans. For instance, one autobiographer in the Abel collection opened by announcing "My ancestors were of Aryan lineage."[59] Assigning oneself this status does not lead to other discrete events, so no matter how loudly this sentence and its placement speaks, its network position might be marginal. Another writer defined Jews as self-seeking, only to define the German future by contrast as "laying aside egoistical striving to strive for the folk community."[60] The Nazis supported "brotherly love," a term implicitly interworked again with Jews, who were sometimes said to promote the opposite, "brotherly hate" (*Bruderhass*).

To grasp Herr D.'s story as a verbally integrated whole is to suspend universal categories such as "Chaos," "Order," and "Elision," the ones Bearman and Stovel impose [87]. Such terms are second-order scientist impressions from the geometry of figure 2.1. Herr D., who made no use of them, enshrined the peculiar German concept of a *Volksgemeinschaft* as the centerpiece of his life journey, as recalled in box 2.3.[61] The *Volksgemeinschaft* is an ethnically homogeneous fraternity that can also be translated as "racial community." In the lexicon of German nationalism, folk as adjective designated a movement that was ethnically pure, ancestrally rooted, inspired by peasant lore, and familial. By the late nineteenth century, Jews had became the assumed if implicit contrastive twin, for who else represented aptly what was hybrid, mobile, and urban?[62] Explicit references to Jews alone misses this semantic action.

Box 2.3   CHAMPIONING A *VOLKSGEMEINSCHAFT*

- "The day in Verdun at the war graves of thousands of German men became for me the point of departure on the path to the **folk community**" [D 7].
- "I experienced how imperative the so strongly emphasized **folk community** is for our people. I got to know genuine comradeship in the SA-quarters" [D 13].
- "In my departure essay from the advanced school of business, I chose this from among the topics arranged by my German teacher, a Nazi: '**Folk Community**, a Necessity of the Day!'" [D 14].
- "'**Folk Community**' is the goal of our Führer, to make his people so powerful, that through its recuperated unity it is always great and—strong" [D 14].
- "In the S.A. hostels we were all brothers in one great family. Overall I found a Nazi folk solidarity that was one hundred percent in Bavaria and Schwaben more than elsewhere... For the aspired **folk community** is the foundation for a strong, free German Reich" [D 14].
- "[W]henever I put all of my body and soul behind my ideal, I felt obligated to it from that moment forward, as it called for a **folk of brothers** and for destroying everything that would stand as a hindrance in its way" [D 14].
- "Since National Socialism incorporated into itself the state leadership, it was never forgotten in this to work toward a **folk community** and to cultivate it true to the inner wishes of the Führer, so that it would someday include as well every ethnic brother" [D 16].
- "I now know, that our German people must pass through the gateway of the **folk community** to reach the sun, in the way that the Führer wishes it, for in it [*Volksgemeinschaft*] we find the strength to do so, it is the unleasher of the primeval, slumbering German ideals of freedom and heroism in us" [D 17].

The concept of folk community enters Herr D.'s life through hospitality and commensality in an ethnic brotherhood. He is "irrepressibly proud" to eat at the regulars' table with other Nazis [D 13]. In childhood, he consumed nothing given him by a Jew, even a baptized Jew who was a regular visitor to the family. Refusal of nourishment from this alien versus sharing bread with party members (without mention of Jews) forms an emblematic pairing whose intricacy will not be captured by appreciating each incident as a countable unit or by aggregating each into "equivalency classes" [83]. Early events presage much later ones by metaphor.[63] In a humanist universe it seems they function as symbols of a whole, the *Volksgemeinschaft* springing to life.

It is easy for social "scientists" to label an eerily monolithic Nazi party as opposite to traditional family, so sheering clan ties appears requisite for commitment to a cultish movement [86]. For Herr D., however, casting *Volksgemeinschaft* as blood kin writ large initiates mutually supportive interweaving of family and society. In childhood he refers to his sister as a good "comrade" (*Kamerad*), a term that functions in German like the English "mate" [D 1]. It is the same word he uses for his fellow Nazis. And if Herr D. treats sibling relations in family analogously to party bonds, he treats party bonds as sibling relations.[64] Herr D. sees the Nazi spirit as a healing force in his conflicted family: "At home things did not always go so peacefully and I had to be amazed, that the sharpest battles were set aside, whenever we discussed National Socialism. Is that not an unusual power, that resides in our Nazi ideal?" [D 8]. In the autobiography as an interworked whole, national unity and family unity magnify each other, leading us to ponder how Bearman and Stovel calculated the elision of family in the first place.

CODING REVERSES THE BASIC MEANING OF THE STORY

"[T]he new Nazi self emerges from the elision of social relations" [85], Bearman and Stovel compute from figure 2.1. Individuals who become members of a movement that imposes on them one master, totalitarian identity are "not firmly rooted in family" [86]. Bearman and Stovel calculate that for Herr D., "elision of social relationships is also significantly more central than expected by chance" [87–88]. Yet the source itself reveals almost immediately that tabulating the nodes with "elision" creates an effect opposite to the verbal whole. Herr D. hails from a petty bourgeois family in the countryside. His siblings travel to other towns for education and for setting up businesses, but all, including Herr D., circulate continually back to the family hearth. The reason Herr D. demonstrates "mobility" and "elides" kin ties is that he continually returns to the family as well! Unlike many of the autobiographers, Herr D. in his opening barely mentions his parents. His nuclear family does not start out in one piece: the children at early ages are packed off to schools until only Herr D., the youngest of seven, remains home: "When this sister as well went away to boarding school, I was mostly alone" [D 1]. From such a beginning, family togetherness has nowhere to go over time but up, triumphing in the years of Nazi membership.

Supposing elision were overly prominent in Herr D.'s story, how would we norm it against those of other German youth? When Herr D. was a teenager, his family constellation would have tested anyone's emotional commitment:

> To be frank, I have to say that with us in our family it was not any different than in most others. There were often blowups at home, which would even lead—more than once—to violent acts. My brother, as the only son at home, was of course party to them also. Whenever I was at home during [school] vacations, I as well was drawn in more often than not and naturally always took the side of my mother and sister, since to me it seemed to be truly dastardly to beat girls. Despite this however I got along with my brother well when it came to our outlook. [D 6]

Upon dedicating himself to the Nazi cause, Herr D. structures the plot by family relations. As we know, after he joins the party, he decides to *leave* his Nazi colleagues for Italy, probably to escape the family pressure cooker (judging by his description of "family issues" and urgent need of fresh air). Sister in tow, he changes course to return to his mother, as noted earlier. Box 2.4 shows the continuing importance

---

BOX 2.4   HERR D.'S INTENSE FAMILY TIES WHILE "BEING" A NAZI

- "At the end of February the first [Nazi] meetings in my own home town emerged. My brother led them, and it was a pleasure to be able to attend them" [D 8].
- "In the next months I remained at [the family] home. Now I could with all my strength help my brother, who in the meantime had become the [Nazi] political leader of our county" [D 11].
- "At this time I was often in Saarbrücken. Here I helped my sister out with her store" [D 11].
- "Because I was often over at my sister's, I already knew some party comrades in Saarbrücken" [D 12].
- "One ought not speak about such family issues" [D 12].
- "My sister accompanied me, as on many journeys..." [D 13].
- "If we travel on, our mother dies..." [D 13].
- "When we returned home, and we visited our mother in Trier, she was already on the way to recovery" [D 14].
- "When I came home with my brother late on election Sunday..." [D 14].
- "At the end of January I traveled to Saarbrücken again to my sister" [D 15].
- "Exactly as I was walking across the railroad street from my sister's shop..." [D 15].
- "Everywhere there was new, fresh life, new courage and new hope. At the end of October I went back to [the family] home. Here a great deal had already changed. Here, too, new movement!" [D 16].
- "One of the first new laws [after 1933] that was decided was the temporary suspension of the forced auctioning off of farming establishments. Ours fell under this provision. Now I did not need to travel back home, the miracle had taken place" [D 15].
- "In the middle of November I went with my brother to the Nazi county leadership meeting. Also for this I had learned on my great journey to always remain natural and to never lose the way to one's ethnic comrades" [D 16].

---

of family ties after Herr D. is accustomed to "being" a Nazi.[65] More important is the emplotment. On the eve of Hitler's seizure of power while the family awaited eviction from the homestead due to collapsing finances, it rallied in a sacramental gathering under the *Tannenbaum*:

> Thus was the execution of the death sentence delayed by eight weeks. In that case we would have been driven out of our parental home! Only the occurrence of a miracle could prevent that from coming to pass. I will not easily forget Christmas 1932! A National Socialist Christmas celebration in our family! Under the Christmas tree through consecration by a homespun, earnest ceremony a German family found new courage again and firmer conviction." [D 15]

This high point of revival of faith and salvation by Hitler is narratively interwoven with the final Nazi surge to power, doubling the "miracle" as familial and political at once.

Bearman and Stovel report that the tearing of kin and other social attachments is a distinctive precondition for being "biographically available" [86] for Nazi recruitment, and that this breakage accelerates in the process of becoming a Nazi [89]. Yet Herr D.'s ties to family as a Nazi seem compelling for a young man proceeding through his twenties. How could Bearman and Stovel square evidence such as that in box 2.4 with their report of "drifting in a world stripped of social relations" [85]? From the framework of ritual, it is as if they reified the outputted "facts" as more secure than the context from which they were extracted. But if we look at the social trajectory in the evidence itself, the eliding of relations seems to be part of a middle-class route to adult maturity. Boarding schools, graduations, successful medical treatments at the town of a relative—all produce frequent severing of ties, hardly a feature distinctive to the process of "becoming" a Nazi. Herr D.'s departures from the remote family vineyard are often family-organized, take place with other family members, or transport him to extended family. Unless reunions are measured, how could an analyst in the abstractive key of "science" create such a measure of elision without inadvertently cooking what the departures signify?

From their calculations of "elision" nodes, Bearman and Stovel compute that "[t]he characteristic features of the NSDAP becoming story is decreasing centrality of relational elements and traditional bases of identity (e.g. kin, church, school, and work) in the narrative of becoming" (86). But an ordinary reader of the original is likely to notice instead how these customary social relations incubate and reinforce Herr D.'s Nazi affiliation. Herr D.'s father is apparently a nationalist conservative, a disposition that often favored eventual Nazi allegiance. In this milieu, Herr D. overhears family consternation over loss of old symbols and the humiliations of Weimar [D 1–2]. The cliché about manly character imparted to him hearkens to the Kaiser's era: "[T]here, that man is still out of the good old days before the war" [D 4]. Such conversation, Herr D. recalls, carried "political undertones." Herr D.'s brother initiates him into the Nazi articles of faith [D 7]. Herr D.'s family also seems to have volunteered refuge to 14 traveling Nazis proselytizers for three days, although this harboring caused police to search the premises [D 10]. Herr D. uses secondary school as a base from which to learn more about the Nazis when he befriends an older classmate:

> Since his parents had a hair salon, I always went over there. At that place I often had a chance to talk with him. I must say that these discussions, if they were only a few and brief, were of great value to me and gave an answer to me about much, although on the other hand they also raised to mind many ambiguities, which occupied me once again and in fact continually more than before. [D 6]

When Herr D.'s brother guides Herr D. to his initiatory Nazi ceremony, the event is an homage to fallen soldiers, coinciding with the period of All Saints Day and Armistice Day. The memorial laying of a wreath seems little different than services conducted by veterans' organizations in town. Herr D.'s attending might be interpreted as participating in the homegrown associational life of civil society.[66] In sum, the institutions that steered Herr D.'s route to Nazi belonging—family, school, barbershop, neighborhood—seem like "traditional bases of identity." They are not obviously different in kind than those leading a teen toward Catholic or Social Democratic affiliation.

Which is only to ask: What *should* be the baseline for judging with quantitative indices whether a young person severs ties unusually frequently? If "shearing away from the dependencies of childhood and adolescence" [86] accompanies becoming a Nazi, it also accompanies becoming an adult. Without a contrast group of nonjoiners, the statistical summary on Herr D. is beside the point. In the scientific framework the need for comparative measurement with non-Nazis is patent and unavoidable. Only a switch over to the symbolic meanings of the outputted statistics as ritual expressions permitted such a lapse in logic. Then selective use of Herr D.'s autobiography from the humanistic perspective, such as Herr D.'s mention of travel and meeting up with Nazis on the road, let the scientific researchers gloss "the meaning" of their deracinated "facts." The blurring of scientific variable analysis with free interpretation makes findings appear portentous even when they lack referents and conventional sense.

THEMATIC CENTRALITY AS EFFECT OR CAUSE OF MEANING?

From the scientific perspective, we know, a text is an assemblage of sentence clauses that comprise the unit "facts" of the story, given first. From these data bits emerge by computation the secondary qualities of the text, the frequency and mathematical centrality of certain nodes.

> [T]the nodes and sequences concerned with mobility [travel] in this narrative are the nodes that contain Nazis...The consequences of his mobility are quite evident, since each time he travels, he encounters other Nazis. In short, his mobility experiences make possible encounters with NSDP supporters, all of which draw him closer to the movement. [86]

Here the units of travel are primary, for they make "possible" the accumulating encounters with the Nazis.

From the humanistic perspective, in reverse, the autobiography as a verbal whole is a structure of paradigmatic themes, which meaningfully configure all the way down how incidents come to feature in the story as facts. The narrative clauses admitted and how they are figured concretize the *Volksgemeinschaft*, the telos of the German people. Thanks to the power of this model, imagined communities create linkages to "real" ones. For example, Herr D. introduces the folk community as a formative guide at the Verdun battlefield in France, where he dreams about "hearing the bequest" of "the unknown soldiers of our fatherland" [D 7].

Now when Herr D. emplots his life as an iterated encounter with a gemeinschaft, what are appropriate vehicles for its unfolding? The template of familial collegiality with relative strangers is activated most vividly when community bonding takes place with strangers beyond one's locale. The intimacy of a *Volksgemeinschaft* in a vast modern society is concretized by telling of family-like bonding with Nazi out-landers met in transit. The incidents of communion with strangers while traveling do not lead to the Nazi folk community, because it is just the reverse: illustrating the Nazi folk community leads to the incidents of communion with strangers while traveling. From the suppressed paradigmatic viewpoint, the travels do not "induce" the contact with Nazis, they are the setting that makes relations with Nazis suf-ficiently emblematic of a *Volksgemeinschaft* to be worthy of inclusion. It is not dif-ficult to surmise that many of Herr D.'s linkups with Nazis in local contexts went unmentioned, whereas encountering Nazis while traveling qualified to stand for the *Volksgemeinschaft* in formation. Only the blurring of scientific and humanist views led travel to be ensconced as a fact, first (in Bearman and Stovel's phrase, a raw "good"), to be cognitively glossed by the researcher, second. From the human-ist perspective, the story is not an interwoven map of facts, but a fact exists because it is properly figural for the verbal plot. If so, events precipitate out of themes, not themes out of events.

Which of the two perspectives on this issue, the figural or the scientific one, has truth on its side? At the least, coding of the individual units in the scientific perspec-tive is impractical, because for consistency it must presume there are "facts" separate from the way they are told—in Bearman and Stovel's vocabulary, univocal "events" separate from "cognitions" upon them, or at least no uncodable conflict between the two [84]. In the Nazi autobiographies, however, stalwarts explicitly respond to the issue that investing in the party detracts from some of their family obligations. When an autobiographer self-consciously writes this up, how can we associate the withering of ties with becoming mechanically unreflexive, as Bearman and Stovel suppose? And if a party activist in the telling bemoans the weakening of family ties in the present but is supported by family agreement that party engagement is the way to unite the family in the Nazi future, there seems to be no correct way to differentiate between the saying versus what is real. Herr D.'s father warned him against overinvestment in the party, but in Herr D.'s commentary, distancing from his father encourages greater family unity and closeness with his Nazi brother. Do we code the told or the telling?[67] The reality of the father's disapproval versus Herr D.'s intentions for family togetherness and the family's peak coalescence? Herr D.'s dedication to the party or his conscious placement of family needs above the party if the two conflict in his view [D 15]? If we seek to measure the self-reflexivity of a Nazi, do we not find this in the believer's explicit reflection *upon* events rather than in the network of events themselves?

Both literary criticism and tests of reading comprehension suggest that cen-tral paradigms govern events more than evental facts generate paradigms. When Christians read Gospel doings as fulfilling climaxes of the Hebrew Bible, the coherence they find takes successive events as actualizations of a figure.[68] When Marcel Proust composed *Remembrance of Things Past*, he put the syntagmatic streams of recalled events "at the service of metaphor and not the reverse." By most accounts, readers in practice take illuminated paradigms, not the cause-effect chains, as decisive.[69] Such models create the environment for human agency, as Jenna Baddeley and Jefferson Singer underscored: "Thematic coherence pulls together multiple episodes of the life story under the auspices of an overarching value or principle. This is perhaps the most sophisticated form of coherence—it requires the ability to summarize and interpret and synthesize multiple episodes from one's life story."[70]

"POWER CENTRALITY" AS LEG-PULLING

Blending *scientific* measurement of network position with *interpretation* of the results as metaphors for "power" cannot help but look absurd on reinspection. To appreciate the artifice, take these three clauses as offered by Michael Toolan, then rearrange them:

> Original Story: John fell in the river, he got chilled to the bone, and he had two large whiskies.
>
> Rearranged Story: John had two large whiskies, he fell into the river, and he got chilled to the bone.[71]

The connector in the first story is getting chilled, in the second it is falling into the river. The joke is that the *content* of the nodal intersection may have nothing to do with the humanistic moral given by the emplotment as a whole. Most readers would agree with Toolan that the original "John in the River" story is about assuaging oneself after misfortune ("poor guy!"), whereas the rearranged John story is about the consequences of unwise drinking ("he should have known better").[72] Nothing varies except connective positions, so I believe we have isolated exactly what Bearman and Stovel would have us highlight, "sequence" and "betweenness" [83]. In granting everything Bearman and Stovel idealize, we see how preposterously unchecked it is for them to blend numbers with metaphors so that statistically "power centrality grasps the importance of each element in the plot that is unfolding" [86]. However you might like to tinker with indices of centrality, the scientific criteria of a gauge's range of application and its ability to cut through context is only a license for liminal play. Conversely, making up stories to lend centrality to a preassigned, thematically trivial kind of connector—such as "a ringing telephone"—could make for an entertaining parlor game.[73]

Measuring "power centrality" in a network is based on a graphic snapshot, so it cannot register the one-way flow of plot in a verbal appreciation. For example, to assess the plot of Three Little Pigs, no child would count the number of times the wolf blew down a house and the network ties of those mentions versus the number of times a house remained standing to decide which action was more central. Likewise, tallying family conflict and elision in Herr D.'s tale is irrelevant in light of the climaxing reunion.

Inside the scientific frame, Bearman and Stovel compare networking of nodes without confirming the positions have a useable verbal meaning back in their humanistic context [86]. Every tool of uncorrupted science emerges out of shared criteria of intelligibility that decide whether formalization is serviceable. Only the blurring of science with interpretation in an anomalous no-man's land let Bearman and Stovel present verbal meaning apart from the standards of one realm or the other. I doubt the incongruence between the gravitas of the historical material versus the abandon with which a researcher engages it can be resolved by a blurred, therefore easygoing genre such as social "science."

THE PERCEPTUAL LOGIC OF THE LIMINAL PHASE

"Liminal phase" is more than a label for anomalous mixing. In the most concrete of ways, it discloses sources of creativity in "Becoming a Nazi." Victor Turner emphasized that orchestrators in the liminal moment recycle material sign-vehicles in "grotesque ways." From the perceptual elements in the ritual arena they launch all manner of conceptual associations and attribute these reworkings to the makeup of the world.[74] Similarly, let me suggest that once Bearman and Stovel dissolve Herr D.'s text into graphed points, they use fresh physical resemblances to reimagine what the text means and why. Bearman and Stovel (a) create a separate arena of diagrammatic representation, which never reconnects to the evidence; (b) associate the perceptual makeup of the diagram with the makeup of the world itself; (c) blur the logic that links the parts of the diagram with eternal logic in the human mind as such; and (d) code for themes that are metaphorical projections from the graphic shape of their own diagram. The unsettling challenge posed by each case of ritual in the present book is to explain why sociologists, when they highlight their empirical method as something like data analysis of texts, instead seem to return to the ancient womb of circularity.

As Bearman and Stovel underscore, their permutations of the "data" in the universe of statistics reveal meanings that are nonexistent in the humanistic universe. "[E]lement centrality may be invisible in the unfolding narrative, as the most important nodes are those that bridge sub-sequences" [88]. The real process of change governing a text, they reason, may "differ from the explicit theory proposed by the author" [88]. From Marx to Lévi-Struass, however, bold theorists of underlying structures have dug beneath superficial appearances for the sake of *returning* to explicate how appearances on the surface are produced. A revelatory model of the hidden should lead us back to otherwise inexplicable detail, not construct merely an alternative reality. Only the cordoning off of an arena for experimental positing can explain why Bearman and Stovel do not check or relativize their final interpretation of the story in relation to Herr D.'s text, whose own constructions are almost never admitted into the research write-up. The discussable fit of the explanation to the evidence is the only check on the proliferation of vacuous methods. Even so-called impressionistic literary theorists hold that there are shared understandings of a narrative that its interpretation should illuminate.[75]

CONFOUNDING THE STRUCTURE OF
THE DIAGRAM WITH THE UNIVERSE

The mute shape of a network cannot get the observer back to a statement of verbal substance except through the license of what "Becoming a Nazi" calls "visual impressions" [79]. In their introductory rationale, Bearman and Stovel remark upon "obvious similarities" [71] between linkages in a social network (in olden days a living metaphor) and ties between events in a story network (after you agree to the metaphor they advise). Connections in representations of either network can look "dense," "knotted," or "cyclic" [71]. In the revelatory arena of ritual, similarity turns from coincidence into warrant: "The key development is recognition that narratives and social structures have similar features, and that these features provide insight into the social meanings generated and reproduced within each" [88].[76] Converting everything into a network representation indeed makes it plausible to apply a network perspective to everything.

LOGIC OF THE HUMAN MIND

The material of social "science" does not appear in entities or definitions. In our experienced world it exists only as it is performed to convey discovery—a telling. Social scientists in the register of ritual go beyond deploying the scientific outlook to narrate it. In "Becoming a Nazi," the clauses of the story are conceptually unorganized stuff tagged as "goods," "facts," "raw materials," or "iron filings" to be connected by "magnetic influence" [75].[77] Such imagery treats the nodes as lacking in "cognitive glue" [84] except as they are pulled together in cause-effect chains: "The absence of connections between elements or sub-sequences implies the absence of theory..." [79]. Only by building networks does the mind "weave together otherwise unconnected components of the story" [86]. All this makes Herr D. and social scientists philosophical twins: both could start by "reporting the facts, but nothing beyond the facts" [89], and then these cogitators may allot theory the delimited role of glossing the unit givens with a theoretical portrait. In adopting a phrase such as "scientific worldview," therefore, I scarcely exaggerate. The coherence of the ritual process depends on enunciating this outlook as a unitary package. The reduction of the world to data points, dichotomous variables, and correlations cum causes is narrated as inhering in the documents themselves as an inescapable, transhistorical model for understanding. Otherwise, the original formation of the documents' elements by verbal metaphor and theme, the repressed context from which data units were distilled, the absence of "facts" prior to their interpretation in tandem, all this and more resurface to disrupt the proceedings.[78] In every ritual performance, how the social scientist cogitates is necessarily confounded with how agents under scrutiny express their lives, uncannily guaranteeing that what is uncomfortable about these similarities that the scientists themselves labored to create must in turn be partially denied before the ritual closes.

CONTENTS FROM DIAGRAMMATIC FORM

In coding the contents of the nodes, how did Bearman and Stovel settle upon the categories of "order" versus "chaos"? They adumbrate a rigorous criterion: "A more fundamental requirement is that our data reflect the elements that organize the [narrated life] process, as versus those selected from the analyst's hat" [76]. Returning to the text one finds that Herr D. never applies the word "order" and at best uses a cognate (*Ordner*), crowd attendant, in describing a Nazi rally. Nazism as a revolutionary ideal seems to activate transformative *movement* (*Bewegung*) and energetic mobility rather than fixity. Herr D. endorsed violence and thuggery. The concept of "order" as an organizing value strikes me as analytically artificial, whereas Bearman and Stovel believe the concept comes straight out of the narrative process. How might they have gathered this experience? From the optic of a ritual, it is not the makeup of Herr D.'s tale, but the formalism by which Bearman and Stovel *represent* the tale's structure that makes order and chaos emerge as naturally relevant categories. The visual graphing of narrative coherence "stands for" the order-imposing narrative mind. When the nodes are disorganized and no structure mathematically precipitates out of the story, the self of the narrator disappears graphically in a "chaos" of facts. Likewise, the theme of elision of social relations is not taken up by Herr D., who emphasizes instead the maintenance of family ties as a constituent and mirror of the folk community. Instead, elision seems like a natural category for which to code because the network diagram of the story is visually already "about" the erasure of linkages over time. Coding, I have proposed, creates an intrusive symbolism of its own. Such a resort to resemblance between the perceptual quality of sign-vehicles and the "concepts" to which they refer is the anthropological hallmark of voodoo or of self-absorbed conjuration.[79]

The projection onto the data of one's own visual and mathematical devices for formalizing the text occurs again when Bearman and Stovel characterize Nazis as simplistic coders. Becoming a Nazi shifts the activist over to a more primitive form of cognition in which an agent categorizes features of the world by highly abstract distinctions:

> Meaning is attached to the Nazi movement by organizing and resolving reality in terms of simplified binary oppositions [86]...The simplification of the world in terms of basic oppositions to which any content can be ascribed is the process that unites biographical availability with the contact afforded by mobility. This unification depends on the negation of particular social relations (for simplification rests on the denial of difference), and allows the author to attach meaning to the movement he bumps into. [87]

It looks as if Bearman and Stovel are the ones to create basic oppositions "to which any content can be ascribed" and to create virtual facts about rows of graves. Nature and society, inner clarity and marching parades, beauty, mere mention of a cemetery, ending Weimar confusion, who knows what can be coded as "order"? The words "order that is distinguished from..." are those of Bearman and Stovel, whereas no such reflection ("distinguished from") is to be found in Herr D.'s story. Appreciate the discordance as in all ritual process: the empirically exact methodologists project onto the text the simplifying formalism of their own codes to discover, aha, it is the Nazis we study who resort to such primitive and ideological ways of meaning-creation! It is not we the methodologists who project such richly mythic binaries as order versus disorder or fluid "becoming" versus static "being," instead those are inscribed in the text and in the perceptible "data" display.[80]

How are the irreal transactions of the liminal phase mistaken for scientific method? To be hardheaded, Bearman and Stovel carry out an epistemological rupture, turning a document that was a coppice of theme and emplotment into a series of points. After they effect this rupture to extrude "data," they never look back to test for goodness of fit. The conclusions of "Becoming a Nazi" seem resolutely empirical only because the "facts" let one break with all constraints on generating meaning out of the text.

The Phase of Integration: A Conjecture

The phase of integration channels the extraordinary energies of the ritual back into ordinary social life. The network structures in "Becoming a Nazi" fuse how we humans make meaning (narrative networks) with our sense of a self brought into existence through bonds to others (social networks). When Bearman and Stovel place us amid their theory of a master identity, they suggest how we as audience participants fit into its universal framework but also how "we" thankfully avoid a disturbed identity. A readily imaginable master identity for sociologists or academics today would be one in which we interact with all others as a scientist: "It is a poor father who acts as a scientist to his children" [75]. An individual in the grip of a master identity has a "self empty of the usual relational markers of distinction that *we* have—*our* roles as fathers or husbands or mothers or workers and what not" [75; my emphasis]. Whereas Bearman and Stovel's modeling might look like methodological formality, the sociological audience saw more. As the communicant Mohr remarked upon "Becoming a Nazi," "Questions about the nature of identity, social action, and the intrinsic narrativity of social existence are all *brought to the fore*."[81]

Every coding rite creates a scapegoat onto which the morally unsettling implications of the encoding process are projected. The scapegoat is a surrogate victim to whom the violence committed upon texts in the coding process and the coder's own fear of intellectual wrongdoing is ascribed. It is not *we* the network methodologists who in our lives are insensitive to context because we remove interpretation from the circumstances of historical time and place. No, it is the impoverished, mechanical Nazis we study who do this in *their* lives. It is not *we* the network methodologists who lack a theory to discover thematic coherence in the document in the period of "being" a Nazi. No, it is the Nazis we study who lack such a theory because it is *they* who lack the multiperspectival thinking that characterizes a rich human self. It is not we who take social relations out of the picture by preferring the abridged version of a life story. No, it is the Nazis who abridge the complex tapestries of life. Once the dark side of coding and of the ambiguous roles coding creates for communicants is unloaded onto the scapegoat, the ritual process crystallizes the moral standing of those remaining in the participant community.

Bearman and Stovel adopt the same vocabulary to describe their own scientific outlook as they apply to a Nazi. They feature "abstraction" for converging on the essential: "Comparison within and across narratives necessitates abstraction... This is accomplished by grouping elements into equivalency classes" [83; see also 20]. When the researchers present the Nazi cognitive style, "abstraction" is again the key feature, but now using it to "order experience" is a character defect [85]. It is not we as network reductionists who have a rigid response in analyzing qualitatively incomparable situations, it is the Nazis with a "master identity" who do.

The eerie doubling of features between coder and scapegoat, pronounced by the researchers themselves, is a constant in social "science" as ritual. "We should not conclude, however, that the surrogate victim is simply foreign to the community. Rather, he is seen as a "monstrous double," René Girard wrote of ritual. "The victim must be neither too familiar to the community nor too foreign to it."[82] The life story of a Nazi is similar to that of a character who is inside and outside American society, that of a member of Alcoholics Anonymous, Bearman and Stovel repeat [5, 7]. Any of us could be reductively defined as similar to a party member, for what Bearman and Stovel analyze are "the pathways through which ordinary men and women became Nazis" [70]. It is no coincidence when Bearman and Stovel close with a stirring sentence that limns a Nazi as the perfect sacrificial object: partly still acting, maintaining the status of a human, yet partly deactivated, a zombie unable to narrate:

> When the process is completed, when the author is a Nazi—the self disappears. Nothing is left to operate the story, except for a mechanical agency. This mechanical agency is the agency of a thermometer that in its very essence can only tell you the temperature: that is, an agency completely built into its being as a thermometer. [89]

The "thermometer" to which Bearman and Stovel oddly compare a Nazi in their conclusion is a passive instrument, reliable and valid, like the ideal reader-coder in social science. Perhaps ritual sacrifice of a rigid coder as a "Nazi" reaffirms the moral purity of the inquiry's handiwork.

Genuine liturgies do not represent or transcode the social or economic orders outside. They are about themselves, how to present and variantly repeat their form of expression as sovereign.[83] "Becoming a Nazi" stages the discovery of network theory as the model of intelligibility for all facets of social experience.[84] Sociology in the key of ritual crystallizes the meanings of social life not because it takes society or anything in society as a referent, only because it has honed the tools for performing cosmologies of human interrelatedness. This conclusion directs us toward a follow-up question: To what if anything does a rite then refer? Addressing that question is the unsettling theme of the next chapter's demonstration.

"METHODOLOGICAL CANONS IN MY FIELD"

First, methodological canons in my field require that I not only read texts, but "code" them, essentially categorizing paragraphs as referring to certain themes, in order to look for insights in the relationships between paragraphs and between texts...I obtained the most cited text from each most cited author and interpretively read and coded it as described above, focusing on the substantively/formally rational distinction that my critics have described so well above...To determine the content of each of these influential authors' work, I read their most cited text during each time period, and coded it descriptively and interpretively. The second most cited text for each author was also coded it if had more than 50 percent of the citations that the top-cited text had. In cases of ties, both texts were coded.

— John Evans, reporting on thousands of pages from about 100 books and articles classified for NSF Project 97–01966, "Playing God."[1]

DEEPER PARADOXES OF "THE MODERN FACT"

This chapter progresses to show that the question "How do 'facts' refer?" becomes more vexing when the facts are coding results for a "representative sample." Mary Poovey's allusive definition of the modern "fact" reminds us that investigators begin by supposing that there are theory-neutral grounds for assembling the unit facts that are subsequently ratified as a collection.[2] This scientist framework of the modern "fact" lands researchers in an untenable regress when the visited evidence is an assemblage of texts. Whether a sample is appropriate for representing a culture's expression of opinion or not cannot be established until after a researcher interprets the coded "facts" and, behind them, the texts themselves in the compilation. We cannot ascertain if sampled texts suitably respond to a question until after we appreciate them in relation to what landed outside. Since outside texts brought into relation with texts inside a sample generate fresh meanings overall, a "scientifically" insulated selection knows not of what it speaks. This chapter explores how investigators who sample texts with systematic (therefore meaning-configuring) criteria beg the questions they would like to address.

Uncertainties over what "data" extracted from texts stand for become more acute for other reasons in coded samples. Given illimitable variety of expression, there is no check for whether the coding across texts taps into similar distinctions and adduces equivalents suitable for being aggregated as units. Social scientists mandate arbitrarily that it seems appropriate to numerate meanings as "the same." Of course, inside the scientist framework, it is feasible to discount error to the degree that multiple researchers reliably arrive at the same coding for each sampled text.[3] This consistency evades the issue, for there is no prior definition of the targeted "meaning," therefore no standard for setting up what it would entail for a coding to nearly hit bull's-eye. Coding may proceed predictably only because researchers inculcated to follow a protocol as "commonsense" equally miss the mark. Opposite the stereotypes of replicable "science," the subtler the imposed codes, the more it seems like quibbling to demand mechanical coding standards and the *less* questionable the data become.[4] "Facts" become totemic ciphers.

PROGRESSING TO A SECOND DEMONSTRATION CASE

A century ago in *The Protestant Ethic* Max Weber bequeathed to sociologists an evidentiary riddle whose solution, many believe, might reveal the dawning of "modern" Western societies. The challenge Weber posed was that of deciding whether texts as testaments to springs of human action are constituted primarily by value rationality or by an opposite, instrumental rationality. Distinguishing each kind through words of the agents themselves would enable sociologists to appreciate whether scrivening among entrepreneurs who inaugurated Europe's economic expansion since the seventeenth century was moved by a novel "spirit of capitalism." Weber believed the spirit did not originate in utilitarian adaptation to circumstances, the mark of instrumental rationality. Instead, he exhibited how business ethics were organized by a revolutionary commitment that transcended means-end efficiency. Representative literature from the seventeenth and eighteenth centuries, Weber said, recommended ascetic labor as a categorical duty, an earmark of value rationality, his term for actions subordinated to elaborated systems of ultimate values.[5]

For his prototype of the "value rational" business culture, Weber focused on the Yankee author Benjamin Franklin. On the surface Franklin's adages breathe with instrumental rationality. "Now, all Franklin's moral attitudes are colored with utilitarianism," Weber acknowledges. "Honesty is useful, because it assures credit; so are punctuality, industry, frugality, and that is the reason they are virtues." Weber nonetheless suggests that Franklin's pursuit of credit and profit is embedded in value rationality ("the spirit of capitalism") because Franklin "ascribes his recognition of the utility of virtue to a divine revelation which was intended to lead him in the path of righteousness."[6] Yet several sociologists who have revisited Franklin's precepts find Weber's attribution untenable. As Jere Cohen summarized from exegesis, "Hard work and redeeming time were not advocated as lifelong principles, but as temporary stratagems..."[7] Work opened the path to prosperity. Franklin advised correlatively that virtues led finally to greater leisure, not to divine salvation. It remains difficult to ascertain how passages in Franklin's writings betoken a revolutionary ethical culture (for value-rational action) versus how they betoken money grubbing (for instrumental-rational action).[8]

Cohen's scrupulous reading continues to unsettle investigators who appraise Weber's primary evidence. Analogously, in the history of labor movements, sociologists have found it difficult to distinguish between workers' demands that are instrumentally calculated versus those shaped by categorical ideals. "Many examples defy attempts to periodize or categorize instrumental (material) versus ideal (identity) ends," Margaret Somers concluded in her review of workers' expressions in the nineteenth century.[9] Social theorists have concluded that Weber's rationalities are so problematic, they operate as metaphysical concepts rather than as tools for research.[10] Gordon Marshall entitled his book that critiques Weber's classifying *In Search of the Spirit of Capitalism*.[11]

Sociologists' enduring campaign to distinguish between rationalities verifies the importance of John Evans's coding in his 2002 book, *Playing God*. Evans classified about a hundred articles and books on bioethics for whether they tended toward value or instrumental rationality.[12] Evans assessed five "components" that arbitrated to which of the two kinds of rationality a text in the main belonged. When he sighted these "objectified versions of instrumental versus value rationality" in bioethical texts, he limned them by their cognate terms, "substantive" versus "formal" rationality, as Weber did for sociology of law [G 229].[13] Like other German scholars in his era, Weber defined his task as that of merely illuminating the iconic meanings that he already "knew" powered capitalist expansion.[14] Evans assumed a greater burden, the quasi-quantitative task of gauging *whether* there is relative change in his sample of texts over time between substantive (value) rationality versus formal (instrumental) rationality.

As a revisiting of Weber, Evans's book, subtitled *Human Genetic Engineering and the Rationalization of Public Bioethical Debate*, could not have been more auspicious. For many today, escape from capitalism's "iron cage" seems even less feasible than Weber pessimistically forecast. Critics fear that human genetic engineering (HGE) may chain us inside the cage by extending criteria of efficiency into our corporeal makeup. Deeper cynics see these technologies as the only means by which human transformation remains imaginable, given the immutability of capitalism.[15] In any event, *Playing God*'s concern for the effects of technology on human character and its solution to Weber's coding riddle qualify it as momentous. Evans proved legions of theorists wrong: they had rejected as unworkable Weber's analytic distinction between formal and substantive rationality. For example, Roger Cotterrell wrote that "[t]he development of contract shows a *blending* of rational and irrational elements and formal and substantive concerns sufficiently complex to cast doubt on the utility of his [Weber's] classifications even as an admittedly ideal typical formulation."[16] The proof in Evans's pudding, his classifying by codes, lends *Playing God* its gravity.

THE SOCIAL "SCIENTIFIC" FORMAT

In *Playing God*'s methodological appendices, Evans elaborates how he guarded against "potential bias" in selecting publications on HGE [G 205, 211]. To "develop a more objective method of determining the content of [bioethical] debates in different eras, without compromising on depth or generalizability," Evans constructed an initial "population of 1,465 texts representative of the professional debate about the ethics of HGE (human genetic engineering) from 1959 to 1995..." [G 43]. His sweep of sources and his whittling of them to the most representative helped him "observe subtle changes in the form of argumentation" over decades [G 42].

As bioethical guidance on HGE becomes specialized, it fosters calculative, dessicating linkages between means and ends. At least this is Evans's finding after he purified 1,465 texts to 345 linkable texts. Then he impressively examined 16,020 citations from 6,614 cited authors. He checked each text to identify the most frequently cited authors [G 208, 279]. In each of four separate time periods up to 1995, he used cluster analysis to group "influential" authors into "communities," according to whether authors tended to be cited together by "non-influential" authors in the larger sample. Evans thereby diagrammed leading ethicists who transmuted substantive (value) arguments into formal (instrumental) rationality. This conversion was inseparable from an ominous separation of elite writers from dialogue with the citizenry [G 55, 57, 70–71, 178, 213]: "In practical terms, the shift to formal rationality in the HGE debate has meant that the professionals who write *to* and for the public have severely constrained their debate at a time when the technology [for HGE] is actually becoming possible and decisions are becoming more critical" [G 181; my emphasis].

To explain this progression Evans invokes the ethicists' adaptation to funding institutions—a default to pragmatics often recommended for interpreting coding data. Up through the 1960s, Evans shows writers treating the educated public as their audience. By the 1980s, federal advisory committees had become powerful consumers of specialized bioethics: the "radical transformation in the debate" was "caused by these advisory commissions" [G 36]. To serve federal agencies, bioethicists adopted a vacuous means-end vocabulary that cast moral goals as so neutral and indisputable, the state could govern by routinized consensus. Due to this decoupling of intellectual legislation from democratic contention, Evans reasons, "[t]he health of our public sphere will be put to the test. Will we be able to have a debate that considers the full richness of the moral question before us?" [G 7].

IDENTIFYING SOCIAL SCIENCE

Such massive coding and computer patterning comprise the fare of rigorous social "science," maximally resisting my protestation that ritual is the operative matrix. To prepare the frame-switch to ritual, let me reconnoiter whether putative causes and effects dovetail in *Playing God*. My determinations, possibly one-sided, suffice to sharpen the puzzle, "Why did few sociologists consider bare explanatory logic if this be social 'science'?"

Is there variation in outcomes, the "dependent variable"? The unit of explanation is the US polity, whose reliance on advisory committees promotes technicist rationales for federal policy. To identify variation in national bioethical debates once the manipulations of HGE become operational, an international perspective across polities seems requisite. Given the global advance of biotechnology, has *any* contestation of HGE culminated in substantively rational policy? How can disparate religious idioms join in dialogue about ends *without* resorting to a facilitative meta-language? *Playing God* clarifies no cases in which technologies for HGE are at hand, but policies importantly differ. Without a comparative benchmark for assessing the US response, finding that discussions of the means of HGE coincides with the availability of those means seems uninformative.

Is there variation in the "independent variable," the cause? Does public participation in the regulation of genetic engineering vary across nations or across US regions? If US abortion controversies remain substantively rational, what shows this results from democratic engagement, as Evans postulates [G 178], not from the qualitatively different biological issues abortion poses? Nor from relative stability in abortion technology compared to that for genetic engineering? About a hundred publications appear annually in the catalog Medline on "induced abortion" in relation to ethics.[17] It would have been easy to apply to abortion the same measuring device, keyword-based sampling from the elite Bioethicsline database, to see if this indicator is sensitive in the first place to the rationality of public debates.[18]

Comparisons are also necessary for Evans's extraordinary supposition that bioethics as a writing profession is defined by distinctively formally rational arguments across life issues. Formal rationality, exemplified in the school bioethicists' call "Principlism," is "the form of argumentation of the bioethics profession" [G 7–9, 30, 34, 72, 73, 83, 89, 92, 137].[19] A variation-seeking question would be, "In policy debates for which no federal advisory committees emerge, do bioethicists diverge in rationality?" If, as Evans contends, there is broader participation and less committee delegation in abortion policy, writers in this field should select more frequently for substantively rational arguments [G 179]. But Evans does not compare bioethicists' publications across moral issues, as comparative demonstration seems to mandate [G 71, 179]. Medline catalogs exhibit *overlap* between discussion of HGE and abortion.[20] But if bioethicists are characterized by monolithic formal rationality, it becomes contradictory to seek variation in their stances across issues, and Evans forbids such variation tautologically: "Although all those who engage in bioethical debate are popularly identified as bioethicists, it is important for this analysis that the only professionals considered to be bioethicists are those who use the profession's form of argumentation" [G 34].[21]

Does the cause, installing governmental advisory committees with a preferred format, temporally precede the effect, the rise of formally rational architecture for bioethics? What Evans calls the "order of events" is crucial: "First came government advisory commissions, which needed a formal rational type of argumentation," *then* came the rise of professional bioethicists with formal rationality [G 175].[22] Evans's chief text illustrating formally rational commensurating [G 17] is from an ordained Episcopal priest who published it before the advent of advisory commissions, however. Formal (instrumental) reasoning had long been rooted in liberal Protestantism and its supporting institutions.[23]

If the issue is whether advisory committees preceded bioethics as an institutionalized profession, some evidence suggests not.[24] For example, the Hastings Center, which for a spell called itself "The Institute of Society, Ethics, and the Life Sciences," was founded in 1969. Georgetown University's bioethics center opened in 1971. The

Encyclopedia of Bioethics was organized in mid-1971.[25] These earlier articulations of bioethics and their institutionalization via encyclopedias and centers are not surprising, given the spectrum of topics, from assisted suicide to environmental justice, which inspired the new discourse.

Supposing there is covariation in readings of the independent and dependent variables, is there a robust explanatory mechanism clarifying the linkage? If bureaucratic committees of experts prefer formal rationality [G 37, 178], should we not show this mechanism defies changes in the ideology of the political administrations appointing the experts [G 41, 83]? Can Evans's mechanism be upheld as explanatory given the dramatic shift in the reasoning style of reports on bioethics under the Bush administration, once conservatives such as Leon Kass [G 189] took its helm, a turning that some foresaw before *Playing God* entered press?[26]

No social research can be expected to address all explanatory difficulties. The question is why a study without any explanatory format would just the same be received by sociologists in the register of causally illuminating social science. If you suspect I unfairly decree the criteria for demonstration, Evans himself anticipated nearly all my comments as pertinent. In his NSF grant proposal "Playing God," Evans installed excellent defenses: a parallel process of classifying for a US bioethical debate in which available technologies remained constant over time; documenting individual bioethicists' careers to reveal the cause-effect sequence underlying their style of reasoning; study of a US debate without intervention from advisory commissions; indicators of the publications' intended audiences, and more.[27] This textbook-perfect design was never implemented, as happens with the best of us.[28] If the design was inconsequential for *Playing God* to qualify as social "science," what organized the presentation? Let us pursue another framing.

THE RITUAL PHASE OF SEPARATION

To complete the first of van Gennep's ritual phases, that of separation, *Playing God* executes three maneuvers: it isolates a body of texts to erect a platform; it strips the texts' relations down to line figures; and it levels the audience down to roles that are morally ambiguous.

THE RITUAL PLATFORM

A sample of texts about a controversy across decades is useful if it reveals the constitution of the debate, but that is to presuppose the result, for the purpose of the inquiry is to discover the debate's boundaries, which neither start nor end in a particular forum or medium. If we blindly rely upon a database's keyword tags to decide which publications comprise the debate, we circularly discover only what we stipulated in advance without comparing the messages that lie outside. The "representative sample" approach of science cannot accommodate the pursuit of exchanges of cultural significance. In the era of blurred genres, the ritual orchestrator reverses the relation between a compilation and what it represents. As Wolfgang Iser remarked of such moments of experiment: "This makes mapping into a performative activity by reversing the map/territory relationship. Instead of denoting a territory, the map enables the contours of the territory to emerge, which will coincide with the map because it has no existence outside its designation."[29] The cosmic frame implicated in Evans's proper labeling of the sample as "the universe" is scarcely coincidental.

CREATING TRENDS

To compile publications about HGE that would extend from 1959 to 1995, Evans was obliged to merge dozens of bibliographies by varying search strategies. For the period 1973–1995, Evans culled 989 items from the Bioethicsline database of the National Library of Medicine that featured four "primary topics": genetic intervention, gene pool, gene therapy, or germ cells. For the years before 1973, he used "numerous and overlapping bibliographic sources" [G 205]. In all, "[t]hirty-eight very diverse reference tools and databases were also searched for possible items." How did Evans decide which entries in these happenstance bibliographies symptomized the later emergence of HGE? Personal guesswork was a necessity. Had Evans discussed the difficulties in this selection process, the sample would manifestly be an artful rendering, as in the humanities, rather than an impersonal registry of a "population." Since HGE as defined today did not exist in 1959, Evans's choice of topics from the early bibliographies leaned toward the philosophical. For example, from the cumulative Hasting Centers' bibliographies 1973–1984, he took in "Historical, Legal, and Philosophical Material" under "General Readings." Likewise, from The Library of Congress Bibliography of 1973, he included "general references" and "clonal propagation." Just as broadly, from the 1973 Fogarty Center bibliography, Evans took as many as 99 items from the heading "genetics and philosophy" [G 277], which featured books with expansive titles such as *What is Life?* and *Social Responsibility of the Scientist.*[30] Similar items were fished from *The Philosopher's Index* [G 206].

Evans's search across later years was differentially constricted. In Bioethicsline for the succeeding period 1973–1995, Evans no longer used terms that would have highlighted philosophy or cloning in a similarly broad way as *before* 1973. By dropping "cloning," for example, he probably omitted a hundred documents (perhaps many more, could anyone access his NSF data). Due to cloning's threat to personal identity, sources about cloning were often richer in speculative discussions and, one would predict, more likely to include philosophy or life purpose, favoring substantive (value) rationality.[31] Among the work Evans shut out was that of influential theological authors such as Richard McCormick. Likewise, by discontinuing earlier headings such as "philosophy" in relation to genetics, Evans likely excluded another hundred Bioethicsline documents. Instead, after 1973 Evans selected sources only if they had been tagged with the four "primary topic" words about genetic engineering in the Bioethicsline database. It appears probable, maybe obvious, that directing the probe away from philosophical references toward more specific, technologically sensitive keywords (such as "gene therapy") would be mirrored self-fulfillingly in a narrowing of content over time. It would create the "observed" trend away from broad spiritual concerns toward formally rational application of technology.

If assembling an instructive sample maddeningly postulates what each text can mean before we examine it, how may researchers acknowledge this dilemma?

The weakness of combining bibliographies different in kind is perfectly typical. Historically evolving discourses, *what* we seek to sample, are bound to generate incomparable registries, the *means* available to us for sampling. It is puzzling Evans ignores this root contradiction in sampling meanings, whereas he underscores minor sources of "bias" in the tradition of quantitative sampling: "One source of bias I share with studies using the ISI data is that only the first author in multiply authored items was compiled..." [G 279]. Did the Bioethicsline bibliographers at Georgetown University include publications and apply their keywords in a consistent manner? Evans asks [G 205]. Given the unavoidable wholesale picking of sources before 1973 and therefore the altering of selection guidelines over time, Evans's concern for other sources of "bias" looks almost ceremonial.

Were the kinds of bioethical publications that Evans retrieved from his four "primary topics" the only type in which bioethicists expounded upon ultimate values bearing on HGE? Most likely not [G 34]. Bioethicsline developed separate keywords for writings on foundational values after 1973.[32] Their exclusion from the sample when they did not crown HGE as the "primary topic," a reviewer of *Playing God* noted, operated by "methodological fiat," whereas my additional point is such decrees always emerge as important after the fact.[33] "Foundational bioethics discusses how the debates about issues such as HGE are related to broader societal concerns, such as systems of ethics, democratic practice, and the like," Evans wrote. "This book will conduct very little analysis of this debate"—then its absence is the conclusion [G 34].

A GHOST SAMPLE NOT ADMITTED

In more intricate ways yet, the sampling excludes substantively rational works whose marginality is then touted:

> Since substantively rational authors are ultimately arguing about ends, they are typically not interested in the means themselves (such as HGE). They are interested in specific means only to the extent that the means point to a larger or deeper problem in the ends. This assumption can often be recognized in a text by the sheer volume of different means being discussed. For example, some substantively rational authors discussing HGE simultaneously consider abortion and in-vitro fertilization to be "part of" the same problem—that is, all these means are consistent or inconsistent with the same end that they are debating. [G 19–20]

Paraphrasing then, in substantively rational argument writers are "typically not interested in the means themselves (such as HGE)," because the means are subordinate to a broader discussion of ends. A work in the Bioethicsline database can garner only a handful of "primary topic" designations—in the main under six or so. A substantively rational argument is more likely *not* to feature as "*primary* topics" exactly the things Evans required them to feature if they were to enter his sample: genetic intervention, gene therapy, gene pool, or germ cells. For if those four HGE topics are just parts of umbrella moral concerns about biotechnologies generally, and if the discussion of HGE is subordinate to religion, narrow HGE terms may appear as keywords, but likely *not* as "*primary* topics." By Evans's own logic, one would expect substantively (value) rational works to feature those four terms among its lesser, catalogued "keywords," and to feature at the helm religion, values or the more general term "biotechnology" as the *primary* topics." The criterion for formal instrumental rationality is that it isolates HGE as its principal topic [G 20], which is what trawling texts for HGE as "principal topic" will net![34] Only science that reifies the sample as a ritual universe operates this circularly.

Let us unveil the artificially excluded items. Repeat the search Evans specifies, yet bundle texts in which HGE terms are keywords, not primary topics. Alongside Evans's actualized 969 items, a phantom opposite rises: 933 items catalogued by Evans's same four terms, such as "genetic intervention," now as keywords integrated within overarching themes, as substantively rational argument favors. In the cockpit over a hundred have as primary topics "morality," "moral obligation," or "moral policy," dozens of others put the term "values" as primary, not to mention "religion," "religious ethics," "Roman Catholic ethics," or "Protestant ethics." It is striking how a religious and philosophical specter resurfaces, with prototypes in box 3.1. This includes the texts Evans claims other people, not himself, increasingly excluded from the debate after 1974.[35]

BOX 3.1   GHOST EXAMPLES

Includes "moral policy" as primary topic and "genetic enhancement" and "genetic intervention" as keywords:

> Daniel Callahan, "Manipulating Human Life: Is There No End to It?" in *Medicine Unbound*, ed. Robert Blank and Andrea Bonnicksen (New York: Columbia University Press, 1994), pp. 116–131. "But consequentialism cannot provide us with any solid guidance—at best hints and warnings, at worst the illusion of wisdom but none of the substance…Emotional repugnance should be taken seriously" (122, 127).

Includes "dehumanization" as primary topic and "genetic intervention" as a keyword:

> Nancy Davis, "Morality and Biotechnology," *Southern California Law Review* 65 (November 1991): 355–371. "The new biotechnologies may not be unique in posing risks to our values, attitudes, and self-understanding, but because they may radically change the way people can and will live their lives, some of the risks they pose are special. It is not clear that such risks can be adequately assessed, or even properly understood, within the confines of a consequentialist framework" (357).

Includes "common good" as primary topic and "genetic intervention" as a keyword:

> Roger Dworkin, "Medical Law and Ethics in the Post-Autonomy Age," *Indiana Law Journal* 38 (Summer 1993): 727–742. "Now, developments in genetics raise serious questions about the scientific validity of the assumptions on which autonomy-based law and ethics rest, and new attention to the values of civic republicanism, community, and inclusiveness raises questions about the extent to which the dominance of autonomy is desirable" (727).

Evans assured his critics that major streams of works were not omitted: "So, as I outline in the methodological appendix to the book, I created a list of 1,465 texts that had been published on the topic of the ethics of HGE between 1959 and 1995—and defined it as 'the debate'—a list that I consider to be *fairly exhaustive*"[36] [G 205, my emphasis]. Evans encountered dramatic clues that his list was incomplete. Consider Evans's 22 most influential authors for 1992–1995 [G 156] and from there, view these authors' most cited works from 1989 onward [G 224–226], by which time Evans describes Bioethicsline as his only sample source [G 205–206, G 277]. The following authors had top (cited) works listed by Evans himself as central to the debate that as far as we can tell were *not* in Evans's winnowed Bioethicsline (citing) universe: Dorothy Wertz, Neil Holtzman, John Robertson, Peter Singer, James Watson, George Annas—6 of the 14 authors in his last diagram who published in 1989 or later.[37]

It may also swirl the senses to consider why an investigator could not have checked from the wellspring, Bioethicsline, to see why so many works could be extraordinarily influential but expelled as citing works, for this 1992–1995 period as for others. Instead, Evans suggested in a symposium with intellectuals party to the "debate" that resorting to documents offered "more objective 'proof' of why things changed" than could personal experience of the HGE debate by renowned participants.[38] Publications, in their guise as unchanging objects, appear more suitable for generating "facts" about influential ideas than does human testimony. When an expert questioned the validity of Evans's summary by suggesting that a work pivotal for bioethics had fallen outside the sample results, Evans's defense was that it had fallen outside the sample.[39] The ritual arena has to remain its own theater. As a rite to detach and simplify, the sampling systematically excluded publications exactly by the meanings most pertinent for addressing Evans's own question about meanings.

MERGING SCIENTIFIC AND INTERPRETATIVE
APPROACHES IN SAMPLING?

The self-fulfilling defects of text sampling are irreparable. The scientific method of defining a population, downloading it, and classifying its units is supposedly a module that one can transport across any population of creatures. But in the study of meanings the procedure requires a schizophrenic stance: the criteria (such as *primary* mention of an HGE-related theme in a catalog) for delimiting the sample population, as variables in the framework of "science," are detached from their original meaningful contexts. That is the rationale for treating the sample as a container capable of outputting coding "facts" representative of an objectivistically generalizable population. If with humanistic "interpretation" you return the variables triggering the sampling to their home contexts, you see they circularly preconfigure the population and the coding results together. As Evans explained,

> Because a substantive debate is about ends themselves, there is no limit to the number of ends that can be forwarded...The means in question is representative of a deeper or larger problem. The means is therefore often linked to other means that are argued to be consistent or inconsistent with the same end...The debate then seems

thicker, more fundamental or important, because one means seems to be connected with many other means... [G 16, 20, 22]

But if a substantively rational debate is defined by its lack of topical concentration on HGE in isolation, and if it is marked by its tendency to move beyond the arena of HGE debate per se into myriad means and ends, there is an irresolvable problem in sampling *style* of rationality via a *topic* such as HGE: the texts that are most substantively rational in style will be least focused on HGE-affiliated terms as topic. Other way round, by including only texts that focus on HGE by "primary topic," Evans could not help creating the result that his texts focused on HGE, the mark of formal rationality: "For example, while in previous eras texts linked abortion, in-vitro fertilization, HGE, and other issues into one deeper problem, such as human control over 'natural' processes, the literature in this community discusses only HGE" [G 145].[40] The interworked context of meaning is what the ritual brackets to make the sample appear objective, but that mundane context is what scientific sampling by variables always mobilizes behind the scenes to determine what can be seen in the reified survey, "the universe."

The quantitative downloading of prelabeled units naturally *requires* a researcher to define the population by topic—only such units are retrievable under subject headings in bibliographies or databases. But a style of argument necessarily drifts outside any unified subject matter. No wonder it turned out that Evans in the 1992–1995 period lists as one of the most influential works in the sample driving the HGE debate Peter Singer's book *Practical Ethics*. This work, Evans says, "never discusses HGE," although he classifies it as mostly formally rational.[41] More tellingly, Singer authored many a work more immediately focused on HGE—including an article titled "Genetic Engineering"—that did not make it into the HGE debate sample as influential. Singer's work on genetic engineering was trumped in the HGE debate even by his *Animal Liberation*.[42] These citation habits suggest that HGE lacks integrity as an independent debate topic. Myriad factors exogenous to "the debate" create the sample, which has to be ritually cordoned-off from this real-world contamination to sustain the illusion of a system.

The issue is that to track objects of cultural significance such as a mode of organizing arguments, an investigator has to move off topic to disambiguate the subject matter from that transposable style of arguing. Correlatively, anyone who wishes to explain an author's approach to a particular topic as an instance of the application of a schema of rationality will do so by showing that the author had the schema at hand because the author used it elsewhere, "off topic." For instance, the theologian Stanley Hauerwas, in his critique of Evans's portrayal of Paul Ramsey as morally "thick," sought to identify Ramsey's disposition over a relatively thin, consensual mode of argument. "Ramsey, I suspect, thought utilitarianism was so institutionalized into our habits of thought that any attempt to raise issues of ends would have results he wanted to keep at bay," Hauerwas wrote. "I think his stress on questions of discrimination in *Just War* reflects this tendency in his thought."[43] Evans in response nearly disciplines Hauerwas by invoking the scientistic worldview: Ramsey's writings on "just war," outside the sample, are irrelevant to the exercise.[44] But irrepressible humanistic interpretation forces Evans to commit over and again the infraction for which he chides those who question his sampling as scientific demonstration. For example, Evans identifies an author's overall commitment to a form of rationality by demonstrating it in operation in publications *outside* the mono-topic selection.[45] He lengthily clarifies the position of Ramsey, his iconic figure of substantive rationality, by coding in detail a work of Ramsey's that seems to have fallen outside the final sample.[46] From the interpretive perspective such a move outside the sample is illuminating, while from the perspective of a scientific "universe" it is transgression. As Evans in the scientific perspective explains, "everything an author has written is not relevant. Rather, I have considered only what the broader members of the community thought was relevant as indicated by their citation of it" [G 44]. To launch the sampling and coding ritual, we have to take up a schizophrenic consciousness

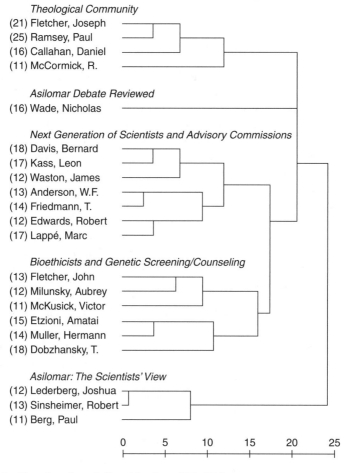

Figure 3.1   Clustering of most influential authors, 1975–1984.

Notes: The scale at the bottom is the rescaled distance at which the clusters combine. The number of texts that cite the author is given in brackets (N = 71).

Source: John Evans, *Playing God?* (Chicago: University of Chicago Press, 2002), p. 75.

between the quantitative-scientific and the humanistic-interpretive perspectives. We cannot acknowledge in one frame what we do in the other. Evans wrote that "the two foremost proponents of the form of argumentation in the bioethics profession as I have defined it," Beauchamp and Childress, are not among authors charted as statistically influential.[47] Indubitable knowledge from the humanist frame does not impinge on the "scientific" procedure for equating influence with citations.

The disjuncture recurs when *Playing God* projects the interpretive concept of an intellectual "community" onto a statistical artifact: writers who are clustered into groups by cocitations, as in figure 3.1. Rev. Richard McCormick moves from the community of theologians in 1975–1984 into that of the overall formally rational bioethicists in 1985–1991 [G 75, 138]. It is vexing to consider whether the ritual vehicle, diagrams of cocitation "communities," at all guides the articulation and receipt of ethical opinions.[48] The sense of the clustering depends on dovetailing the scientific and the humanist perspectives, yet it is demonstrably unfeasible.

Nonappearance as Nonexistence

Once a social "scientist" brackets a corpus as the universe, all that an individual writer intends in public engagement outside the sample is irrelevant to the system. Evans concludes that a topic not mentioned in an article in his ceremonial sample was considered unimportant by its author [G 64, 149]. For example, from one source Evans concludes "since Anderson did not report any possible objections to germline therapy except safety, he seems to have meant only that society must agree to the risks involved" [G 143]. To the contrary, in outside sources (as well as in one retained in the sample at that) W. French Anderson expressed unusual concern for the technology's threats to "important human values" and "an increase in inequality and an increase in discriminatory practices."[49] Only in liturgy is the truth of expression decided in such a fashion, by whether the outside world fits the ritual, not by whether the ritual fits the outside world.[50]

Contents Excluded, Then Found Absent

The circular exclusion of what is then "discovered" as missing is bewildering when one reconsiders debaters' relations to the public. As we have seen, Evans's conclusion is that bioethicists have fallen silent in addressing the public with the rise of formal rationality [G 181]. To support this verdict, he analyzed publications by six authors in a cluster from 1985 to 1991 [G 144]. By contrast, in the earliest era, 1959–1973, Evans found scientists in his sample addressed the public as "the target audience" [G 69, 70]. For example, he remarks, "Medawar's most influential book was actually first read over the radio in Great Britain" [G 243–244]. This is the kind of address that goes missing by the 1985–1991 era [G144]. Instead, the contributors with growing influence in the sample "tend to have government advisory commissions as their ultimate target audience" [G 145].[51] It seems manifest that Evans uses the sample contents to gauge authors' relations to the public.[52]

For a self-fulfilling prophecy *Playing God* filters out the epistles most pertinently aimed at the public. "If an item did not contain four or more citations, it was not included in the sample, because the primary technology of a citation study is measures of association between citations. I examined 765 randomly selected items from the universe. Of these, 345 fit the parameters for inclusion" [G 208]. If one examines sources in the unexpunged HGE sample, it is difficult to understand how the "news stories from newspapers, popular magazine articles, and editorials" [G208], the majority of sources, could have been jettisoned.[53] Authoritative scientists and ethicists in the unpurged sample disagreed severely with each other in forums such as the *Washington Post* and the *New York Times*.[54] Those items "were removed from the data" [G 278] even when the prime issue was how many texts by elites had a popular orientation [G 34, 55, 70–71, 178, 181, 213]. Make no mistake: the very technicist who is supposedly indifferent toward social approval, W. French Anderson [G 143], in reality continually sought to legitimate his activities by winning the public. He appeared on Sunday Television Talk with Reverend Michael Hamilton, wrote a pop editorial for *Newsweek*, and articulated the moral complexity of HGE at Washington National Cathedral.[55] The government advisory commissions on bioethics that Evans says were dimming public controversy appear front and center in letters and newspaper editorials discarded from the sample.[56]

Picture the variety of items excluded in principle. From 1966 to 1971, the Nobel Prize winning biologist Joshua Lederberg issued approximately 194 essays in the *Washington Post* through his regular column on the social implications of biotechnology.[57] Putting technique first, *Playing God* barred this kind of nonscholarly column aimed at a general readership [G 206], whereas the book's moralistic finding is that the public tended not to be addressed as the target audience [G 57, 70–71, 180–181]. In his content summary of the period 1959–1974, Evans writes that "[l]ater scientists, such as Joshua Lederberg...had stopped being explicit about the ends of their research..." [G 64]. In reality, Lederberg, in twin roles as molecular biologist and generous public intellectual, ardently clarified and advocated ends, although *Playing God*'s ritual technology ignored the publications by which he did so. Lederberg warned in the solemn tone of a theologian how short-term reasoning about biotechnology may transfigure the long-term human prospect.[58] "The first step in constructive self-education is a more specific critical foresight as to the substantial dangers of misapplied biology," Lederberg wrote.[59] Judging by real-world publications, Lederberg, whom Evans portrays as formally rational and remote, was possibly more explicit in deliberating with the public about goals than was Paul Ramsey, among Evans's purest cases of substantively rational public engagement [G 69].

By ejecting nonfootnoted items, Evans eliminated publications that may have exercised a more decisive effect on *both* elites and the public than items remaining in the sample. News articles quote experts afresh rather than "cite" published tomes.[60] For example, influential experts in Evans's selection as well as some outside it recall Lederberg's provocative newspaper columns as drivers of scholarly debate but do not cite these columns. Leon Kass, Chair of the US Bioethics Commission under the junior President Bush, even said that the publication of Lederberg's 1967 news column on "Unpredictable Variety" was the event that motivated Kass to switch from biology to philosophy.[61] But such an historical landmark without the apparatus of footnotes could not survive in the sample. Inside the scientific perspective on texts, a decline in addresses to the public via one medium, footnoted print, misleads us as tunnel vision unable to grasp changing media and the status of public intellectuals at large.[62]

CREATING A PURIFIED DIAGRAM

The second task in the ritual phase of separation is that of organizing meaning as if it came from a supra-human source. The aggregation of citations serves this function: if each footnote is seen as equivalent independent of context, we can from the scientific perspective mechanically measure relative intellectual prominence and depict which publications tend to be cocited, as in figure 3.1. The cluster diagram sketches which influential authors tended to be cited together [G 156]. The exact "look" is key to the discovery process, yet in a blurred genre, diagrams can change shapes in murky ways.

Evans in the 2002 book *Playing God* produced importantly *different* diagrams out of the *same* data inputs as in the 1998 dissertation "Playing God." How did this change transpire? For the 1992–1995 interval of debate, Evans raised the threshold for inclusion as an influential author in the cluster diagram from nine citations in the dissertation to ten in the book. This chart trimming changed the storyline significantly. For instance, the sociologist Troy Duster, whose work seems to run contrary to Evans's thesis for the final period, 1992–1995, is among several other authors who dropped out of the diagram. Duster had emphasized the need to debate multiple biotechnologies in tandem; he had insisted on a long-term view based on categorical values; he had taken society as the unit of analysis; and he had accented the role of group mobilization rather than that of individual decision-making. All these features seem to mark Duster as a fresh substantively rational voice. Evan's conclusion in *Playing God* is that this kind of writer is waning, not emerging anew among the influential writers during 1992–1995. Above all, Duster called for critical public discussion on values *while* he depended on funding from federal agencies such as the National Institute of Child Health, a somewhat unlikely conjuncture by Evans's theory of resource dependency [G 194]. Evans propounds [G 165–173] that by the culminating period of 1992–1995, it required a rabble-rouser of the street such as Jeremy Rifkin, or at least someone who circumvented academics, to revive social values: "Rifkin in his ethical writings speaks directly to the public, bypassing…the debate now dominated by bioethicists and scientists" [G 170]. Duster disconfirms Evans's message that substantive rationality can be sustained only by theological or antiacademic populist writing after 1992. "In the book I say that theological and other comprehensive perspectives were squeezed out of the debate that had influence on what actually happened with HGE," Evans writes, "because the proponents of these perspectives wanted to discuss ends."[63] But that is exactly what a whole series of authors who qualified as influential for the dissertation "Playing God" did, who were excised from the write-up in *Playing God* the book.

RAW DATA CHANGES

More intriguing is how the charts change Rifkin's objective citation count between the dissertation "Playing God" and the book. Rifkin would have been expected to fall below the threshold to remain in the book's 1992–1995 diagram, just as Duster dropped out, for in the dissertation Rifkin and Duster started out with equal citations.[64] But sacrificing Rifkin might have weakened the final evidence that resurgent substantive value rationality depends on populist intervention [G 170, 194]. Surmounting the newly raised threshold, Rifkin's citing texts for 1992–1995 increased from "9" total in the dissertation to "14" in the book [G 138]. It is uncertain how such an increase could appear while Evans reported the contributing citations from Rifkin's two most-cited works as unchanged between the dissertation and book versions of *Playing God*.[65] Perhaps Evans decided to convert the Ted Howard coauthor citations for *Who Should Play God?* to Rifkin citations,[66] but were this alone the explanation the Howard/Rifkin book would probably show up among heavily cited works listed for this 1992–1995 period in *Playing God* [G 225]. This bailout of Rifkin would also have violated Evans's crediting rules, since both dissertation and book specify that only first author weighed in the diagrams.[67] The computer procedures and inputs are verbatim identical between the dissertation and book, yet the outputted numbers—in one critical instance alone—differ. Why is the only raw number change a crucial one that let Rifkin remain inside the revamped clusters?

Curious as shifting numbers may appear, they are trivial in relation to the disarrangement at bottom: to play the role of marginalized protestor, Rifkin had to remain as statistically influential to qualify in the narrative about sample contents. On consideration, it seems instead that the debaters truly sidelined would not enter the club of the statistically influential in the first place. How many formally rational writers with extensive government funding and how many substantively rational ones were in this fashion invisibly marginalized by the ritual process?

The lesson is, depending on where it pleases you to set thresholds, the cluster diagrams mutate. Rifkin in the dissertation had formed a separate community with Duster, Daniel Kevles, and Arthur Caplan, all nontheologians, but in the book this community evaporates and Rifkin joins a cluster of theologians, a group that Evans spotlights as "a distinct community" [G 165]. Given the same data inputs, seven communities now collapse via the same "jump test" as before into a new set of five with a simpler storyline. The output follows preferences for an arresting look [G 209]. "Although the strategy of clustering may be structure-seeking," one of Evans's referenced handbooks summed up, "its operation is one that is structure-imposing."[68] Evans's quantitative diagrams reflect interpretive decisions very far down indeed.

To be sure, Evans endorses two heuristics to assure generating his clusters is not whimsical. First, he reminds us that he sought natural break points in the data where the similarity between the clusters makes the largest "jump." Second, he indicates that he tried to keep the total number of cases between time frames approximately equal.[69] Somewhere both guidelines may have become irrelevant between dissertation and book. If I comprehend, raising the citation threshold for 1992–1995 looks deviant, since the slice of data for this period already featured the fewest cases.[70] Second, the natural "jumps" in the data were the same for the dissertation and the book, but Evans judged differently when he drew new communities in diagrams for 1985–1991 as well as for 1992–1995.

The revised diagram for 1992–1995 drops influential Sheldon Krimsky, who in a cited piece invoked the absence of "a strong consensus from an informed electorate" to prohibit not only application of germline engineering, but "initiating such experiments."[71] The subtitle of Krimsky's widely circulated book—*The Rise of Industrial Genetics*—conveys his radical concern for the ultimate purpose of technology in relation to society.[72] Or consider authors David Suzuki and Peter Knudtson, retained as statistically powerful for the period 1992–1995 in the book but absent from the narrative report. In *Genethics: The Clash between the New Genetics and Human Values* they wrote that they hoped to

> have demonstrated a process by which nonscientists—armed with an understanding of basic principles of heredity and a sense of some of the uncomfortable lessons of history—can join in a dialogue about critical genetic issues that is too often reserved for individuals with special privileges, powers or expertise…We can also draw on the wisdom and humanity embodied in our traditional religions, political parties, professional organizations and courts of law.[73]

They virtually require a ban on germ-line therapy: "Germ-line therapy, without the consent of all members of society, ought to be explicitly forbidden" (346)—the very opinion that Evans tells you would scarcely have been maintained by statistically influential authors in his sample [G 4], let alone someone prominent enough to enjoy, as Suzuki did, 24 honorary degrees.[74] If you recognize the statistically paramount Duster, Krimsky, Suzuki, Kundtson, plus the activist Rifkin, you have in Evans's dissertation data a sizable, institutionally ensconced group of fresh dissidents, as viable as formally rational bioethicists. It is difficult to reconcile them with the claim that elites who deliberate on collective values are depleted and marginalized [G 153, 155, 165]. Put together these biotech critics and the theologians, as originally diagrammed in the "Playing God" dissertation, and they seem to equal the individual bioethicists whose works were highlighted as stifling moral contention.[75] The complete information in my view upends a streamlined tale about the dominance of formal rationality.

Chart trimming is not unusual, according to self-reports from investigators. In a survey of over 3,000 NIH-funded scientists, 15 percent acknowledged something more serious, "dropping observations or data points from analyses based on a gut feeling that they were inaccurate."[76] By comparison, in *Playing God* the most that goes on is revamping diagrams and improving raw numbers. If there is contrived mutual adjustment of "the data" for better fit with a model, this is objectionable only when the process is invisible.[77]

THE COSMOLOGY OF THE DIAGRAMS

The final challenge in the ritual phase of separation is to subsume the spectator into a morally ambiguous role. In *Playing God*, Evans accomplishes this by recasting the intellectual producer (possibly a sociologist) as a strategic agent who creates publications for the sake of competing for scarce resources. Evans brings this theory to life by mixing the verbal and the pictorial: he projects his social theory onto the brute numbers and names in figure 3.1. Once we "see" the diagram in this light, it returns novel statements about social relations. There are three components of the social projection and reimagining: the data comprise the arena of a social game, the purpose of writing is to accumulate resources, and citing another writer's work in this game activates that writer's symbolic importance.[78]

The data comprise the arena of a social game: The diagrams of citations call a game board to life—"As texts to learn from, or to be used as persuasion, cited texts are 'important'; entrants to the debate must familiarize themselves with these texts before they begin" [G 207]. Thinking and writing have sense once located as strategic moves in a fixed arena. Via the visual representation one can learn there is such a thing as a bounded "debate about HGE" or a system of texts with autonomous dynamics. The succession of text contents, culled from different locations under different intellectual circumstances, is imagined to occupy the same perduring arena although the citation links are recreated for each time slice and do not correspond to fixed institutions or forums. Only the theory-laden description of the assemblage of citation-linked works as "the HGE debate" suggests that aggregate citation patterns, not intellectuals using texts for more specifically meaningful purposes outside "the debate," decide a writer's position in the diagram.

The purpose of writing is to accumulate resources: The purpose of writing is to accumulate resources, and this entails looking agreeable to those who can dispense resources.

> For example, if the primary resource a young bioethicist at a Catholic college is competing for is tenure, to obtain that resource he or she must achieve a certain status in the field. Perhaps thirty-five years ago the pinnacle of status was to have your magnum opus used by the Church's marriage classes, but today the goal is to be cited by the government bioethics commission. This implies a difference in the preferred form of argumentation, which in turn will tend to change the form of rationality used by professors in similar structural locations. [G 26]

Thus basic changes in the form of argument reflect changes in the dependencies between authors and the resource-granting authorities, in this example the church versus federal offices. The exogenous control of resources, not just the signifying force of arguments in the texts, causes the dominant forms of argument in the arena to change: "Explaining in a cumulative sense why the supporters of formal rationality 'won' in this competition and why the supports of substantive rationality 'lost' requires examining the factors that allowed some actors to disseminate their arguments, while others could not" [G 26].

Citing another writer's work in this game activates that work's overall symbolic importance: If authors tend to be cited together in a piece and therefore tend to cluster together in figure 3.1, it indicates that the authors—not selected useful subportions of their texts—are seen as similar or related overall. "For example, the average debater in this era thought that the work of Kass and Ramsey was more closely related than the work of either of these authors was to that of René Dubos" [G 46]. What makes the citations meaningfully comparable objects for counting? In reality, a cite may be polemically chosen to present the weakest version of an opposing argument.[79] Yet the theory standardizes the purpose of citing to that of referencing another's influence on the game board.

For the phase of separation, the reductive casting of social relations in "the debate" strips the identity of intellectuals down to attention-seeking: "one would be naive to think that writers do not make compromises at the margins in order to obtain what is often the greatest resource—being listened to" [G27]. That reduction not only gives each "participant" a morally ambiguous role as an opportunistic peddler. It also echoes richly the primary divide between instrumental and value rationality. Who represents values of substance for the public and who to the contrary exploits careerist formalism to cater to funding sources? That question is acutely applicable to members of the ritual audience, sociologists. In the phase of integration, Evans clarifies the conditions under which members of the sociological community may hope to adopt a secure outlook.

WHAT DO CITATIONS REVEAL?

To equate cites as an index of influence requires us to wipe off the chart—through blank diagrammatic space—the real places in which writing comes to life. Authors are embedded in diverse intellectual traditions, each with its own citing purposes. What a cite "is" varies by styles of argumentative exchange. The purpose of the social theory applied upon the data is to reimagine from the standpoint of "science" that there is a standard causal system that generates citations independent of specific meanings. The motives for citing have to be treated artificially as undifferentiated, since they are subjective and off the chart [G 209]. Then Evans uses the mechanically outputted citation "data" to rediscover, *now* from the totally different standpoint of interpretation, what cites in the diagram verbally "mean" overall. This *blurring* of the rigors of the interpretive and of the scientific lets mannered imagining play a role in proceedings. For 1959–1974, Evans projects onto the clusters the conclusion that "[i]f we look at the commonalities across the influential members of this [theological] community, we can see what was important: to push the debate, which had become somewhat formally rational with the younger scientists, back toward a more purely substantively rational form" [G 64].

Only erasing history and culture in ritual separation from mundane reality makes it conceivable to locate all citations in blank space as if they were exposed in a single system. If a sliver of producers cites copiously from another sliver, whatever class of works they cite will appear popular although it is *not* receiving such a thing as generic "attention" from authors at large.[80] Evans himself demonstrates that reconsidering quantitative results in their individual contexts discredits the diagrams as net tracers of rationalities. For the 1985–1991 diagram Evans disposes of the anomaly that the Catholic theologian Richard McCormick of Notre Dame is affiliated most closely with the formally rational bioethicists. "To ensure a correct interpretation I reexamined the citing documents to determine what part of this edited volume authors were citing and why McCormick was cited in general."[81] Evans discovered that cites of McCormick referred to McCormick's narrow treatment of issues such as informed consent. "The more broad-framed components of McCormick's work were referred to much less often, thus explaining why McCormick is located here [with bioethicists] in the diagram."[82] The unexpected result led Evans to discover by old-school interpretation that McCormick, whose work appears to be primarily substantively rational, was being *used* for "narrow frame," instrumental reasoning. But if texts house "a *correct* interpretation," imputing a generic default meaning on each citation is misleading since, as Evans insists, every publication houses components of both formal (instrumental) and substantive (value) rationality.[83] If a citation can select either from any work, there is little rationale for Evans to treat the numbers of cites as indicators of the dominance of a particular rationality [G 155, 268].

Just as the Azande selectively invoke context to certify divinations, only the cocitations that reinforce what we think we already know matter in *Playing God*. Were Evans correct in classifying W. French Anderson as emblematic of formal rationality, a theologian nonetheless quoted Anderson's passages (to which I also once happened to call attention)[84] as expressing the substantive value rationality of the church. Reverend Brian Johnstone highlighted one of Anderson's passages as confirming allegiance with the church's overriding value concerns for social justice, humility, and collective responsibility in decision-making, and protection of human dignity, not at all for the consequentialist, individualist decision-making that Evans espied in Anderson's work.[85] Cites typically propagate misleading readings of positions.[86] Pierre Bourdieu as a theorist of cunning argued that tracking citations is a "supremely naive representation of cultural production."[87] Citation traffic in the scientific worldview in *Playing God* is unconnectable to its interpretive interest in how styles of reasoning operate.[88]

Most fundamentally, there is no rationale from the humanist perspective for taking citations as comparable "units." In Evans's account, substantively rational authors broad-mindedly weigh alternatives, which might lead them to cite intensively the formally rational authors they criticize. By contrast, formally rational authors, focusing on narrow means-end calculation, might have needed to cite less and to do so more exclusively from those similar to themselves. Variation in the *type of argument used in the debate ("meanings") undermines the use of frequencies of citation (quasi-scientific "variables") to measure the relative dominance of types of rationality.* Substantively rational authors could produce in our eyes their own quantitative marginalization (measured by citations) even when as speakers the substantively rational authors are as viable as their competitors.[89] Since argumentative rationality is *defined* by Evans as a way of positioning oneself in relation to other authors, rationality has to skew citing practices. Evans's citation analysis mobilizes the "scientific" worldview to assume fantastically that the causes of cites are unrelated to the genre of argument in which they occur—as if the context-specific purpose neither precipitated the cite nor bore a considerable relation to the cite's meaning.[90]

If we imagine that in vigorous contestation there may be a handful of authoritative writers who testify about applying a biotechnology and that there may be a wider spread of moral spokespersons who testify about values guiding HGE in general, then writers about competing values will be less able than those focusing on means to have their citations combine into peaks to qualify as "influential." This might hold even if the writers on ends direct discussion. If dispersed legitimacy reigns in controversies about human ends, the ends-focused writers will appear less "influential" by *Playing God*'s statistical measure. In the 1980s and beyond, each religious denomination developed its own tradition in bioethics, as indicated in the compilations by denomination at the Kennedy Institute of Ethics in 1994, the end of Evans's reporting period.[91] Paul Ramsey, for example, could command the field of cites early in the day because he wrote prior to Protestantism's fragmenting and prior to deeper recognition of spiritual diversity. Surely we ought not reason quantitatively that debate about ends is "stronger" the more it is concentrated in a handful of luminaries. As differentiated religious traditions nurture distinctive stances toward biotechnology to thicken substantive rationality, their works and citations might disperse, making intellectual diversity appear as weakness due to the threshold for appearing in a cluster diagram. Citations that grant authors entry as "influential" into the diagrams have no standard causal generator permitting comparison over time.

These incongruities originate in the crossing of scientific and interpretive perspectives. In the phase of separation we strip citations of contextual purpose to create "units," and then we pretend their raw occurrences do not depend systematically upon the very meanings we appraise in a subsequent ritual phase. We pretend a style of rational argument is unrelated to citation culture so that we can use citations to estimate a style of rationality—an operation whose absurdity is obscured only by fetishizing a method as if it worked outside our powers as cultural agents. The error looks self-made whenever we try to unite "scientific" counting protocols with interpretation. "Influence" has to concern rich messages for it to carry intelligible sense. It is a philosophical error to apply the term to empty forms of citation traffic, without determining first, "influential" with respect to which meaningful features?[92] "In my research," Evans wrote, "the question was which top-cited authors were most similar to each other based on the texts that cited them" [G 209]. Similar how?

Decades ago the analytic philosopher Nelson Goodman convincingly showed "similarity" lacks sense beyond particular and incommensurable practices of contrast and comparison.[93] Whatever might we be talking about when we demonstrate what relative "influence" *means* by frequency citations *and* when we have no operative concept of influence outside this arbitrary measurement? As with ritual process, the models of citation counts merely bring to life a visual experience of a symbol's use and substitute for the symbol's conceptual definition. Likewise, as anthropologists know, ritual practice summons worlds of totemic enactment that are irreducible to a religion's verbal "theology." The vehicles in coding rituals move like tokens in their partial independence from both the world of intelligible concepts and from the world of meaningfully denotable objects outside the ritual.

Of course, like inescapable predictions announced by ancient oracles, the theory that writers triumph in debate through net citations bears a message that dooms anyone who would contest its point of view. Attending seriously to an opponent by referencing them only ratchets up their credits for "influence."

THE LIMINAL PHASE

The free-form part of the ritual takes off when Evans codes the prime publications making up the diagrams "to determine the content" [G 211].[94] This coding solves the riddle of classifying rationality that we saw Weber bequeathed to us from the Protestant Ethic. Fortunately, Evans underscores the systematic character of his coding:

> The content of the arguments of both the influential and common members of the communities is critical. To determine the content of each of these influential authors' works, I read their most cited text during each time period, and coded it descriptively and interpretively. The second most cited text for each author was also coded if it had more than 50 percent of the citations that the top-cited text had. In cases of ties, both texts were coded. [G 211]

> First, *methodological canons* in my field require that I not only read texts, but "code" them, essentially *categorizing paragraphs* as referring to certain themes, in order to look for insights in the relationships between paragraphs and between texts. Coding all 1,465 texts would have been far too time-consuming.[95]

> I obtained the most cited text from each most cited author and interpretively read and coded it as described above, focusing on the substantively/formally rational distinction that my critics have described so well above.[96]

In response to critics, Evans affirmed that his coding gauged frequencies of types of rationality:

> Childress states that I greatly oversimplify principlism and exaggerate its role and influence. I respond that I am just reporting what I see among the common and influential writers in the debate about HGE. One of the reasons I set up my research as I did, with such concern for representativeness of texts in the debate, was to be able to respond to criticisms such as this... I do not doubt that there are people who consider themselves to be doing bioethics who are following this framework (and would then not be bioethicists by my definition), but they are few compared to those who are following principlism.[97]

Phrases such as "they are few compared to" suggest quantitative estimates.[98] "I would have classified all of James Gustafson's work into a one-word category," Evans wrote.[99] "Once one analyzes a large number of texts, simplified classification is necessary."[100]

To indicate concretely how this coding was recorded, Evans refers us to instructions in Matthew Miles and Michael Huberman's *Qualitative Data Analysis*:

> Codes are tags or labels for assigning *units* of meaning to the descriptive or inferential information compiled during a study. Codes usually are attached to *"chunks"* of varying size—words, phrases, sentences, or whole paragraphs, connected or unconnected to a specific setting...Codes are used to retrieve and organize the chunks mentioned earlier. The organizing part will entail some system for categorizing the various chunks, so the researcher can quickly find, pull out, and cluster the *segments* relating to a particular research question, hypothesis, construct, or theme.[101]

Evans would have produced many hundreds if not thousands of coding observations when he was "categorizing paragraphs" and looking "for insights in the relationships between paragraphs and between texts."[102] This guide referenced by Evans also emphasizes that in such coding "clear operational definitions are indispensable,

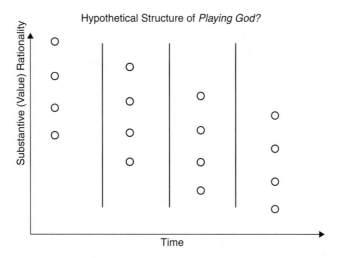

Figure 3.2   Summary of coding results.

Source: Adapted from John Evans, "Two Worlds of Cultural Sociology," in *Meaning and Method*, ed. Jeffrey Alexander and Isaac Reed (Boulder: Paradigm, 2009), p. 219.

DIMENSION	SUBSTANTIVE RATIONALITY	FORMAL RATIONALITY
Debating ends	Ends are defined and defended.	Ends are implicit or considered outside the decision-making process.
Number of ends considered legitimate in the entire debate	Unlimited	Limited in number
Universality of ends	Ends are not believed to be universally held by individuals, although the author may want them to be. Different ends may be relevant to different means.	Ends, particularly when translated into a commensurable metric, are considered to be universal ends of all persons in society or even the world. The same ends should be applicable to all problems.
Commensurability of ends	Ends are not commensurable.	Ends can be translated into a common end or a limited set of ends. Ends that cannot be translated are bracketed as unimportant.
Link between means and end with which to evaluate argument	Means consistent with system of ultimate values or ends are ethical. Means that are inconsistent are not.	Any means that maximizes ends is ethical.

Figure 3.3   Components of debates dominated by substantively or formally rational argument.

Source: Wording from *Playing God?* (Chicago: University of Chicago Press, 2002), p. 19.

so they can be applied consistently by a single researcher over time and multiple researchers will be thinking about the same phenomena as they code."[103] Evans aggregated his codes for paragraphs by text and community: "You have to look at all the passages of text to describe the overall message of the text (and, cumulatively, all of the texts in the community)."[104]

The coded descent of substantive rationality in the sample appears in figure 3.2, with four positions on the x axis corresponding to four sliced periods of debate over

HGE. It shows an ordinal ranking of the texts by rationality, with substantive value rationality highest at the top of the y axis. For a large fraction of the sample across time periods, it looks as if texts overlapped in the overall degree of formal (instrumental) rationality. It is all the more critical, then, to discriminate relative substantive and relative formal rationality in the texts accurately.

Playing God presents the five criteria Evans used for "parsing arguments in a particular debate into substantive and formal, thick and thin" [G 14], reproduced in figure 3.3. To operationalize the contrasting rationalities by developing such local indicators is ingenious. It deserves extension to much of cultural sociology—if we are able penetrate its operation to reapply it.

CODING AS DIVERTISSEMENT

In his NSF proposal "Playing God," Evans highlighted his need for "comparable measurements of the past and present culture."[105] All the more befuddling, then, to discover that the coding results seem not to correspond to text contents in a retraceable manner. Where else to begin than with the most prominent author on Evans's list? That would be the paragon scientist Hermann Muller. In the opening era, Evans summed up, Muller "had been the most influential author. His ends, form of argumentation, and means had set the tone for the entire debate" [G 74]. According to Evans, "The HGE debate of the 1950s and the 1960s was dominated by reform eugenicist scientists, such as Hermann Muller, Julian Huxley, and Theodosius Dobzhansky. To them, HGE was synonymous with what was later called germline HGE. This debate was substantive and thick—and largely about ends" [G 179]. Examining Muller's two top-cited texts offers a crucial glimpse of how the coding works.

Muller's primary documents are perplexing, for by each of Evans's five criteria they appear formally rational, opposite Evans's report of Muller's substantive rationality. Follow each of the "five components" that Evans listed in his original menu [G 19][106]:

A First Criterion of Instrumental Formal Rationality: "Ends, particularly when translated into a commensurable metric, are considered to be universal ends of all persons in society or even the world." This criterion seems perfectly exemplified in Muller's condensing of ends in his top-cited work:

> Despite the carping and quibbling of some philosophers, the most generalized rational formulation of human aims that most persons concerned with the subject can agree upon is the promotion of the greatest overall happiness. We need not define happiness more precisely here than as the sense of fulfillment derived from the attainment, or from approaching the attainment, of whatever is deeply desired. (Any one of a number of other terms might, of course, be substituted for "happiness" here, provided that it is defined in this way).[107]

Muller acknowledges that sadists who wish to poison others would dissent, but he places such deviants outside consideration. Dismissal of opponents as unreasonable incarnates formal rationality, Evans notes, because it squelches contestation over ends [G 157], making Muller inescapably formally rational. Similarly, in the other publication by Muller that Evans coded, Muller posited the goal of "genetic improvement of the population" as so obvious for human welfare, it need not even be debated in the present.[108]

Note that Muller's definition of the final end, "greatest overall happiness," is so vacuous, hardly anyone could contest it. For Evans this is the absolute fingerprint of formal (instrumental) rationality: "a fairly thin, safe assumption that is probably universal, or nearly so" [G 18]. It is "defined in such a thin way that almost no one could disagree with it (e.g., 'it is better to do good than to do harm')" [G 18]. More exactly, Muller's end of "happiness" is what Evans lists in his dissertation as the prototype of formal instrumental rationality[109] and in the book as formal rational utilitarianism: "In utilitarianism, unlike the bioethics profession's form of argumentation, there are not four ends but one—human happiness. This end is justified because it is universal" [G 270]. More interesting still, in *Playing God* it is difficult to find footnoted counterevidence in favor of the substantively rational character of ends for Muller. How Evans could have coded Muller so discrepantly as illustrating substantive rationality will become more puzzling still.

A Second Criterion of Instrumental Formal Rationality: "Ends are limited in number: Ends can be translated into a common end or a limited set of ends." Again, Muller's text fits perfectly. Muller endorses a single goal, and this unification, an aid to efficient means-end calculation, is the benchmark Evans adduces as advanced formal rationality. Muller writes that

> [t]he will to self-development—hedonism—the urge to achieve—functionalism—the ideal of service—altruism—and a spiritual attitude toward existence—consecration—all these modes of approach to living, when followed up logically, become *finally resolved into the pursuit of the same objective*...The final objective, likewise, may be thought of and designated in different ways, such as human happiness, richness of life, increasing survival, or advancement, since these are all diverse aspects of *one* great combination that in practice remains inseparable.[110]

As Muller says, following his formal means-end logic, "[t]his question must then be raised: What genetic and cultural backgrounds are conducive to the highest success, as judged by the ulterior criterion of their promotion of over-all happiness?"[111] To answer, Muller explicates the proper constituents of culture for the sake of strengthening the "drive to coordinate the elements rationally."[112]

It was foreseeable that Muller would have had a fixed number of formally rational ends (in fact, one). As Evans writes in his book, the scientists with Muller at the head had "a formally rational link between means and ends," and such a link drives one to reduce the number of ends. "The ultimate force behind this reduction (as I shall argue below) is the need to make arguments more calculable...Of course, the debate would be even more calculable if there were only one end to be considered" [G 16]. Furthermore, the ends in substantive rationality are of a fundamentally different character (thick and nonuniversal) than are those for calculative means-end reasoning [G 18]. By Evans's definitions, it would have been difficult to find the slightest evidence Muller's texts were substantively rational.

A Third Criterion of Instrumental Formal Rationality: "Any means that maximizes ends is ethical." Muller's two texts designate the maximal promotion of genetic improvement as the only relevant criterion. For "genetic upgrading," Muller recommends that "couples of high native endowment" (breeders) bear more children than they can raise. Their excess will be farmed out to other families,[113] removing from most males the wish to procreate, the better to become "love fathers."[114] The selectively bred offspring should be tagged publicly, to convince prospective child-rearers to adopt superbabies.[115] Sperm donors would serve a "probationary period" while their progeny were tested.[116] All such tools considered abhorrent must nonetheless be mobilized for utility.

Fourth Criterion of Formal Rationality: The "number of ends considered legitimate in the entire debate" is "limited in number." Muller stigmatizes those who would oppose maximally efficient pursuit of genetic betterment as if they held onto an "inviolable taboo" or protected "sacred cows."[117] But this is precisely the rhetoric Evans crowns as the hallmark of formal rationality [G 157]. Muller rejects sacred prohibitions: "The obstacles to carrying out such an improvement in [genetic] selection are psychological ones, based on antiquated traditions from which we can emancipate ourselves."[118]

Fifth Criterion of Formal Rationality: "Ends are implicit or considered outside the decision-making process" [G 19]. In Muller's second-place publication, the end of "significant genetic improvement of the population" is not even justified as a goal, but is posited as guaranteeing "unexpected benefits."[119] Likewise, in the top-cited publication Muller writes "But before discussing these questions of biological means, it is important to consider ends—or rather, objectives."[120] Then Muller legislates the answer with the "greatest overall happiness" of the population as the only "rational formulation," putting other ends outside the sphere of ongoing deliberation.[121] "The classic commensurable end metric is the 'utility' of utilitarianism," Evans wrote in *Playing God*, where all ends are translated or reduced to the scale of the "greatest good for the greatest number" [G 17]. It is bewildering that Evans marks Muller's specific type of expression as the epitome of an instrumental formally rational end, but codes Muller exactly opposite. Muller scorns citizens rather than addressing them: "most of the human beings" in the world today know so little of scientific equations, Muller writes, "they have hardly a glimmering of what is involved—while seeking to turn these forces chiefly to such purposes as broadcasting television commercials, football games, burlesque shows, and revival meetings, or seeing Europe in a week or accurately dropping H-bombs nine thousand miles away."[122] According to Evans, such elitism is a hallmark of formal rationality, in which the writer legislates ends and looks past the ends actually held: "Using ends like these enhances calculability because the ends actually held by the individuals in questions do not have to be consulted, only assumed" [G 18].

Muller disparages public deliberations: "even if the government is of some democratic form" it should be treated with suspicion, Muller insists, because "governments, including relatively enlightened ones, represent in some respects the lowest common denominator of progressive thinking."[123] Instead, Muller wants to keep decision-making in the hands of scientists, Evans's insignia of formally rational writers [G 55]. What a riddle for Evans to write that the eugenic scientists such as Muller took the public as "the target audience" and as the "decision-maker" [G 69].

By each of Evans's five operational markers, it appears we have a remarkable discrepancy between coding criteria versus outputs. Imagine how difficult it would be for Muller to fulfill the substantively rational standard that "the number of ends considered legitimate in the entire debate" is "unlimited." Of course any reading can be destabilized if we insert texts into a new meta-frame, as Weber did for Benjamin Franklin when Weber subordinated Franklin's utilitarian reasoning to a hypothesized religious ethic.[124] Coding by "paragraphs" yields clues but cannot "determine the content" of texts for a Weberian model of rationality.[125]

Let us consider an equally surprising reversal, an outstanding author who Evans classifies as formally rational [G 161] but who seems by the evidence to fulfill opposite criteria. To concretize the flux between substantive and formal rationality, Evans contrasts Muller with the philosopher Jonathan Glover. But the coding again looks topsy-turvy upon revisiting Glover's statistically prominent *What Sort of People Should There Be?*[126]

When you espy texts as "data," the standards for reading them are prone to weaken. In *Playing God*, monstrous riffs that Muller uttered prior to World War II are attributed to Glover instead. Of Glover's book Evans writes:

> In this dream of species improvement he [Glover] reaches back to the vision of Hermann Muller, and quotes extensively and approvingly from his [Muller's] 1935 book. In the first, "preparatory phase of history," humankind was the "helpless creature of its environment, and natural selection gradually ground it into human shape." In the second state of history, according to Muller, humankind reached "out at the immediate environment, shaking, shaping and grinding to suit the form, the requirements, the wishes and the whims of man." *In Glover's vision*, in humankind's "long third phase," humankind "will reach down into the secret places of the great universe of its own nature, and by aid of its ever growing intelligence and cooperation, shape itself into an increasingly sublime creation—a being beside which the mythical divinities of the past will seem more and more ridiculous, and which setting its own marvelous powers against the brute Goliath of the suns and the planets, challenges them to contest." [G 165; emphasis added]

Here Evans credits Muller with the second phase in the sequence of human development. Depending on how you limn it, Evans portrays Glover as authoring or endorsing Muller's third phase—"*In Glover's vision.*" The monomaniacal words about jettisoning divinities in the third phase are only Muller's parlance, however, not Glover's. Glover quotes a three-sentence remark of Muller's, so in this sense it is true the phrases occur "in" Glover's vision. Yet Glover instantly distanced himself from Muller's exposition: "The case for positive engineering is not helped by adopting the tones of the mad scientist in a horror film," Glover mocked. "To find a distinguished geneticist talking like this after the Nazi period is not easy."[127] To be sure, Glover recognizes the logic behind Muller's scary rhetoric. Whether Glover quotes Muller "extensively and approvingly," as Evans concludes, seems doubtful [G 164–165]. More baffling is how Evans coded Glover's book mostly formally rational [G 161, 165]:

First Criterion for Substantive Value Rationality: "Ends are defined and debated" [G 19]. Whereas Muller decreed one end and devoted his text to implementing it,

Glover compares ends extensively by bracketing questions about implementation: "I shall also assume that we can ignore problems about whether positive engineering will be technically possible. Suppose we have the power to choose people's genetic characteristics. Once we have eliminated genetic defects, what if anything, should we do with this power?"[128] Such expository sidelining of the feasibility of means is the essence of substantive rationality in *Playing God* [G 21], so Evans's apparent inconsistency looks strange from the get-go.

Second Criterion for Substantive Rationality: "The number of ends considered legitimate in the entire debate" is "unlimited" [G 19]. Evans portrays Glover as having only one fixed and ultimately vacuous end, autonomy, to avoid any collective setting of substantive goals: "While authors such as Ramsey, Huxley, and Muller had debated in order to convince others to accept their ends, Glover thinks that this debate will not be possible in our newly pluralistic public culture. We can get around this problem, he argues, by forwarding only the end of autonomy" [G 161]. Could Glover have reasoned so? Glover entertains a spectrum of technologies, including the far-fetched possibility of invading individuals' thoughts via their brain waves. By radically rethinking technological conditions for deciding what is valuable in human existence, Glover excavates *multiple* ends: "to ignore the subtle values can be philistine and stifling," Glover concludes.[129] For him, the "aim of the thought experiments has been to bring these unnoticed background values into the foreground, and to bring them into sharper focus."[130] For other authors Evans highlights such experiment as the sign of substantive rationality: "Indeed, for the substantively rational author, speculating about technologies that may not be operative for hundreds of years is a good way of arguing for ends" [G 21]. How Glover was coded the reverse is bewildering.

Glover chaired a European Union Commission inquiry on the Ethics of New Reproductive Technologies that included a section on "positive genetic engineering."[131] Evans quotes Glover as follows: "What he [Glover] envisions is a 'genetic supermarket,' which would meet 'the individual specifications (within certain moral limits) of prospective parents'" [G 161]. Here again, findings appear to emerge by mischance. The words Evans attributed to Glover occur in a passage of Robert Nozick's libertarian *Anarchy, State, and Utopia*, which Glover happened to quote before advancing toward a different position.[132] Once Glover elucidates the alternatives, Glover prefers a "mixed system" with parental initiative and central oversight and, potentially, government planning. Glover recommends that the state orchestrate "some centralized decision for genetic change" if the benefits become substantial or if government control would overcome social dysfunction. Glover justifies this state intervention by the criterion of collective desirability, not just "moral limits" on the character of individual acts.[133] Glover sees the mixed system he advocates as appropriate for "Western European social democrats," by contrast to a "supermarket," which appears to him as "an 'American' model."[134] If Glover rejects a genetic supermarket as belonging to a foreign political culture, it can scarcely characterize his position properly.[135] For these cumulative reasons, the report in *Playing God* that Glover "advocates autonomy to avoid the setting of ends" appears implausible [G 164].

Confounding Nozick's words with Glover's is how testimony arose in *Playing God* that Glover made individual autonomy trump the need for collective debate and policy intervention. Glover crowns as decisive other ends for human life, above all its quality, conceived apart from autonomy.[136]

> It is not just *any* aspect of present human nature that is worth preserving. Rather it is especially those features which contribute to self-development and self-expression, to certain kinds of relationships, and to the development of our consciousness and understanding...If these are some of our values, we can be guided by them in welcoming or opposing the developments scientists offer us. We may for once have some idea of what we do and do not want before the technology is irreversibly with us.[137]

No wonder the National Library of Medicine's Bioethicsline counted "quality of life" as a keyword in its entry for Glover, but not "autonomy." To me, the National Library of Medicine's labels, on which Evans relies, run counter to *Playing God*'s reports about text contents.[138]

Third Criterion of Substantive Rationality: "Ends are not believed to be universally held by individuals, although the author may want them to be." Glover wrote in his introduction that

> [t]he aim is to bring out some of the underlying questions of value more clearly. The intention is to describe the possibilities in ways that separate out separate values, and to say, "these values rather than those are what matter, aren't they"? Of course, in a way I hope for the answer "yes." But, because people have different outlooks, the answer will quite often be "no."[139]

In keeping with substantive rationality, Glover postulated his values were not universal, and he advocated only "thinking coherently about kinds of life as a whole."[140]

Fourth Criterion of Substantive Rationality: "Ends are not commensurable." Glover rules out an expert calculus to balance between competing values. For him, only conflictual public decision-making can decide how governments should intervene in HGE.[141]

Fifth Criterion of Substantive Rationality: "Means consistent with system of ultimate values or ends are ethical." For this indicator the results look mixed. With his large-scale vision of ends, Glover does not highlight the means for efficiently formal rationality. Instead, Glover focuses on consistency with a value system, substantive rationality. But neither is Glover a deontological ethicist who categorically bans means, illustrating tensions in Evans's indicators.

Apart from these five sorting criteria, Glover reiterates Evans's other keynotes of substantive rationality. Glover adopts an indefinitely long-term perspective and privileges effects on societies as wholes for assessing policies.[142] Unlike Muller, Glover endorses ongoing debate on ends in their own right and foresees their resolution by political "elections."[143] By calling for "*unmediated* public opinion" [G 57; emphasis in the original] to decide policy, not expert panels, Glover reaffirms what Evans labels everywhere else a substantively rational stance.[144] In "Playing God" the PhD dissertation, utterly contrary to the book, Evans emphasizes that Glover shares the "broad frame" characteristic of substantive rationality because Glover defines the "deeper and larger problem" posed by biotechnology for "the nature of humanity," which puts Glover "in opposition to the [formally rational] bioethicists and scientists."[145]

Exceptional changes occur between the basic observations in Evans's dissertation "Playing God" versus his book rewrite. In the dissertation, Evans wrote that Glover articulated values like the eugenicists and "shares the *end* of Huxley and Muller," aligning Glover with substantive rationality.[146] This appears contrary to the book, in which Evans *contrasted* Glover to Muller and to Huxley: "While authors such as Ramsey, Huxley and Muller had debated in order to convince others to accept their ends, Glover thinks that this debate will not be possible in our newly pluralistic culture We can get around this problem, he argues, by forwarding only the end of autonomy" [G 161]. It is puzzling to conceive how Evans shifted from asserting that Glover shares the end of Huxley and Muller to asserting that Glover wants to avoid setting societal ends [G 164]. What motivated such an overturning? It is also difficult to discern passages where Glover opines genetic debate "will not be possible." Instead, Glover foresees possibly raucous electioneering over HGE policy, as with populist disputes over economic policy.[147]

Reviewing sample sources, it seems more accurate to put Muller in the role of hyperinstrumental scientist whereas Glover scrutinizes the whole human condition by including passages even on dreams and moods. Placing these two side by side— Muller, a prototype for the 1950s and 1960s against Glover, a prototype for the 1980s and 1990s—it appears that Evans might have confused the basic import of his data over time by classifying Glover as formally rational overall and Muller as more or less substantively rational. As a reviewer for the *American Journal of Sociology* commented, comparing the texts coded as formally rational to their contents, "almost all these documents (including the commissions') take great pains to express substantively rational points about the goal of protecting humans and human dignity, the ends of science as a human pursuit, and so on."[148] How did Evans, who informed humanist critics that his method was different than mere reading because it followed sociology's "methodological canons" in coding, apply criteria to weigh relative formal and substantive rationality consistently?

Comparing the dissertation to the book *Playing God*, it emerges that Evans produced diverging classifications of the same items. Researchers are apt to shift their impressions, but to me Evans altered reports of basics. Whereas I once expressed astonishment at how Evans in *Playing God* classified Muller as setting multiple ends,[149] taking the dissertation in hand revealed that Evans originally had ascertained a single end just as I had. In the dissertation write-up, such a coding output did not yet pose an anomaly for neatly aligning authors' components of rationality. Evans had not yet signposted multiple unlimited ends as a tracer of substantive rationality.[150] We have landed upon a trial in which Evans and I independently read the prime texts of Hermann Muller and of others in his community, and we spontaneously received the same impression: we originally agreed there was one final end subsuming others.

In the dissertation a single shared end was consistent with the indicators of substantive rationality Evans had in place then[151]:

> Although the authors in this community differ in the details, the shared *end* (inference assumption) is that humans should control or even perfect their genetic and

cultural evolution...This community of discourse also contained authors who were critical of the advocated eugenic *treatments*. It is critical to note that they were not opposed to the *end* of controlling their genetic destiny. Rather, the fight internal to this community was not over whether it was desirable, but whether it was possible through the advocated *treatment*.[152]

Evans seems not merely to report, but to buttress the observed agreement over ends in this largely substantively rational community. There are neither competing ends nor controversy over their significance.[153] For example, in his report on Theodosius Dobzhansky, Evans wrote, with his own underlining: "Although an intellectual rival of Muller in debates about genetics (Beatty 1987; Paul 1987), he shared Muller's *ends*."[154] In the book's write-up by contrast Evans accentuates disagreement over ends among these same scientists:

> The HGE debate of the 1950's and the 1960's was dominated by reform eugenicist scientists, such as Hermann Muller, Julian Huxley, and Theodosius Dobzhansky. To them, HGE was synonymous with what was later called germline HGE. This debate was substantive and thick—*and largely about ends*. The ends pursued were not only what later came to be called beneficence (the concern over the "genetic load" of the species) but also ends that are best described as theological [G 179; emphasis added]...In sum, the scientists were conducting a largely substantively rational debate *about the ends* that should be pursued with HGE. With the exception of species self-preservation through the avoidance of the genetic load, *no one* thought the large number of other ends suggested were universally held or commensurable. [G 54; emphasis added]

Where is the newly appreciated evidence in *Playing God* supporting this revised observation that among scientists "no one" thought ends were universal? Finding it may test readers.[155] To my mind, in "Playing God" the dissertation Evans mandates the nonexistence of such evidence from scientists in this period:

> Regarding the commensurability of ends, since they have not yet encountered any external opponents—those outside of their community—*they do not evaluate anyone else's ends: thus making their approach to commensurability difficult to judge*. In their form of decision making they are clearly focused in that the treatment is selected because it is the maximal means to achieve their *end*.[156]

Both write-ups reference the same handful of texts, but in the first version their authors are so insulated from rivals that raising the question of alternative ends is an historical impossibility. For these eugenicists "have not yet encountered any external opponents." In the book write-up what was naturally "difficult to judge" from evidence becomes clear cut: there is active debate about incompatible ends. The elemental observations that change for the book happen to keep the eugenicists neatly aligned with the book's revamped definitions of substantive rationality.

What then caused the change in the coding "to determine the content"? In his NSF Proposal "Playing God," Evans references the exact same page from Miles and Huberman as he references in the book *Playing God* to indicate what it entailed to have "coded" qualitatively. In the NSF Proposal, this is accompanied with an inventory of the categories that were applied to five transcripts of governmental commission meetings and accompanying materials: "The 46 'claims' coded in the data are all of the effects (problems or benefits) that participants think will happen with the use of human genetic engineering. Finally, 23 arguments supporting why a problem is a problem or a benefit is a benefit were catalogued."[157] This candid detail contrasts with how Evans presented coding of the influential publications in *Playing God*. For this more decisive corpus, it is almost baffling that Evans abandoned his initial format of reporting even in reply to questioning.[158] If I understand, he maintained contrary to his prior practice that cataloging or enumerating categories is antithetical to qualitative coding.[159] Only the final documents coded in *Playing God*, the decisive measure of change over time, seem to lack itemizable categories.

The reversed assessments of Muller and fellow eugenicists resemble other apparent inconsistencies between dissertation and book. In *Playing God*, Evans singled out Lederberg's two coded texts from the 1959–1974 period as publications that stood in contrast to Muller's: "Reform eugenicists such as Muller and Huxley had been debating ends. Later scientists, such as Joshua Lederberg and Edwards, had stopped being explicit about the ends of their research" [G 64]. In the dissertation by contrast Evans seems to have reached an alternate finding from coding the same two texts. Instead of contrasting Lederberg to Muller and Huxler, Evans comfortably fit Lederberg into their group: his "frame is largely the same as that used by Huxley, Muller, Dobzhansy and others considered above."[160] Contrary to the book write-up, Evans indicated that Lederberg explicitly identifies values because they are the same as those of Huxley and Muller. Lederberg "continues to operate in this community of discourse."[161] How could one advise that Lederberg (in the book) is *unlike* Muller in discussing goals whereas one initially found (in the dissertation coding) from the same texts that Lederberg was *similar* to Muller in discussing goals? The revised report for *Playing God* supports a theatrical view of scientists' thoughts and intentions: "But instead of facilitating a debate about ends in public, they [the scientists] quickly realized that such a discussion would not be in their interest" [G 55]. As for Muller, we might ask, "Did the coding change between the dissertation and the book or did different narratives emerge from the same coding records?" How could Lederberg's two influential works for 1959–1974 move from largely substantive rationality in the dissertation to approach "purely formal rationality" in the book [G 64]? To me this exceeds a difference in shading. Classifying or qualitatively coding the texts is necessary "to demonstrate that the cultural change…actually did occur," Evans wrote in his NSF proposal "Playing God." More broadly, Evans insisted "systematic cross-time comparisons can be made."[162]

In the liminal phase of ritual, social scientific discourse functions exactly by subverting its referential function. Evans deployed umbrella principles of large-N social science to defend findings in *Playing God*.[163] It turns out these formulas do not index real-world objects, such as actual units of analysis. They stimulate imaginative associations.

"As if" epistemology of social science: *Use large-N samples to generalize about populations*. For a sample to become "large," the traits of the units in the sample must be observed independently from each other. Therefore sociologists should be able to confer on how to compare Muller on his own (or anyone else) to

Evans's benchmarks of formal-versus-substantive rationality. Evans seems to dismiss double-checking as impossible, because categorizing one case depends on categorizing dozens of others *interdependently*. Each case must be compared to all others in its host community, to outside communities, and to cases across eras. "Therefore my claims are from comparing the dots [data points] to each other," he wrote "not only within a time period but also across time periods" (figure 3.2).[164] With each observation dependent on every other, this operation could scarcely get off the ground as instructed by the coding guide, Miles and Huberman. Operationally, there is only one gestalt—a "one N" study. The humanist historian whose interpretations are backed by footnotes to individual documents has greater claim to "large-N" study in reality than does the genre-blurring investigator who presents an undecomposable mass.[165] As Evans explicates his principles, first person, "I am analyzing a very large number of cases and...I am not focused upon the meaning of any one individual text..."[166] Yet, as this chapter's opening quotation reminds us, the dominant author in a period may be represented by a single coded work: "The Ramsey I am making claims about," Evans explained of the leading theologian, is "the one who wrote *Fabricated Man*."[167] To sample and then not dissect individual texts in particular looks like a way that scientific "generalizations" may be set free from evidence.

"As if" epistemology of social science: *Estimate traits in a population by aggregating observations of their frequencies.* Evans started by classifying "paragraphs" of texts and then cumulated them at least approximately.[168] That need to estimate frequencies explains why Miles and Huberman in *Qualitative Data Analysis*, Evans's preferred handbook, naturally included "content analysis" in *qualitative* method:

> However, a lot of counting goes on in the background when judgments of qualities are being made. When we identify a theme or a pattern, we're isolating something that (a) happens a number of times and (b) consistently happens in a specific way. The "number of times" and "consistency" judgments are based on counting.[169]

In my view Evans emphasized flexibility over procedure in aggregating codes: "the location of each of the points [figure 3.2] is a generalization from many texts (although *not necessarily* a quantitative generalization)," he wrote.[170] Without a method for weighing many hundreds, if not thousands, of paragraphs, a "large N" cannot generalize about these texts' "*central tendencies*" when they are complexly mixed in tenor.[171]

"As if" social science epistemology: *phrase sample results as estimates of tendencies.* To understand the character of his generalizations about the distribution of rationalities in his sample, Evans directs us to read his chart (figure 3.2) as analogous to the following individual-level data:

> Let us say I was interested in biblical interpretation in the United States during the period from the 1950s to the 1990s, and I had nationally representative survey data from every year. The dots in my graph would be regions of the country, and time would still move from left to right. Let us relabel the Y axis "literalist" at the top and "nonliteralist" at the bottom. We could still say at the first time period that *compared to the people in the South*, the people in the Northeast had a less literalist take on the

Bible. This would be conducted by making an *average* claim about the people in the Northeast (e.g. 33 percent literalist) and an *average* claim about the South (e.g., 55 percent literalists, p. 21).[172]

The premises of this "suppose that" are: (a) there are individual-level data from respondents on whether they are literalist; and (b) an individual-level response is observed and entered (let us say "coded") independently of what other respondents have to say. As we have seen, neither of these conditions seems to hold. No individual-level data presented in Evan's study correspond to the individual-level survey responses to questions about biblical literalism. If I understand him, Evans contends at best that codings are comparative from the ground up, each coding relative to all others from its point of origin. The unit of comparison—paragraph, text, community?—is avoided. In truth this is a world away from opinion surveys, in which each respondent's signal stands on its own as a countable unit.

Ritual subverts everyday sense: allegedly a claim about a relative tendency in a large-N study establishes standards to ensure the claim bears weight. Evans wrote that the bioethicists who did not use Principlism were "noise in the data."[173] As he explained, "The 'noise' is how many cases do not fit into the signal...With surveys, 'noise' is lessened by surveying more people."[174] But descriptions of noise and signal for "large-N quantitative cultural sociology"[175] reference something only if there are discrete codes for each text, whereas Evans bewilderingly suggests there are not. Compare: "To put it starkly, on page 145 [of *Playing God*] I did not write that I coded this text [Grobstein] *as* formally rational."[176] There Evans wrote: "For example, Grobstein suggests that 'an oversight body might consider drafting a first-round set of principles' for HGE, which he outlines. Given that the influential authors in this community tend to have government advisory commissions as their ultimate target audience, their form of argumentation is highly formally rational" [G 145]. To review: Grobstein is one of the four "influential authors," Evans coded each of their texts "to determine the content," he coded "focusing on the substantively/formally rational distinction," he classified these four authors as using argumentation that is "highly formally rational," and he quoted Grobstein to illustrate in particular *why* the group qualifies as formally rational. Yet, paradoxically, Grobstein's text is not coded as formally rational, apparently only categorized as formally rational. Here social "science"—"data" with "noise" versus "signal"—is born of its reverse, inscrutable guesswork.

"As if" social science epistemology: *The exact indicators of rationalities are peripheral, because approximately the same gross "central tendencies" will emerge in a large population no matter*. The quantifying imagery of "central tendencies" makes classification of any individual inconsequential. Only this license of science leaves serious-looking problems in the coding definitions unresolved. Ponder two competing criteria: explicit cataloguing of discrete ends indicates formal rationality,[177] and, second, reasoning based on conduct's consequences is formal rationality as opposed to reasoning from inviolable duty (deontological absolutes, which are substantive).[178] Principlism, the bioethical approach that Evans limns as a paragon of formal rationality, features four ends, of which two are deontological and inviolable [G 90, 248]. So criterion one trumps criterion two. Then the reverse: in Evans's eyes the

National Council of Churches, in its ethics report on HGE, finalized a limited set of enumerated ends with a mixture of deontological and consequentialist ends.[179] In Evans's eyes Principlism did the same.[180] But the churches were categorized one way (substantively rational) and Principlism very much the other (formally rational) [G 88–89, 117–119, 262]. The inconsistency seems challenging.

No classification system is perfect. But inside the humanistic perspective, unlike a crossed genre, usage may force greater clarity. Ponder how Evans responded when readers thought they found Evans's indicators in conflict. As Jeffrey Stout imagined it,

> The trouble is that this way of thinking about rationalization creates confusion. It conflates three distinctions that are not equivalent; think and thick, formal and substantive, means-oriented and ends-oriented...It is a mistake to identify [formal] rationalization with instrumental reasoning. The bureaucratic settings that Weber associated with rationalization are often preoccupied with the adjudication of rights-claims—that is, with explicitly formulated side-constraints intended to establish limits for instrumental reasoning.[181]

Bioethicist James Childress found similar unworkability:

> Principlists may hold utilitarian, deontological, or mixed views...These examples are sufficient to indicate that Evans's means/ends analytic framework fail to illuminate most principlist positions. Indeed, Evans tends to reduce formal rationality, attributed to principlism, to consequentialist reasoning. Consequentialist reasoning is a "hallmark of formal rationality." Because of his reductionist interpretation of principlism, Evans can use the metaphor of calculation to replace the principlists' metaphors of weighing and balancing principles. In short, Evans's analysis oversimplifies and distorts by making formal rationality consequentialist and then assimilating principlism to this model.[182]

All that matters is how Evans responded. He invoked "as if" scientific principles that stand outside the world of interpretations:

> By way of foreshadowing, I can say that most, although not all, of the criticism of my book results from theology and philosophy being more precise than social science. This is not how these fields are usually portrayed, but I mean something distinctive here. Social science is less precise because it tries to make grand claims where precision is impossible, such as "the debate about HGE changed from substantively to formally rational from the 1950's to the 1990s." Theology and philosophy typically do not try to make such claims, and instead are more likely to conduct close readings of texts, avoiding generalization.[183]

The perspective of "science" converts profound issues about the feasibility of coding multipolar texts into quibbles about exactitude. Expressing himself in the first person, Evans suggested it is relatively incidental whether synonyms in his coding—instrumental, thin, and formalized—harmonize: they "strike me as empirically being three overlapping circles in a Venn diagram," he wrote. "I described the overlap of the circles, but Stout says I would do better to look at the circles separately."[184] Only in ritual does the symbolic output, "empirically…overlapping" codes take precedence over the sense from which they were derived. The as-if metaphors of social "science" that take us to the realm of sample units as mute objects preempt the question whether distinctions are cogent in the realm of textual meaning. In the object-world of a Venn diagram, classificatory issues are imagined to be about mergeable colorings, not meaningful logic. A humanist question about cogency of thought gets blurred when it is translated into a "scientific" question about estimates.

WHAT KIND OF SENSE?

For liminal exploration, Evans remixes indicators of formal and substantive rationality in ways their inventors had seen as illogical [G 197]. He crowns "thin" as an obvious synonym of formal, utilitarian rationality, "thick" as a synonym for substantive, deontological rationality, but Michael Walzer—originator of the concepts—seems to proceed in the opposite direction.[185] For example, Walzer associated "thick," culturally specific discussion with "distributive complexity" that weighs the consequences for the social distribution of goods—closer therefore to formal rationality in Evans's scheme.[186] Evans touts protection of individual autonomy as a component of consequentialist, formal rationality, whereas many in the philosophical community understand a concern for autonomy as protecting rights absolutely, independently of consequences.[187] Most interpret the philosopher Robert Nozick as emphasizing "deontological commitment," whereas Evans references Nozick to claim, much the opposite, that Nozick's protection of individual rights (e.g., the right to shop in the "genetic supermarket") is formally rational [G 161].[188] Classic histories of bioethics trace concern for autonomy to the rise of deontological commitment to protect individuals from harmful testing, however beneficial the consequences for society at large might be. This aligns professional bioethics *against* consequentialism, reverse from Evans.[189] The number of axes that tell against Evans's components of rationality are so ramifying, it is a puzzle to envision a coding process coherently scaling the texts.[190]

In sum, Evans's coding may not conjure sense when viewed as referential assertions about texts. The inchoate categories succeed instead by triggering a web of liquefying reassociations. Weber had assumed that political discussants amenable to dialogue start from the means at hand to consider "various possible ends" that come into view.[191] In the modern public sphere, Weber lets the means-end relation govern choices, not establishing ends as supremely precursory. Evans bests Weber in capturing peculiarly modern dilemmas, because he establishes as prior the following question: "Which technological means should we put in our hands?" This contemporary question forces a debate over ends anterior to all means in public life, an option that Weber found difficult to imagine in public life except among sectarian fanatics. Even if no one can debate ends as purely as Evans imagines for substantive rationality, via Ramsey and others he offers fragmentary glimpses of how reason incarnated in tradition illuminates dialogues about ends, a possibility Weber erased as irrational, thus unanalyzable in his means-end schema. "Liminality is the realm of primitive hypothesis," Victor Turner wrote, "where there is a certain freedom to juggle with the factors of existence."[192]

THE INSIGHT GENERATED FOR THE PHASE OF
INTEGRATION: A SPECULATIVE CODA

Ritual arenas in contemporary society are anomalous spaces, heterotopias for deau-tomating routinized perception.[193] *Playing God*'s graphic reduction of "debate" into positioning on a game board engages us in "savage thought" as Lévi-Strauss charac-terized it.[194] For if you return to the cluster diagram (figure 3.1), one of the multista-bile messages is that published dialogues superficially based on verbal reciprocity are simultaneously a unilateral effort to flood the arena with publications of potentially nugatory content, so long as publications get cited and attract funding.[195] This crude underpinning of ethical cogitation could not be exposed more powerfully than by the graphic symbolism, which builds the citing game into the elemental makeup of the universe.[196] "The critical determinant of resource extraction—and thus ulti-mately of the ability to produce arguments—is then the degree of fit between the form of argumentation used by the writer and the form preferred by persons in the environment who have the power to decide what to do" [G 26]. Subjected to Darwinian struggle, writers share the same problems and roles.

This is how *Playing God* creates a "monstrous double," an intellectual both like and unlike audience members in moral standing. Whatever the overt content of a publication, its intellectual producer instrumentalizes thinking for "resource extrac-tion."[197] Sociologists engage in "resource extraction" from federal agencies and taxpayer-supported universities. Like the ambiguously compromised writers on the game board, sociologists publish for tenure and grants [G 26]. It follows that "one would be naive to think that writers do not make compromises at the margins in order to obtain what is often the greatest resource—being listened to" [G 27].[198] Above all, the compromised bioethicists use reductive rationality as sociologists do when sociologists pigeon-hole debate into a fixed coding system. As Evans acknowl-edges, "it is ironic that this method [of sampling and coding], as well as sociology itself, is part of the rationalist impulse of modernity."[199] As we have seen, when coding texts we lack external checks for judging whether a code hits its target, and thus we lack yardsticks for judging the size or centrality of the unique meanings that have been omitted reductively. In an insidious reversal, sociologists can also cham-pion substantively particularistic arguments for the instrumental purpose of getting cited. How then do we know who adopts an authentic stance in our community? No wonder a reviewer interpreted *Playing God* as a moral drama: "Evans's book is espe-cially welcome; for in his drama theological ethicists are not merely buffoons and sideline attractions, but rather rise to the level of authentic heroes and villains."[200]

From Renè Girard's standpoint of ritual sacrifice, Evans purifies debate by removing the formally rational authors who imperil ethical dialogue [G 202]. They would adopt a universal language by which citizens may reach consensus, but trans-lated ends become so empty and sophistical, such ends cannot steer the development of the life-threatening means, biotechnology. As Evans puts it, "Trying to 'speak for' everyone, as bioethicists do with their universal ends, is hopeless and a viola-tion of the separation of church and state" [G 196]. Therefore he recommends that elite experts, those who comprise the citation diagrams, be expelled from commit-tees that reach collective decisions about ends. In their place, citizens should speak to each other about ends directly, perhaps via citizens' commissions [G 201–202]. Exactly what the new verbal exchange over values will look like, the ritual does not disclose, except that it will be passionate and large as life. As Evans reminds us, "'it is but a thin friendship that remains harmonious only so long as the friends never touch anything that really matters to them.' This concern rings true in the HGE debate" [G 197].

If my framing of *Playing God* as a ritual affirmation were plausible, we would predict that the policy recommendations with which the book concludes, while impracticably "utopian" [G 198], would impart an essential verity. That happens when Evans dismisses the need for real-world brakes on how elites would match particular means to an array of ends, once those ends were chosen by the public:

> If an ends commission decided that its ends to forward in genetic research were benef-icence, nonmaleficence, and maintenance of the current specificity of genetic change as possible in the reproductive act, I have no doubt that bioethicists could determine which, if any, forms of HGE advanced these ends. [G 203]

As you might suspect given the abstractness of "ends in themselves," it seems unlikely their implementation is a neutral technical job entrustable to special-ist intellectuals. The experts in deciding how to pursue a mandated goal would, by concretizing it, subject it to reinterpretation. Would not the means that elites chose to institutionalize populist HGE policy have ramifying implications for practice, and thus values, in other spheres of life, short-circuiting public delibera-tion? Dealing with these practical issues in ritual is beside the point of affirming the transhistorical message that deliberation over ends should be protected from instrumental degradation.

What role remains for the sociologists in this solution? If I have unsettled the assumption that conventional social scientific explanation commands the presenta-tion, perhaps I have license to speculate further. As with the properly named *Playing God*, the services a sociologist provides to society are not those of constative diag-nosis but those of ritual demonstration. *Playing God* conveys that the sociologist, in parsing and coding the modes of deliberation in texts, carries out an elementary social act around which other conduct can be organized. The sociologist turns the means-end schema for analyzing human conduct, the talisman of Weber's analysis of rationality, into the inviolate, constitutive basis for moral deliberation and action. Weber as we know claimed that the means-end schema comprised "the ultimate ele-ments of meaningful human conduct."[201] Nowadays, academic writers have become more skeptical whether or not the means-end schema is needed to ground the analy-sis of action or ethics. But the alternatives that social theorists formulate can seem mind-bending in their complexity, ill-equipped therefore for inspiring an alternative consensus.[202] By contrast, in a coding ritual about means and ends, Weber's basic schema is activated as a metaphysical truth. It functions as the self-apparent frame-work that sociologists can endorse without debate, the only framework therefore that does not undermine sociologists' authenticity by conforming to instrumental reward.[203] The formalizing means-end schema, potentially a dangerous mark of an overly rationalized academic agenda, is embedded and enacted in the ritual as if it were outside human making, an enchanted and mystified given within which articulate subjects necessarily conduct themselves. However erratic the coding as a representation of the world may appear, the execution of the coding successfully binds sociologists and their audiences to this extrahuman, eternally recurring framework for moral choice.[204] Sociologists restoratively emplace the discord of modern deliberation inside a cosmic consensus.

CHAPTER 4

"A QUANTIFIABLE INDICATOR OF A FABRICATED MEANING ELEMENT"

LAST PARADOX OF THE "MODERN FACT"

To extract messages from modern "facts"—expressed in sociology as coding labels or data points—the facts typically are arrayed to help us perceive nonrandom patterns. Why should one suppose that when such "facts" are extracted from texts they speak to the meaningful dynamics that led to the texts' composition in the first place? If you bear in mind that coding does not preserve the semiotic operators that generate a text—its verbal "system" of implicit parallels and contrasts—it becomes a nonstarter to imagine abstracted data offer clues to meaningful devices. I chose the research prototype governing this chapter because it discloses there is slight reason to suppose that an *absence* of statistically significant differences in codes between sample populations marks lack of differences in significant cultural mechanisms. Nor ought we imagine the reverse, that *presence* of such sample differences is a tracer of differences in the signifying devices of a culture. Neither pattern nor its absence in coding frequencies from a corpus of texts plumbs social meaning. Texts signify by implicit contrast to what is not mentioned as well as by superseding or negating what they first affirm.[1]

This chapter clarifies such unlikely pronouncements stepwise. To preview, start with James Gleick's *The Information*, a genealogy of concepts of communication in the digital age. Gleick asks us to examine the following numbers as discrete data observations:

---

3 1 4 1 5 9 2 6 5 3 5 8 9 7 9 3 2 3 8 4 6 2 6 4 3 3 8 3 2 7 9 5 0 2 8 8 4 1 9 7 1

As Gleick remarks, in this sequence (as well as in the unending string from which it is excerpted), the world's computers so far have found "no statistical features...no biases or correlations, local or remote."[2] The data lack design or clue, no matter how fine-grained the dissection. Yet the numbers reflect a pure algorithm: they consist of Pi, the ratio of a circle's circumference to its diameter, derivable transparently in any classroom. Penetrating into what we want to comprehend, the meaningful device generating the outcome, cannot in any way be aided or supported via induction or via imaginative inspection of the numerals, the unit "facts," as the bafflement of computers confirms.

Similarly for coding outputs, numbers distributed among cells in a table of coding results may obscure the only thing into which we aim to inquire, the only phenomenon of significance: how the "facts" about texts were meaningfully generated.[3] That paradox becomes evident in the circuit that researchers who try to interpret counts of lexical choices in a large corpus follow. To make sense of weak or inconsistent findings, they remark that the frequencies of words vary by the genres within which they function. How do they reach toward taxonomies of genre-specific subsamples that lend word counts their bearing? They proceed inductively by partitioning the sample according to the lexical trends, circularly presuming that the frequencies of codes are a measure of genre, not that genre lets you interpret frequencies. Once the researchers acknowledge the need for more "fine-grained" study of contexts to explain how signification works in corpora, they descend therefore into a paradox. Their findings about culture seem compelling only to the degree that the generalizations retrieve encyclopedic knowledge of the signifying devices at work in *individual* cases.[4] Why not acknowledge that the motor of inquiry amounts to working upon one potentially unique text and then another, and why not configure the presentation to make transparent this underpinning of generalization?

THE CULMINATING CASE

To penetrate to the bottom of the incompatibility between the scientistic and humanistic perspectives, it is best to adumbrate a preeminent study to have advocated their blending. The purest is perhaps Wendy Griswold's "The Fabrication of Meaning: Literary Interpretation in the Unites States, Great Britain, and the West Indies."[5] This presentation, which appeared in 1987 in sociology's most exacting journal, was greeted far and wide as offering confirmable and generalizable results.[6] It remains probably the most broadly circulated classic whose findings rest on systematic coding of text contents.[7] At least Griswold's powerful article aided the veritable birth of a somewhat positivist version of cultural sociology that still prospers in the United States.[8] In its companion piece published in the same year, Griswold proposed that a "sociology of culture can both subject its cultural interpretations to definitional precision and validation criteria typical of the social sciences and be as sensitive to the multivocal complexity of cultural data as art history or theology."[9]

An advantage of revisiting such an orthodox opus is that we can reappreciate how its findings circulated to unite communities of researchers. Griswold's study focused on literary reviews of the novels of the Caribbean author George Lamming, whose career took off in 1953 with publication of *In the Castle of My Skin*. Griswold discovered that novels by Lamming that stimulated favorable critical appraisals in her sample of reviews shared a noteworthy feature: they absorbed readers in the effort to unravel their multivocality while they did not overly frustrate the readers. "This ambiguity seems to refer to the capacity of a novel for evoking multiple interpretations and the creative tension the reviewer experienced in deciding what was Lamming's likely intended meaning" [1108].[10] Lamming's novels tested readers' experience of deciphering, because they stretched conventional understandings through poetic associations. Griswold proposed that understanding how ambiguity supported engrossment offered sociologists a chance to elaborate "a theory of cultural power" [1105].

In the years since Griswold published this intriguing conclusion about artifacts' "cultural power," researchers across an amazing spectrum of circumstances have adopted it enthusiastically. Rogers Brubaker and Margit Feischmidt, writing in 2002, imported Griswold's proposition into their analysis of historical commemoration in Eastern Europe. They wrote that "[p]owerful cultural objects—whether events, persons, or cultural creations—are always ambiguous: indeed, that ambiguity according to Griswold is a key part of what constitutes their power."[11] Yuko Agasara carried Griswold's finding over to Asia in her book on "Office Ladies" in Japan. "[C]ultural power derives in part from a work's ability to sustain divergent interpretations," Agasara wrote. "It is precisely this ambiguity that provides Office Ladies room to maneuver."[12] Griswold's ambiguity principle has been cited to illuminate Disney cartoons as well as memorials.[13] Given this traction and Griswold's emphasis on the need for "confirmable" and "generalizable" results [1080], is it not time to revisit what goes on in the peculiar texts where the sighting first occurred?

My proposal in the present volume is that the usual constituents of social "scientific" demonstration, such as controlled comparisons, the discovery of structures in tabulations, or inference from entities such as "society," do not govern the proceedings as an explanatory "method." Instead, if you examine these tools in their arena of use, you find their implementation reverses their overt epistemological functions. Method in practice is subordinated to the truth-making of collective ritual. For example, "ambiguity" appears to be a potent explanatory concept that is worth formalizing as a variable so that its occurrence can be systematically catalogued. But the tantalizing promise of a concept so central to our aesthetic experience also makes its registry frustratingly slippery. On examination of the source texts, it is difficult to reimagine how coding for such a concept could be conducted upon sophisticated expression. Or, at the next stage, once "ambiguity" is identified in the reception of an artifact and turned into a datum, should it be interpreted as a feature of personal experience, as a part of the design of a deep-laid text, or as a dimension of the collective reception of an artifact? If the answer is uncertain, so is the proper formatting of the data to search for patterns, we will see. Indeed, Griswold's tables may be incorrectly catercornered for the matters about which they are supposed to speak. Brought to life in social "science" as ritual, familiar instruments of explanation act as if possessed by foreign spirits.

DOES CODING PRODUCE "DATA"?

Professional sociologists appraised the coding of texts in "The Fabrication of Meaning" as displaying a model for how categories of "formal" measurement "should derive from the original texts themselves."[14] Via coding, these experts wrote, Griswold "has

Novel	Reviews Mentioning Ambiguity (%)	Ratio of Favorable to Total Reviews
In the Castle of My Skin	50	.667
The Emigrants	31	.188
Of Age and Innocence	42	.75
Season of Adventure	33	.25
Water with Berries	63	.5
Natives of My Person	40	.467

Figure 4.1   Ambiguity and evaluation by novel.

Source: Reproduced from Wendy Griswold, "The Fabrication of Meaning: Literary Interpretation in the Unites States, Great Britain, and the West Indies," *American Journal of Sociology* 92 (1987): 1109.

sought to develop methodological approaches that incorporate sociology's empirical rigor."[15] Such adjectives mistake the instrument with its deployment. When applied upon texts, coding breaks with the complexities of the empirical order to occupy the mind with purer, condensed vehicles of thought. Figure 4.1 displays one of Griswold's most evocative diagrams, a rank ordering of each of Lamming's novels by frequencies of ambiguity and by favorable critical appraisal. To replicate these results, I contacted Griswold for the list of 95 book reviews in her sample, which she had offered researchers on request [1088].[16] Griswold had originally collected every accessible review of George Lamming's fiction published in Great Britain, the United States, or the West Indies from 1953 to 1976, but it is challenging to guess for sure what comprised a "review" or what was available. The passage of time led her list of sample publications to go missing. I tried to reassemble the 95 items per her search procedure, hopefully reaching a mass of them adequate for opening up the perplexities of the coding.

REVERENCE AND REFERENCE

As figure 4.1 indicates, Griswold *combined* the reviews from each of her three regions—the United States, Great Britain, and the West Indies—to see if she could explain why some of Lamming's novels resonated more powerfully than others in her sample of reviews of his six novels in all. She guessed that "ambiguity" would not only engross readers in disambiguating the novels, but doing so would stimulate appreciative reviews. This just-so account presumes we can know what ambiguity is according to its function rather than by its verbal expression in a review. How exactly does creative engagement by the critics appear when articulated on the page of a book review? What *is* ambiguity on site? The blurring of appealing scientific hypothesis-testing with exegesis of highly compacted reviews produced a baffling gap: Griswold did not offer an example from her evidence to concretize this entity called "ambiguity," yet social scientists propagated news about the abstraction in every direction.

Is ambiguity about superficial contradiction and final integration of polarities? In the introduction to his head-spinning *Seven Types of Ambiguity*, William Epson establishes a Pandora's box of possibilities: "'Ambiguity' itself can mean an indecision as to what you mean, an intention to mean several things, a probability that one or other or both of two things has been meant, and the fact that a statement has several meanings."[17] By refining clear indicators for what is unclear, many a philosopher has tried to manage the concept of ambiguity by verbal algebra.[18] We know only that Griswold tallied "the number of reviewers who specifically mentioned the ambiguity of the novel in question" [1108].

As figure 4.1 indicates, mentioning ambiguity in reviews of Lamming occurred strikingly frequently. Lamming was notable for overloading his readers with poetic figuration and for withholding conventional detail. Even for the novel that Griswold characterizes as the least arresting, a third of the reviews "specifically mentioned the ambiguity." As she summed up the response to a flawed novel: "*Season of Adventure*'s lack of multivocality and ambiguity made it less powerful than most of Lamming's other novels, and its reviews and publishing history confirm its relative weakness" [1110].

Griswold's theory of cultural power posits a relation between ambiguity and positive appreciation within the mind of the *individual* reviewer, expressed in singular critical appraisal.[19] It is "the meaning for them, there, then" that Griswold initially seeks [1081]. But each reader's personal experience of meanings gleaned from a novel can also be aggregated to index to its reception by a collectivity. Thus, novels "that are seen as simultaneously coherent and ambiguous will be most highly regarded by contemporary readers precisely because of their multivocal capacity," she wrote about the cause or trigger [1079]. The response at the level of the individual review is coded as dichotomous: a "mixed or negative" review on one side versus a more consistently "positive" review on the other.

FIRST ATTEMPT AT REPLICATION: THE NOVEL *WATER WITH BERRIES*

When I took reviews in hand, it astonished me to find that at the individual level ambiguity is "specifically mentioned" (to my mind) primarily when the reviewer expresses frustration and disappointment. This dislike of ambiguity more often pushed a review over to a mixed or negative appraisal of a novel, reverse from Griswold's report of correlations at the aggregate level. The diversity of expression is paramount, however, so it is best that researchers have a look for themselves. Start with *Water with Berries*, the novel that by Griswold's measures is most frequently considered "ambiguous," with 63 percent of the reviews coded as commenting upon that feature. Since many reviews are brief, my excerpts do some justice to the body of each.

DECOMPOSING *WATER WITH BERRIES*

Consider how baffling it is to identify "ambiguity" and "positive appraisal" on the ground. Paul Theroux wrote the following review in 1972 of *Water with Berries*:

> The plot is for much of the book unclear, and as soon as it becomes clear it is incredible; the poetic prose of the narrative has a perfect dazzle, but this is about as helpful as an unshaded bulb, distracting rather than giving light. It is when expatriation is

defined and dramatized that Water With Berries takes on a life of its own, for Mr. Lamming is meticulous in diagnosing the condition of estrangement.[20]

Theroux calls the book "unclear" on first encounter but eventually "clear," perhaps meeting Griswold's ideal criteria for ambiguity to have an invigorating effect. Yet, the apparent reverse of Griswold, he dislikes the novel for its ambiguity *all the more* after descrambling the message as a whole, and he appears to offer a mixed or negative review. Perhaps drawing on his years as traveler and teacher in Africa, Theroux seems to praise Lamming primarily for depicting the condition of exile from one's home, not for a deciphered literary effect.

If the youthful Theroux is not a bona fide litterateur, consider Douglas Dunn, the poetry critic for the *New Statesman*:

> Artifice, coincidence, unnecessary characters and details, and Mr. Lamming's dense and turbulent style are asked to do too much; that is, to tell a story. It is too contrivedly enigmatical; the effect is close to the modish American Gothicism; murky pasts, exile, violent rape, secrets, conspiracies, conflagrations, an ambitious nostalgia for a distant West Indian island, probes into racial darkness. Water with Berries is powerful, despite its dismal overworked solidity, its display of props sometimes galvanised by the surprises Mr. Lamming strains after like a middle-aged athlete trying to regain form.

It seems defensible to take "enigmatical" effects as signaling ambiguity, yet the reference to a flagging athlete, the evaluator's last sentence about the quality of the novel as a whole, is dismissive. Overtaxing ambiguity is not registered separately in Griswold's tallies.

When critics mention ambiguity, they often take pains to describe how it is located in the novel's architecture as a whole, allegedly fully grasped. For example, the commentator for the *Yale Review* emphasized that *Water with Berries* did not escape from a "malaise of tendentiousness":

> But it is an intricate and uncommon allegory, its deadends and thoroughfares sufficiently in need of a clue to make a second reading as important as rewarding...The gesture Water with Berries drives toward, the redemptive revolution, remains however as formless as an imaginary conception and its relation to the history that supposedly necessitates it proves nebulous enough.[21]

References to testing of "the reader's concentration and the work's coherence" seem to indicate ambiguity, but the review's complaints disqualify it I think from being "positive" rather than "mixed." Overall the novel is less "satisfactory" than others and displays "a dismal paradox in a novelist."[22] Once more effects of ambiguity probably lean contrary to Griswold's report. Or consider an appraisal from Trinidad:

> An uncharitable commentator might see the novel as a "thriller" in which the right doses of sexual perversion, murder, suicide, arson, mystery, and politics are mixed and saved from banality by the scrupulous severity of Lamming's style. Anyway, what disturbs me is that Lamming was doing so many things at the same time, and doing them well, but he did not emphasize where the stress was supposed to fall.[23]

The multivocality and need to decode the "severity" of the style possibly suggest ambiguity, but the overall critical appraisal of the novel as a whole is difficult to guess.

Where then can the association between ambiguity and cultural power be found? Not in the *Times Literary Supplement*, whose evaluator spurned Lamming's mixture of genres:

> Lamming writes very well, but *Water with Berries* does not entirely convince either as a study of the pains of exile, or as an allegory of colonialism. The book flounders between realism and fantasy...As for the melodrama of Mr. Lamming's *Tempest* myth, it tells us nothing new.[24]

To mention fine writing but a lack of clarity due to straddling between realism and fantasy, or between psychological portrayal and allegory, arguably indicates ambiguity in the "intended meaning or point of view." But the unorthodox straining the reviewer experienced fairly clearly led to disapproval. Conversely, a critic for *Bim*, the literary journal of the Young Man's Progressive Club in Barbados, found the novel's "*juxtaposition*" of styles less jarring and more satisfying: "a happy blend of the simple and the complex."

> Although the action from exposition to resolution encompasses a mere fortnight, it is rich with a variety of elements which all contribute to the definition and illumination of the principal characters...For each scene he [Lamming] has provided the mot juste so that the reader finds himself furnished with a banquet consisting of delicately balanced portions of excellent characterisation, superb narration, and compelling action...This book should bring a great sense of satisfaction to a wide range of readers.[25]

Best I can tell, this reviewer did not describe the style or message as intriguingly difficult at all, yet he seems to rate *Water with Berries* favorably, illustrating the simpler gushing tone typical of adamantly positive reviews.[26]

So far I have assumed that ambiguity concerns *how* Lamming is perceived to narrate rather than the "content" of the novel's plot. This keep faiths with Griswold's description of ambiguity as "the creative tension the reviewer experienced in deciding what was Lamming's likely intended meaning or point of view" [1108]. At least it appears so when Griswold brings ambiguity into relation with her theory of cultural power. Ambiguity at that moment is about avoiding "fitting any formula or pattern too closely," so it is the critic's registry of overall design. But elsewhere, Griswold writes that ambiguity is no longer about remote correspondence to convention, but about a novel's subject matter: "Ambiguity is another, related theme prominent in Lamming's novels. The impossibility of ever knowing the truth is continually restated" [1098]. Here, as Griswold says, ambiguity is a "topic" or category "of content" [1096] that she counted similarly to other "subjects and themes" such as "race," "colonialism," "class," and "revolution." Now we see that it is not the architecture of the presentation, but *what* is represented that matters. Then the "intended meaning" of ambiguity may be so obvious the reviewer discerns it effortlessly. Everyone is familiar with prominent genres that reference ambiguity by rote, just as a reader of a pat mystery novel can "get" the ambiguity as part of an unchallenging recipe. In short, Griswold's various discussions of ambiguity can strike one as evidently at odds with each other when you return to their use on the ground.

With ambiguity as topic, many positive reviews of *Water with Berries* mention it without expressing tension about deciphering Lamming's message. Here is a critic for the College Language Association:

> All three men are artists...all are black, and all are visited by tragedies that occur as swiftly, as neatly, as the proverbial guillotine. However, a Kafkaesque quality envelops the disasters, delaying the shock value for the reader. Only Teeton endures, and rather ambiguously so, to begin his journey back to his homeland. The tale of the three testifies to the catastrophic psychological consequences which lie in wait for the black West Indian who intrudes into colonialist countries, whatever the reason. He finds himself in an atmosphere that becomes more damning, more inescapable, the longer he remains there. Almost like fish out of water, it seems he can never quite catch his total breath until he returns to native territories.[27]

In the four-paragraph review, the critic without much reservation gives a thumbs-up appraisal: "deserves recognition." But this reviewer also seems assured of univocal meaning in the basic action ("neatly"), confident about the genre ("psychological novel"), and certain about the message ("you can't go home again"). A reference to a character's psychic trials—Teeton lives but as a personality Teeton endures "ambiguously"—is an opening for possibly coding the review as mentioning ambiguity, which it certainly does by literal vocabulary. But consider how farfetched the outputted social scientific generalizations would seem if this raw passage were fed as "ambiguous" into tabulations and hypothesis testing. The critic's reference to Teeton's enduring "ambiguously" seems unrelated to tension between the novel and shared literary schemas. Since Teeton suffers from memory lapses, the phrase may refer more literally to the sheer psychological frailty of Teeton before he turns homeward and to the reduced vigor with which he "endures."[28] Only by freewheeling play could sociologists move from this kind of trivially incidental reference to ambiguity toward imagining that the research is tapping into the generalizable processes by which readers experience a text's power.

Likewise, connoisseurs assert their professional status by explaining in their reviews how easy it is to *see through* potential ambiguity, paradoxically ruling out prolonged tension. Is this nonetheless a "mention" of ambiguity? The critic for the *Commonweal* does this twice over:

> Lamming uses the Ceremony of the Souls to create a powerful and mysterious scene with the modern Miranda, but the novel as a whole is a study of the psychology of colonialism in the relation between the sons of Caliban and Prospero's "resurrected wife," the Old Dowager, Mrs. Gore-Britain...Lamming's rhetorical problem is to gain sympathy for Teeton so that his readers, typically British and American, will be willing to accept Teeton's calculated "ingratitude" toward the generous condescension of the resurrected Mrs. Prospero, his refusal to be a "pet nigger," his assertion as a man that what may look like a personal, even sexual violence, is in fact an act of human and therefore political independence.[29]

This critic takes pleasure in analyzing both the appearance of what is going on as well as what Lamming really intends by it, attracting prospective readers by laying bare the composition as a whole. By analogy we may ask, if we observe how a stick inserted into a bucket of water merely appears to bend, but explain that it is a mechanical surface reflection, are we describing ambiguity or ruling it out? That is the dilemma when an accomplished evaluator says a book portrays "mysterious" affairs but really has one structured message. The book no longer resists "definitive analysis" and it no longer "intrigues or disturbs its recipients," Griswold's correlates of the power that ambiguity provokes [1105]. Whichever way we code in such a situation, we doom the measurement process by internal contradiction. If we code ambiguity and its correlative, cultural power, as "absent" in this *Commonweal* piece, we suppress the satisfaction the reviewer takes in paraphrasing the difference between what Lamming describes versus what Lamming ultimately signifies, the decoding that drives the reviewer toward positive judgment ("it is obvious"). This critic praises the "protean principle to investigate every possibility of history and politics." Conversely, if we code the ambiguity as "present," we suppress the univocal resolution that the reviewer offers and we dilute ambiguity into evident intricacy. (If an autumn tree has red and yellow leaves, and we say so, we are not describing its color as ambiguous, are we?) Then ambiguity is not about the strained exercise of literary schemas. It is about richness of content at best or about obviously unmasked allegory at worst. As we saw, the *Commonweal* reviewer easily put himself in Lamming's shoes, dissecting the novel as a well-structured solution to an unmistakable question. The coding choice has ramifying implications either way: do we privilege the reviewer's stance on what is being described (the novel's telling) or do we privilege what is being described (the perceived book content)? Which of these choices gets us back to what Griswold ultimately would like to grasp, the critic's experience of reading the novel? My own answer is presented here in action: it is to lay open the process of forcing the reviews into a Procrustean bed.

For example, another critic of *Water with Berries* described the novel's ironic perspectives on the same events, which might qualify as ambiguity:

> To help put across his points about the disintegration of personality, especially in people who are products of a colonial past, Lamming makes use of a pattern with which by now his readers should be quite familiar...he [Lamming] explores a number of these relationships from various angles. Sometimes his use of this pattern is decidedly ironic. The frequent reference in the novel to another of Shakespeare's plays, Othello, emphasizes this irony.

Irony in its technical sense comprises the trope of multivocal intent. But in the same review, the critic rejects the novels as formulaically contrived: "In his unrelenting faithfulness to this Tempest pattern Lamming loses touch with the characters he is creating...The last impression that this novel leaves, unfortunately, is that the only real thing in it is its reliance on the Tempest theme, and that has been severely overwritten."[30] The critic condemns a trite lack of substance: "the reader fails to be moved by the final catastrophe." Code for ambiguity as a subtopic in the first excerpt and you miss the critic's stance that the ambiguity is empty and feigned;

code for the critic's stance that the novel's "persistent" copying of the *Tempest* theme is pat and unambiguous ("proves its undoing") and you miss ambiguity as topic and theme. Code the first way, and Griswold's theory of cultural power is undermined, since the critic dislikes the novel; code the second way, and her theory is supported, because pat recycling of formulas should lead to disapproval. The entire test of the hypothesis depends on oracular coding results assumed to be easy and given, although they are beset by dilemmas.

The bewildering difficulty of coding is revealed in deciding what constitutes a "positive" review as well. Is it "mixed" or is it "positive" to say of *Water with Berries*, "Despite its weaknesses, this book deserves reading"?[31] Do caveats about weaknesses push a review into the "mixed" category? Or is a review necessarily positive if it declares a book deserves reading, as if "mixed" books never deserve reading as well? Do not striking endorsements also include caveats about weaknesses as rhetorical proof of the reviewer's trustworthy conscientiousness? The reviewer's job is only to establish a critical relation to the book or to indicate points of entry for potential readers. If a resonant review, like a seminal novel, is multidimensional, and if the reviewer therefore does not try to locate the book on a metric of approval, the overall categories "positive," and "mixed/negative" are not there in the text ready for translation. The summary is only a fabrication of the social "scientist."

SECOND NOVEL, *IN THE CASTLE OF MY SKIN*

Two final types of coding issues confirm a possible disconnect between Griswold's quantitative hypothesis about correlations versus the verbal logic of reviewers. What happens when a reviewer judges *In the Castle of My Skin*, ranked by Griswold as one of Lamming's most powerful novels, as *contrivedly* ambiguous? *The Times Literary Supplement* reveals the coding problem:

> The book is difficult to classify. Part of it is written as an autobiography in the first person...The author does not try to identify his symbols. Are these crabs the three boys or the two other groups of three who have emerged in their conversation? The reader knows only that one of the boys suddenly tries to catch them...[32]

Rather than being captivated by the possibilities for deciding, this critic sees the symbolism as a "fault" as irritating as "motes in the eye." To preserve a quantitatively testable proposition you can respecify that ambiguity should tantalize "without utterly mystifying or frustrating" [1105]. With that finessing, however, Griswold's verbal elucidation becomes true by definition, for in the humanist universe expressing dislike for a novel's ambiguity *is* negative appraisal.[33]

The scientific concern for arraying the coding frequencies unhinges these "facts" from any real verbal dynamics. Across Lamming's six novels, the ranking of each novel by the percentage of reviews "specifically mentioning ambiguity" corresponds more or less to the ranking of each by the percentage of reviews coded as lending a positive (rather than mixed-negative) appraisal (figure 4.1). This apparently scientific coding pattern is impertinent for interpretation: rankings at the collective level may reverse the correlations that obtain inside the individual reviews, where meaning originates. More specifically, within the group of reviews that give a novel a high rate of positive reviews (at the collective level), the mentions of ambiguity may nonetheless be concentrated among the negative reviews in that group (at the individual level).

In the humanist universe of the individual text, we have every reason to suppose the quantitative rankings are misleading. The most enthusiastic reviews do not articulate ambiguity because they tend to be humble in conception. The majority of my reviews of *In the Castle of My Skin* demonstrate this dynamic:

- This is an interesting novel, entertaining and well worth reading.[34]
- This powerhouse of a book—moving and gripping—should attract the open-minded and unsqueamish, seriously interested in an honest portrait of another culture.[35]
- This is a unique contribution to world literature that should be in all the libraries. Mr Lamming has the talent, the problems are universal, and it's fun to read.[36]
- Mr. Lamming, whose book has taken its places as an important work of imaginative literature since its publication last year, is here showing in a few lines what his whole work is trying to express...[37]
- [H]is themes are predictable and closely related and he is one of the most committed artists and original talents to have emerged from the West Indies.[38]
- His descriptions, for example, are brilliant, graphic, and functional...[39]
- There is a bursting vigor and energy about that segment of life, which Lamming catches marvelously here...And it is exactly for this reason that Lamming has written so good a novel...[40]
- Lamming has written this first book with a penetrating insight and sympathetic understanding of the naiveté, ignorance, pride, and aspirations of the people of his native island.[41]
- In *In the Castle of My Skin* the outer circumstances of George's life are re-created with vibrant emotion by the author.[42]
- Highly rewarding both as a social and as a personal document.[43]

In a nutshell, these reviews appreciated the novel so unreservedly they seem to have seen it as "too unambiguous to provoke reflection" [1106], opposite Griswold's theory.

Is Ambiguity a Generalizable Concept?

All of which reopens the question, how *did* Griswold operationalize "ambiguity"? Coding ambiguity rests upon such intricate contextual shadings, the codes cannot erect weight-bearing "data."[44] For several dozen more reviews of Lamming, I features examples of coding dilemmas at http://www.biernackireviews.com/. If "The Fabrication of Meaning" were concerned primarily with launching a cultural sociology with the "definitional precision" of science, would it not establish its indicators and offer clarifying illustrations of ambiguity?

Scientific quantifying only heightens the mystery. Codes of ambiguity vary strikingly across regions: in the West Indies, 63 percent of reviewers registered this theme, versus only 32 percent in Britain and 38 in the United States. How does Griswold gloss the exceptional West Indian rate?

> Similarly, one of the pressing problems West Indian intellectuals of this period were grappling with and needed literary tools for was that of individual and national identity…The consensus on the importance of the "What are We?" question appears both in the West Indian reviewers' interest in delineating a coherent body of specifically West Indian literature within which Lamming should be assessed and in their concern with the themes of identity and ambiguity in Lamming's novels. [1104–1105]

If I understand it, Griswold explains the extreme concern of the West Indian reviewers for ambiguity from their social interest in choosing among possible identities—a matter of topical content, not aesthetic form. It is baffling that the questioning of identities as a *content* should automatically run contrary to univocality in communication, however.

It does not take repetitious postmodern talk about indeterminancy to conceive that discussion of ambiguity can itself become formulaic.[45] The reviewer for the *Times Literary Supplement* stereotyped it as a pat ethnographic trait of the natives:

> Uncertainty is a major characteristic of life in the Caribbean; nothing quite certainly is. Truth is the grain of sand within the pearl of conjecture. The laws of cause and effect are held in abeyance. That sense of fittingness and of inevitability which is the western heritage from the ancient Greeks is absent from the West Indies…Mr. Laming has caught this peculiar Caribbean tendency more subtly than Mr. Edgar Mittelhozer, especially in the chapter describing the impact of the riots in the capital on a small village some way out.[46]

Ambiguity as a topic here (as in some other reviews) is enunciated clearly as a manifest feature of culture. For coding this creates an acute dilemma. Griswold attributes the experience of ambiguity to the author's skill at locating the novel near genre categories that it plays with, "instead of fitting any formula or pattern too closely" [1111]. The West Indian critics, Griswold confirms, interpreted Lamming by specific comparison to such canonical authors as Joyce, Conrad, Faulkner, Seneca, Dickens, and Zola, perhaps suggesting they had some of the same specialized literary equipment as their counterparts elsewhere.[47] Either ambiguity is a product of this interaction between the artistry and literary categories of interpretation; or ambiguity is a topic which the West Indian critics hone for identity formation, creating univocal messages in the main. But for these contradictory versions of what she is measuring, Griswold creates *one* count, just as science proceeds by "nominalistically transmuting words into signs which it then processes arbitrarily."[48]

SUMMING UP THE BAFFLEMENT

The parsing of texts flourished in the domain of biblical interpretation after the Protestant Reformation and in the domain of law after the creation of sacred constitutions. The meaning of texts seemed existentially decisive.[49] Now that the coding of texts has become an academic speciality in cultural sociology, few have cared deeply about the solidity of the data outputs.[50] Due to lack of patience in tackling forbidding detail, the boundary between the empirical and the imaginatively construed was elided for all. Only in a ritual does the universal message evidenced in an encoding procedure replace the evidence itself as the sacred.

A scholar operating in the traditions of the humanities would be obligated to display documents in their complexity for transparency and definitional precision. A humanist would identify "mechanisms" by displaying how the book critics in their own words expressed ambiguity and praise. Instead, the blurring of science and interpretation resulted only in an epistemic loss: opacity of definition and unreplicable codes in the aggregate.

The delicacy of interpretation confirms how coding "data" are fabricated: "The meanings attributed to any cultural object are fabrications," Griswold wrote, "woven from the symbolic capacities of the object itself and from the perceptual apparatus of those who experience the object."[51] The mystery is why that lesson is not turned around to consider the coding process as well. When Griswold was challenged in a critical reply by Norman Denzin to open up her coding process as an interactive process of construal, Griswold reinsulated her black box of coding by fiat.[52] "[T]he social scientist," she explained, "operates according to a shared set of procedures based on the initial axiom that the world is indeed as he, or she has defined it."[53] But the "shared set of procedures" is not en plein air, only promised in the background. Griswold's modestly positivist cultural sociology functions as a disguised twin of sacred ritual: in both, the symbolic vehicle, be it a "quantifiable indicator" or a religious emblem, is established by a rupture from the interference of the mundane world. Sociologists are accustomed to thinking of the formalization of data into abstract indices as certifying that a procedure belongs to "science," but for texts these vehicles do nothing more than to form a purified, unquestionable domain for creative reassociation. Such is the ritual phase of separation.

PART TWO: THE LIMINAL PHASE

To show that there is no residuum of "scientific" content left after coding "facts" are glossed, let us consider how "The Fabrication of Meaning" outputs its own "virtual" meanings not easily found in the source documents.

MEASURING THE "DIVERSITY" OF THEMES

In the most interesting test of her hypothesis about the sources of cultural power, reproduced in figure 4.2, Griswold shows that her ranking of novels by the themes that reviewers espied also parallels her ranking of novels by the approval reviewers bestowed. When a novel elicits a wide range of unusual or infrequently observed responses from critics together with some core consensus, she reasons, the novel has appropriately stimulated the critics' ingenuity [1107]. As in figure 4.1, Griswold's quantifying at the aggregate level does not display the correlation *inside* individual reviews—unusual themes mentioned in relation to positive approval. In the interpretive universe, it may be the book critics who most inventively engage a novel in their reviews who *at the individual* level also deliver more negative appraisals.

Least Cultural Power?	Novel	Variance	Mentions in Top Third Categories (%)	Categories in Tail: Lower Quarter Mentions (%)
	In the Castle of My Skin	9.057	57.6	46
	The Emigrants	6.550	56.6	43
	Of Age and Innocence	6.159	56.8	48
	Season of Adventure	9.372	57.1	42
	Water with Berries	10.536	62.3	47
	Natives of My Person	12.023	64.1	59
Most Cultural Power?				

Figure 4.2   Agreement and dispersion.

Source: Reproduced from Wendy Griswold, "The Fabrication of Meaning: Literary Interpretation in the Unites States, Great Britain, and the West Indies," *American Journal of Sociology* 92 (1987): 1107.

DO THE CODES ISOLATE THE "CARRYING CAPACITY" OF NOVELS?

As Griswold underscores, at least two variables converge to produce reviewers' exposition of intended meanings: the novel's composition and the conventions brought to bear in deciphering it—a conjunctural explanation *simpliciter*. If Griswold sought evidence for the capacity of each of Lamming's novels to bear multivocal interpretations—"carrying capacities"—she would I think control for the other variable that interacts with each novel to produce meaning, namely, the conventional expectancies the reviewers bring to bear. Instead we are left with no inkling how much the results reflect a work's own carrying capacity, as Griswold claims, or how much those carrying capacities are constant while reviewers happened to access varying conventions of reading. If the phenomena of interest are constituted by a conjuncture, there is slight rationale for explaining population variances in meaning exclusively by one side of the coupling. Lamming's career spanned decades, so vital history reshuffled the conventions brought to bear upon his successive novels in figure 4.2 [1109].[54]

More generally, is the "carrying capacity," like a physical capacity from the scientific point of view, ever discernable in an opus? Were there for each of Lamming's six novels only one convention on which any reviewer anywhere, anytime could draw to interpret that novel, we still would not know whether the perceived multivocality of those six novels reflected the carrying capacities. For the conventions themselves, as many critics have remarked, vary in their own capacities to convey multivocal effects.[55] (In this thought experiment the conventions of reception vary only according to the novel, not by reviewer.) For instance, Griswold mentions in passing two hypothetically relevant genres, that of the Bildungsroman and of the colonial allegory. The Bildungsroman entails a highly specific plot structure based on personality development of an alienated protagonist. Such an usually self-conscious genre may more acutely intrigue the reader who notices what falls outside the convention.[56] Alternatively, if the novel itself activates particular conventions, why insist the conventions are an independent variable in the conjunction? No matter how tempting it may be to attribute verbal meanings to the numerical spreads in figure 4.2, how do we know those spreads of topics for each novel line up with the creative dissonance readers experienced, since the *meanings* of those mathematical spreads are relative to semantically incomparable prompts and their categorically different conventions for decipherment? As in the present chapter's introduction, it is reckless to infer that patterns in the numbers parallel meaningful generators of those numbers.

Best I can tell, "The Fabrication of Meaning" does not classify the specific literary conventions a critic has put to work. These enabling conventions remain purely suppositional whereas the article invokes them as the crucial explanatory variable. They comprise readers' "presuppositions, their perceptive conventions, their cognitive categories," which coproduce meaning by the logic of social "science" [1081]. Inside the interpretive humanist universe, however, Griswold cannot isolate these conventions in her evidence. Apperception of a novel's themes is inseparable from how the enabling structures that bring the work's meaning to life have been activated: inside a review they will be fused in expression. Evidentially they are not separately codable "variables," whatever blurred social "science" might suggest. To appreciate such coproducing of meaning, one could dissect a review in relation to a total cultural field, but this is painstaking literary criticism, untranslatable to codes. It is remarkable how often Griswold insisted on the need for "empirical rigor" and confirmable precision [1080, 1096, 1115], and all the while she never operationalized her independent variable, the diverse enabling conventions she says coproduced the reading responses to Lamming's novels.[57] The ritual perspective is indispensable: once deracinated "facts" isolated from context were erected, Griswold was liberated to apply her own explanatory forces, or I might suggest, ritual "ghosts" upon them.

The hallmark of liminal play is that the researcher takes advantage of an abstracted symbolism for imaginative experiment. Griswold's figure 4.2 treats the themes mentioned as separate unit equivalents. This purified data at the collective level cancels the real work of reviewers in the humanistic universe, that of describing the merging of themes and their semantic drift. For example, Griswold notes that race accounted for 11.4 percent of subject mentions for *In the Castle of My Skin* [1107]. But reviewers were certain race did not carry a unitary meaning by real-world reference:

> The race problem is in the background more or less; how else could a Negro write a novel of the life he knows? But that is all…the few whites who manage things have never thought it necessary to see that the Negro population understood its "place"…the currently fashionable racial-political dogmas are too thin. There has to be something deeper. For the moment, his castle is the color of his skin. But the young man knows, because he feels it, that he must somehow find an even more profound "belonging," and he leaves the island to begin that search.[58]

Race then seems present but subordinate and transcended.[59] Compare this to a review that states "the thesis of the book is centered upon the tortured, troubled insecure feelings which the Negro suffers as he gropes his way from the dying culture of racial exclusion."[60] The foregrounding or backgrounding of race looks irreducible to "mentions." As O. R. Dawthorne wrote in an essay on Carribbean narrators,

> This expanded introspective study of self is, to my mind, one of the exciting facts about the West Indian novel...if a myopic view of race or nationalism is widened in this much larger vision of existentialist self-inquiry, then the instrument of interrogation has to be magnified as well.[61]

Caribbean reviewers mocked the British predisposition to reify race as a thing, whereas for those who lived on the islands, race seemed a more questionable "now you see it, now you don't" dimension inextricable from many others in the experience of colonial subjects.[62] The West Indians almost protest against coding as simplistically colonial.[63]

In the liminal phase of "The Fabrication of Meaning" we can discern how the perceptual "shape" of the arrayed codes as symbols permits Griswold to imagine an equivalent "shape" of meaningful responses to Lamming.[64] Griswold "examined what percentage of categories were in the tail of the distribution, that is, in the lowest quarter of the mentions" [1108]. If a novel such as *Water with Berries* has a higher fraction of rarely mentioned themes, this marks rich multivocality relative to Lamming's other novels.[65] In the interpretive worldview, however, it is not possible to norm externally the difference in meaning between terms that would make the dispersal and concentration of "mentions" semantically comparable across novels [1107]. A dispersed frequency of mentions among many closely related terms, such as "race," "colonialism," and "social change," may not illustrate multivocality so well as repeated reference to less closely related terms, such as "nature," "colonialism," and "role of the artist." Griswold sidesteps such issues by assuming the "as if" posture of play: "*If we consider* the percentage of mentions included in the top third of the categories for each novel to be a measure of agreement, the greatest consensus appears for *Water with Berries* and *Natives of My Person*..." [1107; my emphasis]. A hallmark of the liminal phase is this subjunctive "if."

The larger issue is how to appraise that two reviews of the same novel express a relative consensus when the purpose of the review is to adopt an aesthetic stance toward themes, not to "mention" themes. When critics' purpose is to discover the functioning of literature, consensus may concern principles for reflection despite "topical" dissensus. Great literature aims at a fresh take on signifying practice itself, so correlatively the business of critical readings is unrelated to countable denotations of "what the book is about" [1107]. The blurring of the scientific and the interpretive perspectives lets a sociologist proceed as if a mathematical spread between artificial units ("mentions") corresponded by metric analogy to a semantic spread in the evidence itself. The formal apparatus *for* seeing creates *what* is seen.

SOCIAL INTERPRETATION OF NUMBERS

Using her model of how meaning is produced by the conjuncture of the novel itself with a socially distributed apparatus of perception, Griswold established an elegant comparative design:

> In order to look at the interaction between a cultural object and its recipients, the analysis needs to exert some control by holding one side of the relationship constant while allowing the other to vary... [O]ne might look at how a single text, symbol, or convention is received by a variety of societies or groups, varying these over time or space. [1082]

Griswold with this design found "systematic" *differences* in the meanings of the *same* novel by Lamming across her three regions when those differences consist of distributions of mentions codes as "sexual behavior," "madness," and so forth. By comparison to British or West Indian reviewers, "Americans revealed their obsession with race by talking about it so much" [1102].

Social scientists in the register of ritual interpret such transnational differences with the assumption that the diagram is emblematic of a standard causal system under the ceteris paribus condition.[66] Codes reflect equivalently widespread concerns in each society, not contingently intervening contexts specific to each author. Like oracles, researchers invokes forces standing "above" the discourse data to bring it to life.[67] For example, Griswold found that only 10 of the 28 British reviews mentioned colonialism as a theme in Lamming's novels, whereas, of the 30 reviews from the West Indies, a higher proportion, 17, mentioned colonialism. From such comparisons Griswold reports, "The British indicated their preoccupation with colonialism by avoiding the subject so persistently and by concentrating on style rather than content" [1102]. British critics responding to Lamming were "conspicuously silent" and "reticent on the subject of colonialism" due to the unpleasantry of "the loss of empire" [1097, 1103]. Notice first off that the probability of the critic getting around to the topic of colonialism will be influenced simply by the available space in the review: the West Indian reviews, which in my experience were a bit more likely to appear in limited-circulation, specialized periodicals for local literary connoisseurs, included long and freewheeling pieces. There is no regular causal system or meaningful generator to ensure the differentials in topic mentions signify very much.[68]

More importantly, in British reviews I retrieved, British critics exposed the predicaments of colonialism with penetrating acerbity:

- Political power has shifted markedly in Barbados during the last fifteen years, from white to black, and these events are portrayed here as they affect the villagers.[69]
- A densely confusing fable about colonialism and conscience.[70]
- Apartheid is the inevitable, hysterical reaction of a fear-ridden white minority... the result of the lessening power of the white man and the comparative emancipation of the coloured man. Some kind of literature must be part of this emancipation.[71]

- What is much more difficult and subtle is to tease out the deeper cultural manifestations of colonialism...But George Lamming is probably the first writer to discuss the Caribbean personality in a way that sensitively begins to establish the links between "the politics of sugar" and the "colonisation of language."[72]
- A statement of what George Lamming's Season of Adventure is about could make it appear respectably well intentioned...It is about freedom—political freedom—in the West Indies...[73]

More subtly, by introducing the binary of colonialism as present or absent, the ritual cordons off the reality that it was daunting for British critics to avoid incorporating the relations of a concept as permeating as colonialism. Griswold never illustrates what counts as mention of colonialism or of any other theme.[74] To my eye, colonial relations were part and parcel of most British reviewers' landscapes:

And then there are the various figures...Shephard, the native leader of the anti-colonial movement...and the colonial officials who plot Shephard's death because they fear his success in the elections.[75]

[Lamming] sets out, to picture childhood in the West Indies, a village changing hands from feudal white man to native speculator.

The West Indians are known for their response to Western education and it is not a parrot-like, glib or brilliant imitation, but a felt and sensitive response...The coloured people had, in fact, little more to do than study the whites all day long.[76]

To encapsulate "colonialism" as a standardized reference, Griswold had to extricate it from its imbrication with property relations, race, and cultural authority. For Griswold's claim is that the British reviews of Lamming "avoided discussion of history and politics in general" [1102].

If the British critics fairly routinely invoke colonial circumstances descriptively, is it a mindset of "persistent avoidance" that blocks them from thematizing those relations explicitly? Or is colonialism so obviously a component that in brief reviews it fails to merit explicit attention, like slavery for the ancient Greeks or like camels for Mohammed? Even within Griswold's dichotomous coding, why does their 36 percent rate of overt mention of colonialism signify "the British were *always* reticent on the subject of colonialism" [1103, emphasis in original]? More fundamentally, mentions of "race," "class," "colonialism," and of every other content depends on how reviewers see one as priming mention of others. Given this contextual interdependency in literary expression, there is no rationale for treating mentions of "colonialism" as an effect of an independent cause, social percipience.[77] If a social scientist can treat frequent mentions as evidence for a topic's weight, as with "race" in American reviews, but reverse gears to treat infrequent mentions as evidence for a topic's weight, as with "colonialism" in British reviews, then guessing the meaning of the numbers is a Rorschach test of whatever the social scientist imagines.

In response to the sociologist Norman Denzin, who highlighted the potential indeterminancy of reviews used for coding in "The Fabrication of Meaning,"

Griswold reaffirmed her preference for a firm "investigative structure."[78] Returning to the primary sources confirms instead that there is irresolvable uncertainty about whether the codes bear significance.[79] Why then have they survived as "facts"? Binaries at least condense matters into what is simply true and what false. "Since Plato, Western thought and the theory of knowledge have focused on the notions of True-False," Nassim Taleb recently wrote. "Commendable as it was, it is high time to shift to Robust-Fragile, and social epistemology to the more serious problem of Sucker-Nonsucker."[80] If overly sarcastic, Taleb nonetheless suggests that validity endures only if formulations are isolated from contexts—demanding therefore a ritual arena.

If you wish to determine what the frequency of British mentions of colonialism signifies, in the humanist frame one returns to the contexts in the primary sources. Griswold instead attempts comparison in the scientific frame. She asks whether across-the-board avoidance of political issues typifies all British reviews, not just those for Lamming. Or are British reviews ready to deal with politics, just not those of colonialism? Griswold's ingenuity shows scientific comparison can never disclose the meaning of coding differentials. She compares British reviews of Lamming to British reviews of a starkly different type of literature, spy novels. From her coding she finds that British reviewers were willing to combine discussions of literary style with political issues in response to *The Spy Who Came in from the Cold* [1103]. Therefore she takes this relative lack of sociopolitical discussion in reviews of Lamming as evidence for a reticence to deal with the politics of Lamming's novels in particular, namely, colonialism. As I see it, Griswold found that it is a constant across the British reviews that they underscore the literary style of the work under consideration. This undercuts her hypothesis that an emphasis on aesthetic style in Lamming's reviews was a way of *avoiding* politics, for the emphasis prevails with or without mentions of politics. To interpret the variation in the mention of politics as support for her interpretation, Griswold still has to assume lesser mention of colonial issues signifies a mindset of reticence, which is to assume beforehand, all over again, the very thing that comparing coding results from spy novels was supposed to demonstrate. Conversely, if Griswold had found that the British reviewers were neglectful of political issues in discussing spy novels as well, who is to say across the board *relative* neglect signifies anything, as if there were such a thing as a normed measure of mentions of "politics" in reviews across different cultures anyway? Further, a literary artifact's own style may pull a reviewer away from politics positively. Lamming's novels have by consensus an intrusively acute poetics that aestheticizes experience—potentially distracting recipients from politics, not forcing them to avoid politics as uncomfortable. The coding frequencies are only a diversion from the verbal makeup of the documents.[81]

Why did Griswold's comparison of reviews of spy novels with reviews of Lamming seem to leverage greater insight? The comparison looks helpful only if we convert the coding results into an index of whole "ways of seeing" as signposts for what is characteristically "found in the societies as a whole" [1083]. We have to *assume* that individual reviewers' mentions of politics in *The Spy Who Came in from the Cold* reflected British society, so that our emplaced observations of what is going on for recipients of a singular novel speak to the readiness of the British to discuss politics "in general." We have to ignore the alternative that there may have been something idiosyncratic about the novel and its formulas for reception that unfettered British reviewers or especially encouraged them to talk politics. By reducing the variables invoked by the comparison down to merely generic "novels" and "society," in the framework of scientific comparison we rule out the cultural specificity that constitutes reception of a novel. Ought we really suppose that, apart from the impropriety of Caribbean imperialism, the Cold-War setting of *The Spy Who Came in from the Cold* is otherwise "equivalent" in its triggers to Lamming's novels? For Lamming, is the code for colonialism really of equivalent meaning to the code for politics in the spy novel?

Such dilemmas for glossing patterns in coding applies to discourse "data" at large. As Aaron Cicourel formulated it, the problem is that of justifying "when the researcher should go to higher or more complex levels of predication to explain the utterances examined," that is, when incidentally triggered words are really tokens of higher-up social forces, such as presuppositions about roles in the society at large.[82] Ritual process characteristically begs this question while also accentuating it. The question is more acute because the "facts" are treated as representing simplified categories, "novels" and "reviews from Britain," which on their own do not provide cues either for moving upward toward or for abstaining from a higher-order predicate, society. However, if we import as natural the assumption that codes from Britain express something essential and widespread in British "society," then we beg the question of how to justify moving upward. A covert alliance between the scientific perspective and the notion of "society" lets an investigator posit a sociocultural explanation for text contents while bypassing the intricate cultural makeup of those texts.

As soon as you concretize the novel and the context in which its reviews were composed, however, the jump to what Cicourel called "higher" orders of explanation looks phantasmal. For example, after the success of his first novel, Lamming's interviews and appreciations of him circulated across English-speaking societies.[83] Familiarity with such commentary shaped reviewers' experiences of Lamming's later works directly. Beyond such contingent influences on reviews, what parametric deviations or consistencies in the coding are so large it is necessary to invoke "society" as the cause? Since the West Indian critics were far from reticent about discussing colonialism, should a differential of 21 percentage points between them and their former overlords count as essential, that is, as evidence of opposite ways of seeing "found in the societies as a whole" [1083]? The liminal phase suspends such considerations in favor of productive experiment.

Even if there had been no differences in coding outputs across regions, such a result does not rule out the effect of regional culture in producing the uniformity. As Jorge Luis Borges emphasized from the humanist perspective, there are diverse reasons why local critics may converge in preferring cosmopolitan responses to literature: due to political offensives against the cult of national particularity broadcast from Continental Europe, due to emotional difficulty with intimate confession, or due to autonomous literary downgrading of local color.[84] In short, the interpretive perspective may reveal that regional cultures express themselves in the *denial* of regional difference, confounding the pattern in the scientific "facts" adduced by coding.

INVENTING "SIMULACRAL FACTS"

The power of ritual to create phantom facts is manifest when Griswold invokes nationally distinctive responses:

> Some suggestive patterns emerge from the preceding data, patterns that may be illustrated by an example: three different responses that a single episode from *In the Castle of My Skin* elicited from West Indian, British, and American reviewers. The episode takes place when G., having finished high school, is about to leave Barbados for a teaching position in Trinidad. His boyhood friend Trumper has been in America for several years, and, before returning to Barbados, Trumper writes a letter to G. that ends with the tantalizing line, "You don't understand, you don't understand what life is, but I'll tell you when I come and I am coming soon." And so he does, wearing American fashions, speaking American slang, and casting a worldly eye on Barbadian politics. Trumper announces that his most important transformation has been in his discovery of his blackness. "'My people,' he said again, 'or better, my race. 'Twas in the states I find it, an' I'm gonner keep it 'til my kingdom come.'" G. envies Trumper's confidence in his identity, but worries about his own ability to make a comparable discovery: "It was like nothing I had known, and it didn't seem I could know it until I had lived it." The question of whether G.'s longing for an identity will be answered by racial consciousness is left unanswered. [1099–1100]

By narrowing the cue to which the book reviewers in different countries responded, Griswold zeroes in on how different "potential meanings might be fabricated from this scene...British reviewers, unwilling to ascribe any fixed social meaning to the scene, seem to regard it more in terms of an elegant literary expression of an adolescent groping with life's mysteries" [1100]. Three British reviews back up this finding.

Return to the sources, and it looks questionable whether two of the three reviews mention this "single episode," the Trumper scene. You may examine the originals at http://www.biernackireviews.com/, part two. An *Observer* review by David Paul is devoted to three other happenings in the novel, yet the Trumper episode seems not to be included among these emphases. David Paul classifies Lamming's *In the Castle of My Skin* as a unique variant on books coming from colonies "where the problems of colour and of political freedom have brought conflicts for which no real solution is in sight"—scarcely an evasive prettifying of social conflict.

It might also be a stretch for Griswold to feature V. S. Pritchett's review as characterizing a distinctive British stance toward the "single episode." Griswold cites Pritchett's verdict that "Three careers will be open to the intelligent: the police, school teaching, and America. And in each of these questions of race, colour and social justice will take, perhaps, an ugly form; but as yet the boys are only groping." Rechecking the passages at http://www.biernackireviews.com/, Pritchett probably alludes to the Trumper incident via the word "America." This scarcely anchors Griswold's contention that the "social context of the reviewer, I have argued, influences which of these meanings he or she will ascribe *to the scene*" [1100; emphasis added]. Far from avoiding a "fixed social meaning," Pritchett seems to inject it by listing three career paths the boys cannot avoid, whether they know it yet.

Pritchett also recounts anecdotes to praise Lamming for describing "politics and social change in the life of a small feudal estate."[85] Too subtly for binary coding, Pritchett concretizes social issues to reaffirm separately that in literature aesthetic experience is paramount.

Griswold's thesis about Trumper places a heavy load on slim references, so it is no wonder evidence leads in many directions. Whereas Griswold quoted British reviews that barely referenced Trumper, she neglected several British reviews that highlighted the scene specifically. They may have escaped her sample, but to me these unquoted reviews emphasize political critique, overturning her summary. For example, critic James Stern singled out Trumper's return from the United States as instructive: "One of the triumphs of his [Lamming's] two books is the picture they offer of the coloured man's position both here and in America." Stern cites Trumper's speech about racial identity: "Race-conscious, the coloured people thus form a united front."[86] Stern did not aestheticize Trumper's avowal, but drew parallels to the racial identity of emigrants to the United Kingdom. Likewise, the critic Michael Swan singled out the scene of Trumper's return from the United States with a sociological frame:

> Liberia, that Israel of the Negroes, would mean nothing in the Barbados of Mr. Lamming. Yet, at the end, "race" suddenly appears. The narrator meets his boyhood friend Trumper..."If there be one thing I thank America for, she teach me why my race wus. Now I'm never going to lose it. Never, never."[87]

This British review seems to insist that racial identity emerges forcefully, irreversibly in the end. Opposite from Griswold's sample report, these unmentioned British cases featuring vivid detail about Trumper seem astute in ascribing a "fixed social meaning" to the scene.[88]

The single British review produced by Griswold that does explicitly mention the Trumper scene, seems to lend that episode the force of social critique, perhaps contrary to Griswold's claim about it:

> The observations of the village boy who returns from the United States at the end of the book form a brief but enlightening comment on the recent American influence on the Negro islanders; what we commonly regard as the exemplary liberality of interracial relations in the British West Indies he dismisses scornfully as the supine complacency of the Negro inhabitants, duped by subtle administration. But Mr. Lamming does not attempt to draw his own conclusions in that matter...

Remarking that Lamming did not impose his own commentary upon Trumper's words scarcely denies a stable social frame. The reviewer writes that an assistant teacher "is finally revealed as the new landlord who has bought the village from its decayed white owner and who launches a programme of evictions."[89] This critic sketched the social dilemmas in extreme form—"supine complacency" about racial indignities—and he indicates the "American influence" extends to the "Negro islanders," not just to Trumper, affirming the collective level of the reference. Finally, this British reviewer's comment that Lamming did not explicitly vouch for a racial identity was echoed in American reviews as well, that is, in the reviews that Griswold maintains had affirmed a fixed social frame most earnestly.[90] As I understand it, what typifies the American reviews is not whether the reviewer discerns Lamming as resolving issues of race, only whether reviewers see "race" as a determinant problem [1096]. In short, Griswold's own examples may abrade claims the British were "unwilling" to see the Trumper episode as imparting a fixed social meaning.

More technically, how could Griswold have laid such emphasis on reviews by Pritchett and Paul that said so little about the Trumper episode at all? From the perspective of ritual, once Griswold interpreted her reductive counts of codes, the texts in their concreteness had to conform to the message she had found. In the reversal of the usual sequence, it was not the theory that corresponded to the raw facts that mattered, but the facts that corresponded to the theory. Reversing the correspondence theory of truth is the essence of ritual, which makes a world rather than trying to reflect one.[91]

COMPARABLE CONTENTS?

To read as significant and essential the cross-national variation in the frequencies with which reviews mentioned topics, each review has to be treated as a "unit," generically like the next in *how* its meaning was produced.[92] Griswold says her data grasp not just contrasts, but "systematically different readings of the same novels" [1082] and "three different sets of meanings" [1115]. When I took the reviews in hand, however, they did not seem to be comparable creatures: reviews written to fit into a few lines of a pop newspaper jumbled with reviews written in whole chapters for connoisseurs at Yale. As a signal of what a small interlocked world the Caribbean literati comprised, George Lamming was in 1955 the editor of *Bim*, a major review forum, affirming a closed circle different than that faced by a critic for, say, the *TLS*.[93] Lamming had dedicated his first novel in 1953 to *Bim*! Across the Anglophone world, did the text-object called a book review really cohere and if so, was this ware produced by a communicative purpose similar enough to make content themes equivalents for coding? Text genres such as literary reviews that continually change shape through transformative questioning of their own essence cannot comprise a delimitable sample of facts, stabile through time for systematic analysis. As Paul de Man remarked of literature, they are constituted by their refusal to petrify into relatively "evident" entities.[94] Stuart Hall, writing in the journal *Bim* in 1955, laid out the peculiar regional agenda for reviews in the West Indies: "If it may be asked why we must make the effort to understand what our native artists are about," Hall wrote, "we may reply briefly with Ezra Pound, that 'criticism is written in the hope of better things.'"[95]

In addition the reviews varied by whether they were intended to portray the critic's experience of a *literary* opus or to offer buying advice to potential consumers of a product.[96] The diversity of the processes generating the appraisals suggests that the enabling schemas that most immediately and powerfully impacted the coding outcomes might be nothing more than the schemas for—what else?—constructing reviews. Appendix 4.1 surveys insurmountable challenges in deciding if writing "should" qualify as a review for the sample.

Among her three regions, the West Indies contributed by far the highest rates of ambiguity and positive reception [1091, 1099]. Lamming himself disjoined Caribbean reviews from others: "[F]or what emerges from the varied contributions of prose and verse [in *Bim*] is a certain unity of concern which an American or a European intelligence would immediately recognise as regional."[97] The sample results sit on this unique literary ecology.[98] By displaying bare numbers after the contaminating background context has been stripped from a table, however, the sociologist is able to extract a timeless global message about "cultural power." The extraordinary expectation for witnessing pure forms that is established through a ritual process bypasses the roadblock of extrapolating to the universal from quite strange particulars.

THE MEETING OF PERSPECTIVES VIA "SOCIETY"

In the liminal proceedings of "The Fabrication of Meaning," the concept of society slides the reader between the scientific and the interpretive perspectives. "The Fabrication of Meaning" uses the pragmatic heuristic that we have seen John Mohr recommending as a default for deciphering data.[99] Griswold proposes that the "facts" are explained by how literary elites addressed shared challenges to their society. Reviewing Lamming's messages is among the "'tools' used by people to grapple with present and pressing problems" [1104]. For example, "[f]or the British the problem was neither the glories nor the brutality of colonialism but rather the end of empire and the consequent need for rethinking the position of English culture in an era of economic and political decline" [1104]. It has become a modern "doxa" that "society," whatever we imagine it designates, is an appropriate resort because it has inexhaustible powers to configure the outcome of human undertakings.[100] Society as a ubiquitous "ether" pertains to every coding pattern.

The arbitrariness of "society" as the decoder emerges from Griswold's gloss of her controlled comparison. Griswold's research design is intended to expose the reviewers' reception of the *same* novel in *different* societies, so differences in the meanings received by the reviewers exhibit the effect of something in society, habits of "socially differential percipience" [1079, 1082]. These social presuppositions for apprehending the novel are treated as givens independent of the novel. Conversely, then, by logical symmetry inside the scientific viewpoint of experimental controls, what does the researcher discover by reversing the comparative design, controlling instead for the society and varying the novels within the same society? Does this design reveal the effect of each *novel itself,* holding the society constant? By scientific logic the answer would have to be "Yes." But from the humanistic perspective this is painfully simplistic. We know a researcher cannot find the effect of the novel itself, for the literary schemas that are activated to generate meaning out of the novel intervene. The elective affinity between a literary artifact and the particular literary schemas the artifact happens to activate invalidates Griswold's talk of isolating overall "percipience" by society or by social group [1081].[101] The scientific method of control never makes full sense when it comes in contact with the cultural world of texts, but interposing "society" papers over the illogic.

This dilemma of incompatible scientific and humanistic perspectives under-mines a rigorous comparative design even when it is an appealing mark of blurred social "science." Can we compare reception of the "same" novel across "different" societies from the perspective of scientific controls? The print that readers apper-ceive is indeed "the same" in the trivial sense that it comprises the same black letters. Griswold's comparative logic assumes nonetheless there is "the same" shared and *meaningful referent across the cultures*, a tale with scenes, before the publishing lite-rati across the globe figure it more complexly in their unique responses.[102] How do sociologists know reviewers are dealing in different ways with "the same" semanti-cally meaningful work, what we signify by "the poem" or "the novel," as contrasted to "the physical black type on a white page"? The overriding difficulty "is that only some events are actually in the text; others may only exist in the mind of the reader," Marisa Bortolussi and Peter Dixon wrote.[103] "Further, readers may or may not infer any particular event based on their knowledge and goals." Informative comparison assumes we specify at what level reviewers had a meaningfully shared referent in their experience, a prompt, before they rhetorically figured it and evaluated it in their writing.[104]

It seems advisable then to seek semantic criteria rather than to mandate extralin-guistically when reviewers across communities reacted to "the same" piece of litera-ture. In mixing the scientific logic of "controlled comparison" with the interpretation of texts, Griswold operationally reduced texts to brute objects. If you recognize that the invoked "variables" are textual creatures, controlled comparison requires one to verify that recipients recognized the basic plots and materials in similar ways. That precondition looks difficult to fulfill, but it is the sort that would have to be solved before the comparative design could remain true to its promises.

The need for semantic rather than physical control in the research design to hold "the novel" constant as a variable is all the more necessary since British and American editions of the books circulated with different editorial Forewards. The first US edition of *In the Castle of My Skin* featured an extensive introduction by the author Richard Wright, known widely for his own novel *Black Boy*. Wright, who had a profile in part as a black nationalist, advised that Lamming's character Trumper introduced a "frenzied gospel of racial self-assertion" into the novel.[105] If American readers digested Lamming with this advisory from Wright, they responded to a "different" novel than did their British counterparts. The problem of sequential contamination in the US sample due to Wright's launching of Lamming's reception could not have been more acute. But how do we determine the basic semantic recep-tion of the novel outside of elaborated reaction to it? This problem appears unsolv-able, so it confirms the requirements for applying the logic of comparative controls may not combine with the cultural universe of texts.

The same problem of mixing scientific controls with texts occurs in demonstrat-ing the theory of cultural power. That proposed theory starts firmly within the interpretive perspective, because it makes categories of understanding the "variable" that interacts with the novel to produce an engrossing experience. As Kenneth Burke emphasized, in an ideology-saturated society, readers deal with a plethora of contra-dictory schemas from which they choose how to interpret a text. Alternatively, much important literature, such as Beckett's plays in the 1950s, from inside its own lines blatantly models unprecedented schemas from which a reader may learn to decipher the work as a whole—"the absurd." To probe the fabrication of meaning, the reading process might be analyzed more fruitfully as a rhetorical operation rather than as a social one.[106] Kenneth Burke intimated that inquiry into the schemas for reading might include syllogistic progression (step-by-step appreciation of a kind of argument pressing forward via the narrative), qualitative progression (the appreciation of feelings post-hoc from narrative action), antecedent categorical forms (such as "the sonnet"), or technical schemas (such as chiasmus and reversal).[107] In any event, by underspecifying the cultural workings of the literary experience, we arrive at "society" as the default explanation of differences in the received meanings of the novels. The more you attend to the critics' professional know-how and to the generative schemas with which they read, the weaker the rationale for leaping to a generally shared "percipience" to explain coding outputs. Sociologists since the nineteenth century have invested so much energy in solidifying "society" as a "cause," they can invoke it without asking whether more tangible but less spirit-like forces may be operating.[108]

Perhaps a more promising use of scientist comparative logic would be to isolate (and to vary or control) the categories of understanding the literati deployed. That strikes me as the best design aligned with the two variables in Griswold's proposed theory of cultural power: the literary artifacts versus the presuppositions brought to bear. As we have seen, however, it is daunting to disentangle the schemas that contingently join with the object-novels to produce significance apart from the expression of that significance itself. The explanatory variables in "The Fabrication of Meaning" seem both untested and untestable via conceivably independent evidence.

The wide circulation of Griswold's primary finding about cultural power may have inadvertently confirmed a prophecy that the social theorist Alasdair MacIntyre set forth four decades ago. MacIntyre challenged the possibility of an empirical social "science" such as Griswold proposed, one that accepted the agents' own texts and practices as adjudicative evidence. He declared that any generalization that rendered local cultural contexts intelligible and that also appeared to be "law like" for most cultures would unknowingly amount to tautology derived from "our general understanding of rationality."[109] The propositions that surmounted the contextual effects of local culture would have to be embedded in our basic human makeup, MacIntyre reasoned, so they would stand independent of the meaning-laden contingencies of fact that make up the subject matters of social and political science. MacIntyre expected researchers to misrepresent continually as "empirical results" what were posited in advance as definitional truths, outside of specific excavations from evidence.

Griswold's apparently fact-driven discovery that cultural power grows from a stimulating fit between an object-novel and the schemas applied to interpret this artifact fulfills MacIntyre's prophecy. Her "finding" seems true by definition, since most everyone has assumed since Immanuel Kant that humans gifted with reason "produce meaning, the meaning for them, there, then" [1081] from the schemas they bring to bear on the objects they confront.[110] As Griswold suggests, it has been a commonplace in literary theory to explain aesthetic engagement and appreciation by a text's tactical challenge to habits of reception [1111]. Commentators since the New Criticism of the 1930s have agreed that an "aesthetic object" differed from those for mass consumption by violating readers' formulaic assumptions.[111] "Even as readers try to pin down what a writer means," a *New York Times* reporter reiterated, "the best authors try to elude them, using all the resources of sound, rhythm and syntax to defeat any straightforward account of what they are doing."[112] Bourdieu named it "frustrating gratification."[113] If Griswold's finding about cultural power could not have derived its originality and influence from explicit statement, perhaps it did so from what remained implicit in the article's execution as ritual.

THE PHASE OF INTEGRATION: A CONJECTURE

I believe the "The Fabrication of Meaning" impresses recipients because it artfully enacts coding as an eternal formula for establishing "interaction" between cultural artifacts and their recipients. "In the final analysis," Valerio Valeri wrote of worship and belief, "ritual contributes to constituting the social community that performs it, to creating a communicative field, and more generally a relational field, among its participants."[114] Griswold wrote to bring cultural sociologists into a community of their own. Knowledge, experiment, science—none in their operation are ultimately about information, only about ways of binding people together.[115] If the performance is what mattered, why was coding so central to it?

Michael Oakeshott wrote of ritual that "certainty is possible only in respect of something we have been 'given,' and not in respect of anything we have ascertained."[116] So it is with the device of coding. Griswold to my mind never justifies her preference for coding in what she calls "provincial positivism" except that coding cements a descriptive sketch (which is to assume a warrant rather than to adduce one).[117] More specifically, I would add, coding for social contents such as mentions of "race" assures us that there are base referents in texts upon which we can agree. Why is it important for the performance that coding creates out of literature a form of expression that is patently direct?

Sophisticated reading today is freighted with what Frank Kermode once called the burdens of "loss and disappointment."[118] When we embark on appreciating a text by its internal figurations, we close the text off from what we share already in the known world. By searching for literary meaning inside a text's verbal construction, sophisticated interpreters lose the possibility of accessing for their community a single truth at the core of a cultural artifact. Only if investigators see a presageful text as referring transparently to the world outside it, Kermode surmised, can they reach a consensus in which meaning and truth coincide absolutely. Such is the lost universe of determinancy and the sacred to which Griswold in my estimation tries to return us by transmuting responses to literature into discrete codes.[119]

In my reframing by ritual, Griswold's performance promises to sociologists that they can restore this unified world of obviousness and consensus by invoking "society" as a secure if culturally reworked referent of literature. The presupposition built into Griswold's coding categories as a system is that the constituent "themes" of the novels are at once linguistic terms as well as extralinguistic social and psychological tensions: "violence," "sexual behavior," "local politics," and so forth, for a total of 11 boxes [1097–1099]. The received meanings of novels are amenable to coding because they are windows on socially categorizable goings-on.

Of course a ritual that crowns coding as a sovereign form of expression for nostalgically uniting a community of researchers around satisfying transparent meaning calls forth a monstrous doppelgänger. Consensus also requires a method that is easily enacted and appreciated. Yet the more formulaic a method and its apperception becomes, the less research is able to unleash a wealth of cultural meanings and, above all, the more the enactment itself moves toward triteness for the communicant. If we as social "scientists" are united around coding for the production of "facts," we are also potentially formulaic dullards, similar to the writers Griswold lists who are mediocre because they are overly pat [1105]. I would hazard the guess that Griswold expels the "monstrous double," as René Girard terms it, when she sets about recommending the community focus on analyzing "the most powerful works": such texts "will generate the most abundant and complex patterns of responses and hence will provide the richest data for the social scientist as well as for the humanist" [1113]. It is possible her advice will not carry much practical import if, other way around, "the most powerful works" can be identified as such only by coding patterns of response. Nonetheless, the communicants in the rite are directed toward artifacts with enough cultural overloading to frustrate simplistic reduction of the objects' form or social bearing.

The threatening "double" that coding includes in an undifferentiated community sets up the more general question, How do sociologists as investigatory virtuosos exercise "cultural power" upon their own audiences? A sociology dedicated to the "definitional precision" of science in the appraisal of texts is apt to insist on overt if reductive clarity, the opposite of ambiguity. Out of such formality of coding, what is left of the fresh polyvalence necessary for engrossment? Ambiguity of course is neither imprecision nor is it the paralysis of someone who cannot move between alternative readings; it is the multiplication of possibilities whose tenability is resolved upon technical consideration—that is, by the act of closure that is the essence of coding. Griswold's advice that cultural analysis be directed toward the most difficult artifacts enables the "rational" procedure to embody a myth of eternal recurrence. The philosophical critic John Caputo expressed such a dynamic:

> On my accounting, clarity and ambiguity should not be viewed as simple logical opposites on a timeless spectrum but different stages in the process of making meaning, of producing meaning as an effect. Clarity is a late product, something that emerges at dusk, at the end of the process, when a belief or practice has more or less run its course and has acquired a kind of distilled, stable, settled, literal sense…Ambiguity on the other hand belongs to an earlier matinal stage, to a deeper stratum of meaning, where meaning is sending up its first shoots, things have an irreducible richness that cannot be definitively laid out or decisively nailed down, finally settled or straightened out.[120]

Coding method in the abstract is perceived as a rational instrument for representation. But dramatized in a larger story about excess possibility and final crystallization of meaning itself, coding brings us home to the modern community's ultimate mythical cycle.

BACK TO THE START

Circling back to the introductory example of the devices producing the number Pi, we have discovered from the ground up how the frequency of codes across texts bears no witness to the *meaningful* processes by which the texts were composed. We have every reason to suspect that a statistically significant difference in coding frequencies can be a misleading artifact of compositional logics unique to each text, not a result from a more general principle in the environment at large. Conversely, a chaotic lack of patterning in the coding numbers may be produced by simpler cultural principles, algorithms one might even say, once you return to the individual texts. As Weber cautioned, "[t]here is a priori not the slightest probability that exactly what is meaningful and essential to concrete patterns would be contained in the class concepts in graspable correlations."[121] Although Weber offers a strictly negative logic (reasoning about that which *cannot* be assumed), his formulation is enough to pin down the contrivancy in the interpretation of correlations. If projecting meanings onto abstracted data seems so alluring yet logically suspect, is it controllable? Why cannot we resist assigning cultural significance to a pattern of "facts"? Hermann Rorschach did not view the inkblots he famously invented as prying into the test subjects' imaginations, only into their automatic perception, lending individuals' responses an uncanny objectivity and lack of reflexivity.[122] Of course patients always cite broader knowledge to show their reaction to Rorschach inkblots is warranted. The first step in critical diagnosis of a coding diagram may be insisting on sheer absence of sense.[123]

APPENDIX 4.1 DEMARCATING THE SAMPLE

Is there such a thing as a unit review to be found? Griswold said she included in her sample "all the published reviews I could find that appeared between 1953 and 1976" [1088]. The question unanswered is this: "What is the essential verbal make-up of a review?" Griswold narrates in her footnotes a "catch as one can" assembly. Items included "a range of materials," from "books on Caribbean writers" to newspaper blurbs [1088]. Quite a few Caribbean reviews were for self-conscious West Indian literati [1084]. They were in style and purpose similar to the literary criticism articles of professors in the United States and Britain in their concern for placing Lamming's works in the current phase of this intellectual game or that. Does one therefore include contemporary university "literary criticism" among the items to be included in the sample of literary "reviews"? If so, biting references to colonialism might become overwhelming by the radical 1960s and 1970s.[124]

The items in the sample already include high literary treatises not intended for lay readers. For example, Stuart Hall's six-page essay feature on Lamming's *The Emigrants* (and on Samuel Selvon's *A Brighter Sun*) appeared in a "little magazine" in 1955, a year shared by most other reviews of that novel. Hall wrapped his words on Lamming's novel together with a larger theory of historically shifting relations between "the Novel" and society. Hall placed Lamming in the context of Zola and Woolf, remarkable polar extremes, and he included more than one pedantic reference to the Princeton literary theorist R. P. Blackmur.[125] In sum, Hall's item, like others in the Caribbean "little magazines," seems similar to professorial writing, but it is also a review, given its quick publication.[126] It is so unlike a brief notice in the TLS, it makes frequency counts of this or that in Caribbean versus British sources an empty diversion. "Each of the three categories [the reviews' societies of origin] contains a few critical discussions from literary journals or books on Caribbean writers; these were somewhat longer than newspaper reviews but shared similar characteristics otherwise," Griswold wrote in a footnote [1088].

If *books* "on Caribbean writers" qualify, given their very different institutional function, is there a demarcation rule excluding any contemporary publication from the sample? Could timely criticism churned out for academic conferences or tenure in US and UK departments count, too?[127] There is no correct solution, but we must try to make transparent the circularity in the process of inquiry: the composition of the sample is based on the meanings we intend at the outset to seek. Since so many quick-release magazine reviews were skewed in their discussion of Lamming by surveying him as part of a larger field of authors, or as expressing a state of play, or in accidental relation to another author's release, these reviews are no closer to the original reception of Lamming than purely scholarly essays.

CHAPTER 5

WARY REASONING

What the signs conceal, their application declares.
—Ludwig Wittgenstein, *Tractatus Logico-Philosophicus*

LET ME ASSUME TWO BURDENS IN THIS CONCLUDING CHAPTER. Let me sum up parallels across the three case studies to show why ritual is indispensable to their operation and why sampling and coding texts cannot be repaired for the rubric of science. As the second burden, let me retrieve an alternative research tradition by which cultural investigators may capture focal meanings. Mary Poovey astutely diagnosed the perversities in reifying "facts," but her postmodern acknowledgment of interlocking theory as "the only source of meaning" justifiably worries archive-tethered humanists in an era of scholarship "after the fact."[1] The unappreciated critical edge of Max Weber's ideal-type approach offers a remedy.

ODD PARALLELS

Add up the quirky samples, sourceless observations, changed numbers, problematic classifying, misattributions, substituted documents, and violations of the sine qua non of sharable or replicable data, and it seems that in some respect, each of the demonstration studies lack referential ties to the outside world of evidence.[2] Most concretely, we saw, none of the sociologists listed their sources. To find Herr D.'s real autobiography, it was necessary to read hundreds of files in the Theodore Abel Collection at the Hoover Institution. Detective work cannot reveal the sample items in the other demonstrations. John Evans has not itemized his mainspring, the citing texts from which he derived the "influential" cited texts [G 208].

Were all coding sheets in hand, referents of the constructed "data" might remain imperceptible. I speak from experiencing my own files. When I collated my published coding results a decade after their appearance with my notations and root documents, I was unsure how each code corresponded to a verbal feature. Likewise, for Bearman and Stovel, the coded linkages are "now you see it, now you don't" imputations of reasoning in the mind of a Nazi. Who can blame sociologists if coding records appears extraneous to the enterprise?

In the infelicitously blurred genre of coding, the term "qualitative" can designate readings so soft as to appear nonsubsistent. Since it is challenging to match codes individually to their source points, we retain only boilerplate promises that a thicket of qualitative codes corresponds intelligibility to anything. In pure humanist interpretation, by contrast, academic tribes retrace and contest evidence, casting the inquiry as both qualitative and "hard."[3] Footnoting each derivation from a text sustains transparency and retrial.[4] As in some natural sciences, the visibility of the interconnections in an edifice puts a humanist's whole building at risk if an anomaly in the evidence leads to ramifying reinterpretation.[5] Only in a problematically crossed genre could there permanently be, as one of our researchers said, "little to debate" about relations of coding results to sources.[6]

In each exemplary study, coding skewed readings where reports corresponded to isolable passages. Bearman and Stovel announced that Herr D. experienced "straight rows of graves in cemeteries" [87], but such columns of headstones did not exist in his story and to me were not suggested. For this key paraphrase, Bearman and Stovel did not index a datum. By the picky standards of a humanist, it looks as if Evans misattributed quotes. Griswold expounded on how several reviews treated the Trumper "scene" in a novel, whereas most of her preferred examples barely alluded to it.

Each highlighted study inadvertently barred evidence that probably should have been considered for the interpretations at issue. In assessing British critics' relative lack of social commentary, Griswold appears to have overlooked book reviews in a prime London journal. Evans's method happened to exclude from his sample exactly the kind of sources he then concluded did not steer deliberations, such as those in the mirror sample. Bearman and Stovel ignored passages from the genuine autobiography and from the *ersatz* that showed Herr D. fully contemplating his actions.

Each study was narrated as a tale of discovery, yet each primary finding was guranteed a priori. Bearman and Stovel knew deductively that a master identity "necessarily" required the severing of multiplex social relations. Evans supposed from unidirectional social theory that bioethicists moved debate from substantive to formal rationality. I think he circularly restated it by deciding which authors qualified as composing "bioethics."[7] For Griswold, legions of theorists have reasoned logically that engrossment results from modest challenging of expectancies. Tautologies have the advantage of being true, but why in ritual do they evince commitment? Or do they? The mystery is similar to that confronted by anthropologists in the field: "When a dancer dons a lion mask to become a lion god," Ronald Grimes asked of ritual participants, "is 'believing' what is going on?"[8] The answer is that the lion is a tool for rethinking one's relations to the world. Ritual creates a community of believers who unite self and society by an extrahuman paradigm, cosmically if tautologically.[9]

The multistabile diagrams in ritual social science perceptually stimulate the articulation of relations between self and society.[10] Taking another look at Bearman's narrative map, we see the elements of personal consciousness, that is, the content of the narrative clauses, evacuated to form empty points, so the "self" exists as pure structure or as a way of conceiving structure. The left-to-right temporal dimension of the map encompasses the personal sequence of clauses in the autobiography as well as the external history of the Nazi movement. Do changes in the patterning reflect different ways of making the world coherent or different ways in which the self and the world make each other? The diagram unravels and then lets us fit back together such diverse realities.

Analogous mirroring between self and social field emerges in Evans's cluster diagrams. Consider the contradictory perspectives combined in figure 3.1. Does cluster membership represent a writer's personal strategies for allying with others who share a similar rationality for the sake of extracting resources from the environment? Or do the clusters show only where outsiders in the social field overall, the citers in the aggregate, place a writer when citers mobilize a text for their independent strategic motives? Depending on how Evans limns the cluster diagrams, he can switch between those two perspectives on the significance of a location. The publishing scholar as independent strategist *stakes out* a position *or* the publishing scholar as defined by their argumentative rationality is *assigned* a position by the citers. The two perspectives are discrepant while visually copresent.

Griswold teases out a more fundamental contradiction through her tables. The sociologist Norman Denzin noticed it when he alleged that Griswold proceeded with the banal logic that "strong objects are defined as those that elicit strong responses."[11] Whether his phrasing was fair, Denzin at least insisted there is or is not an independent indicator for the strength of a novel apart from readers' response to it, but that one cannot have it both ways at once. Griswold discusses why each work has a symbolically constituted "meaning-carrying capacity" [1110]. Her displays of the aggregate coding for each work presumes that this capacity is "recognized, or sensed" [1106–1107].[12] Yet she simultaneously posits that the power of a novel "is itself a product of interaction" with recipients' schemas [1106]. The two assertions appear incoherent when conjoined—there is some built-in symbolic power to a cultural object but that power "is itself" only *relational*? Yes, and both findings can be seen as separate perspectives coexisting in her charts [1107, 1109]. The meaning of the novel may be seen as a collective event, when its carrying capacity gets "recognized, or sensed" [1106] and is then expressed in the aggregate shape of responses [1107]. But Griswold also presumes meaning is created and experienced by individuals when the data do not descend to patterns inside individual reviews.

In each of the three primary cases, the intersection of individual- and collective-level perspectives on meaning-making in the diagrams parallels the "savage thought" in totemic objects.[13] Claude Lévi-Strauss understood that diagrammatic imagery permits ritual participants to unite contradictory perspectives. For example, the Kwakiutl reused animal parts to craft boxes with diagrams of the physically incorporated animal. The artists "reconstituted a new creature, all of whose anatomical points coincide with the parallelepiped plans of the box, thus making an object which is simultaneously a box and an animal," Lévi-Strauss wrote, "and at the same time, one or several animals and a man."[14]

In each exemplary study, the codes and charts do not so much communicate a sharable fact of experience from an outside reality as propose an interweaving of individual self and the social field. We discovered as much in the similitude between inward self and outward networks in Bearman and Stovel; in the eternal means-end patterning of ethical selfhood and competition in Evans; and through creation of individual meaning by social percipience in Griswold. This articulation of self with other defines the distinctive experience of "unitive consciousness" in ritual (and calls forth the need for community differentiation from monstrous twins).[15] Even in pop culture, a paradigm uniting self and world alludes to the sacred. Consider readers' responses to network models. Nicholas Christakis and James Fowlers's recent book *Connected*, a reviewer wrote, offers "[a] *God's-eye* view of social relationships that may make you dizzy. Every business leader, teacher, and parent should see their life from this vantage."[16]

CRITERIA FOR VALIDITY IN CODING?

Social "scientific" talk about method is akin to what Freud called secondary rationalization when the action of research is ritual. There are no standards of validity in coding for choosing *general* indicators of historically *specific* meanings. In some physical sciences, investigators can appraise an operationalization because they have reason to guess there is a natural kind with distinctive machinery that can be grasped by measurement (or "coding"). Whether we identify oxygen with a gas monitor or with a splint test, it is said, the element we guess we have identified works the same way in relation to countless others. In chemistry we can assess the status of instruments, coding devices, by whether they display such convergence.

When reading subtly orchestrated texts, by contrast, coding categories accomplish nothing more than sorting. Sociologists cannot expect that sociocultural meaning they try to identify via general indicators will behave consistently relative to other meanings when texts help us generate sense by violating precedents and by toying with dissonance. The disabling problem for coding is that the literature of the ages has always suggested that the most essential meaning of a text may run contrary to the linguistic devices used to convey it. Sometimes a literal reading is atypical and deep whereas a figural reading more obvious and naive.[17] A narrative may insert "because" to mark an absurd absence of connection, conveying the opposite of what is stated.[18] If we approve an indicator's validity because the indicator correlates with others as expected, all we do is ratify what we suppose we already know.[19] An excellent indicator of the presence of a text theme may mislead us as to what the theme is about: "If 90 percent of the A's fall under the code B, while only 5 percent of the code B's are A's, A is a good indicator for B but a poor referent of what we mean by B."[20] Conversely, the more sensitive our codes are to the local meanings, the weaker the claim that the codes tap into a generalizable characterization that is extractable from the specific correlation it explicates in its context on the page.[21]

If the indicators you choose cannot be winnowed by whether they tap into an underlying causal structure, then you find something of interest in texts or not.[22] There is no external check for accuracy of coding categories unless you dream, little different from the Azande, that finding an interesting variant on what you already know is exactly the point.[23] Perhaps it is. Wendy Griswold was eloquent in aiming for codes of self-consciously limited validity. "By a *provincial* positivism" (emphasis in the original), she said, coining an epistemological phrase, "I mean to suggest that within the discourses of the day—a certain place, a certain time, a certain pattern of local knowledge within and outside the academy—some concepts or theories, provisionally chosen, can get you farther than others."[24] Were it correct that rational adequacy is warranted extrinsically by a village culture, ours, rather than by what is in texts, we may ask: get you "farther" by what kind of locally articulated yardstick? "Further" works only as a placeholder.

The retrospectively elicited agreement of expert "natives" with the coding outputs or with the reasonableness of indicators offers little encouragement. It is commonplace for the outputted corpus data in linguistics as well as the cluster analysis of themes or citations in sociology (or in your discipline of choice) to persuade locals that their prior intuitions are not fully adequate grounds for counter-response.[25] Informants adjust to agree in some part with the "science." Coders themselves lack consensus on what comprises *mis*representation of meaning because there is no mandate to conserve any original information, no requirement to maintain the original semantic framework, and no rule for preserving nomic regularities through the coding categories.[26] My contention throughout has been that coding in the primary studies accomplishes nothing more than separating tokens from context to inscenate a ritual arena.

The premise of coding is that meanings are entities about which there can be facts.[27] But we all know that novel questions and contexts elicit fresh meanings from sources, which is enough to intimate that meaning is neither an encapsulated thing to be found nor a constructed fact of the matter.[28] It is categorically absurd to treat a coding datum as a discrete observation of meaning in an object-text.[29] My preference is to think of "meaning" as the puzzle we try to grasp when our honed concepts of what is going on collide with the words and usages of the agents we study. Describing meaning effectively requires us to exhibit that fraught interchange between cultures in its original: the primary sources displayed in contrast to the researcher's typifying of them.

MANAGING THE CLASH OF GENRES

The frame of ritual is indispensable for grasping what transpires in the head of a researcher who blurs genres, because social "scientists" who conscientiously expound their premises make explicit the incompatibilities between scientific and interpretive worldviews. Let me illustrate how researchers manage the clash. In the quantitative scientific mode Evans wrote that he could not know why an author cited another, because that would demand "a subjective account that the outside observer has no access to" [G 206]. Then in aggregate diagrams the bioethicist Thomas Childress, the co-originator of the package of formal argument in which Evans thinks the HGE culminated,[30] failed to garner citations adequate to satisfy the threshold for inclusion as an influential author. To account for this anomaly, Evans accessed his prior contextual knowledge of the authors' purposeful citation practices that he had said from the scientific viewpoint of "the outside observer" were out of reach. He concluded "*people rarely cite the methodological canon they are operating with.*"[31] As I appreciate him, Evans called upon his interpretive knowledge of discourse to *explain away* what was uncomfortable about the numeric result. At that moment, Evans ascertained by humanist interpretation that the dominant authors are precisely those who do not provoke citation, opposite the purpose of counting citations.

Or, as Bourdieu once announced to show luminaries are omitted, "How can we reduce Plato's presence in Aristotle's texts to explicit references alone?"[32] In social "science" as ritual the interpretive knowledge of citing practices that would disqualify mere counting of the cites as equivalents has to be forgotten to go on pretending the counts produce a defensible diagram, and then this interpretive knowledge in reverse has to be recalled in an advantageously self-confirming way to decide what a diagram actually means.

Only the divides between the three phases of ritual make intelligible this schizophrenic protocol for screening out complex meaning in texts, viewing the "data" results, and selectively remembering and forgetting what one had first learned from reading the texts themselves. From the interpretive perspective, Griswold saw the meaning of a book review being fabricated from the uncertain *interaction* of an expectant schema with the complexity of a novel. Logically, her own coding schema coming in contact with complex book reviews would iterate such a creative interaction. Instead, when she was questioned on the status of her coding as "data," Griswold vacated her interpretive postulate to reoccupy the scientific mode of fact gathering. She upheld her codes as examples of a "quantifiable indicator" given by "provincial positivism."[33]

Since decontextualizing and recontextualizing "facts" in coding rituals allows us to compartmentalize the interpretive and the scientific moments, social scientists have failed to appreciate why crossing them remains radically inconsistent. Let me review the stunning contradictions that make standard sampling and coding unworkable.

SAMPLING "MEANINGS" IS CHIMERICAL

In scientific inquiries it seems plausible to define near the outset the mechanisms that sampling aims to probe. At least we can reasonably delimit a relevant physical grouping as *the* target population. This launching of scientific reasoning is unserviceable when the target is an ensemble of complex texts serving a communicative function. Coding the features of a well-chosen sample is supposed to represent with more confidence what is shared in the population. Population of what? If we pursue questions about the dynamics of expression and communication, there is at the outset no definition of the population that would portray those dynamics and therefore we do not know the boundaries of the texts to sample. Criterially "similar," thus scientifically equivalent texts could be linked to differentially evolving models of composition to generate contrasting meanings.[34] We do not know what we are sampling except by retrospective analysis of the relations of the texts to each other and to what lies outside, the genres and local histories that produced them.

The German novelist and romantic critic "*Novalis*"—of all persons—captured the dilemma of sampling in the world of texts with uncanny precision over two centuries ago. To define by empirical study the essence and role of fine "literature," Novalis reasoned, you would have to establish which works counted as literary.[35] If you were already certain of the criteria for inclusion that reached literature's essence, actually reading literature would be epistemologically pointless, because the identifying *theory* about what literature has to say that you use to count a text "as" literature would itself be the encapsulated truth about literature.[36] This circle is inescapable. When E. D. Hirsch sought to delimit literature as art, he included in his definition the readiness of inquirers—"us"—to evaluate a work *as art*, a circularity that presumes we know that toward which we can take up such an appreciative stance.[37] Blurring the scientific logic of sampling with text interpretation preempts self-examination of this circular autonomy of sampling. For example, Evans had to presume to know in *Playing God* what kind of text belonged in the sample (based on *substantive topic*), whereas the point of understanding texts is to discover progressively which are relevant for one's question (based on *forms of reasoning* in them). Evans kept finding that many "influential" texts lay outside his winnowed sample, but this could not trigger him to respecify the sample once it seemed given as methodologically natural.

Similarly, I think Griswold presupposes that a review is a unitary kind across national contexts, despite their varying purposes. The sample process begs the question of the sense in which such reviews comprise a comparable type. None of the verbal dynamics that created positive reviews can be probed if the sample is the base for "finding variation" rather than the considered aftereffect of interpreting variation.[38] Scientific logic can even let you proceed as Bearman and Stovel did, retrieving any *ersatz* source as "illustrative"—like some lab experiments in which the manipulated materials have never occurred in such form in nature.

Thus sampling in cultural inquiry is unrelated to the business of sampling physical objects in natural science. If we draw blood from a patient, the vial does not just *stand for* the features of the patient's total circulatory liquid, it actually *possesses* those properties in full. The relation between sample and population, like that between a tweed suit and its fabric swatch, is perceptual, not figurative.[39] Likewise, if we have on hand a population of rabbits from which to sample, we have randomizing procedures for warranting that sampled rabbits proportionally *possess* the same features as the population. As usual, the ritual process reverses logic when it mobilizes "sampling" in the conventional image of natural science. The blurring lets sociologists invoke the authority of "scientific" habits to make a large-N something-or-other seem representative, instead of first using criterially satisfactory evidence of representativeness to create authority secondly.

Sampling of natural objects is again inapplicable to culture because the texts that are merely *imagined* as suitable for comparison radically change our understanding of what a text in hand *is*. To recall a legendary example, when the French historian Roger Chartier revisited Robert Darnton's masterful portrayal of *The Great Cat Massacre*, he noticed the sole testimony bore the odd third-person voice of a fictive observer. Rather than read the story of the massacre as an autobiography, a format accessible in our day, Chartier relocated the text as a specimen from the eighteenth-century genre of revelations of the mysteries of craft trades. Thus the unknown author's purpose appeared not to be that of recounting personal experience. It was to act as travel guide to a nether world in which anecdotes normatively "should" unfold bizarrely to entertain the reader-visitor. Chariter switched the events to which Darnton attributed a genuine exoticism over to playful genre-governed contrivances, not necessarily expressions of workers' lives.[40] A "meaning" is never attachable to a text as the predicate "fur" clings to a sampled rabbit.

Text sampling in the blurred genre of social science presumes that texts are meaningful as bundles of attributes, such as "thematic mentions." But texts do not contain communicative features like rabbits possess fur, even if you acknowledge that color and texture of fur results from interaction between observer and rabbit. The premises necessary for sampling cultural meanings from texts collapse once we discern how meaning is deferred and remade. The self-referential paradox, "My utterances are false," is "about" the theme of truth and falsity, but whether the sentence is to be taken as true, false or neither depends not just on a kind of interaction with the text, but on how we *make* the text quite unlike the possibility of making a rabbit's fur. This holds true for the nonfiction we absorb everyday, be it the Colbert Report or Rush Limbaugh's racism-saturated remarks not "about" race. We create what a text is "about" all the way down.[41] If we learn more about an author's definition of the problem to be solved, if we reverse what should be taken literally and what figuratively, then we do more than establish an unanticipated perspective: we cut into a different thing.[42] A body of texts has no fixed attributes that permit a *sampling of meaning* to occur.[43]

This paradox of texts has been embodied most acutely in coding psychoanalytic sessions. The clinicians Harold Sampson and Joseph Weiss found that researchers could code patient transcripts once a metaframe, "the patient's unconscious plan to overcome his problems," was specified and had established what the text therefore concerned. Given this metaframe, Sampson and Weiss wrote, the "ultimate guarantee of freedom from both error and research bias is independent replication of research findings," which they believed they had demonstrated.[44] Other way around, it was impossible to specify procedures for eliciting the metaframe. Their curious split, anchored findings once the text's substance is chosen versus interpretive mystery in making that choice, illustrates how demanding standards in the humanities do step in after we clarify how a text is to be "taken."

SAMPLES ALWAYS CONCEAL A MISLEADING HEURISTIC

The heuristic by which a researcher samples texts always taps into meaning selectively and outputs a *patterned* misconstrual of a cultural field. Consider the whole landscape on which texts in the sample depend for their identities, and you inevitably adduce classes of terribly relevant-yet-excluded texts, as I attempted to demonstrate in chapter three.[45] A text is constituted by its relations to the whole cultural environment, but that environment is exactly what a researcher excludes for focused sampling from a venue or categorical database.[46] A publication forum or topic, instead of measuring "the same" cultural target over time, shifts its communicative functions in relation to an ever-changing field of production. Plowing into the evidence with a mechanical, quasi-scientific delimitation of relevance across time or place (say, reviews over decades at *The New York Times*) is bound to produce a categorical blunder when we move from what, in a scientific perspective, the sample *is* (items surfacing in a venue) to what from an interpretive perspective we would like the population to symbolize (say, the messages transmitted to nonspecialist audiences). Asserting what a sample of texts "stands for" uses a fictive trope from the humanist frame that might be reexamined. But in the crossed genre of social "science," the sample is decreed to be real just by calling it commensensically approximative.

If landscapes of cultural meaning are unique, so is skewing of their samples, and case trial is the only test. If you worry I belabor problems in unrepresentative studies, let me highlight briefly the most rigorous sampling to have come my way, Shyon Baumann's pithy book *Hollywood Highbrow*.[47] To gauge the rise of aesthetic discourse in film appreciation, Baumann registered 684 film reviews sampled meticulously from 1925 to 1985 in *Time*, *The New Yorker*, and *The New York Times*. Baumann concludes by vocabulary counts that in the 1960s the linkup of cultural experts with "the general public" finally legitimated Hollywood film as fine art. Baumann trusts that with statistics he can "empirically document" film critics' relations with the public.[48]

Due to the simplification in imagining what a sample "stands for," it takes only minutes to find massively contravening information about most conclusions sociologists reach via mechanical text samples. New York writers were likely to garner cultural capital by distancing the city's literary business and its high-hatted plays from the movies. In broad-shouldered Chicago, by contrast, Carl Sandburg, "an American in every pulse-beat," wrote in 1920: "I am the cinema *expert*, the critic of the silent celluloid for the *Daily News*."[49] In the two thousand reviews he penned in eight years, Sandburg completed innovations in film criticism for which Baumann thinks Americans waited until the 1960s. Sandburg analyzed technique to treat the director as "the creative artist" who could earn the acclaim of a genius author.[50] "Will school pupils in 6922, or even 1000 years from now, be able to study early examples of the cinema art as pupils of 1922 study Virgil and Homer?" Sandburg asked hopefully.[51] He equated celluloid with sacred manuscripts of the ancients.

The contradiction between scientific and humanistic perspectives consists in isolating equivalent text "units," as in the sciences, when the question of meaning is only about potentialities for creating texts.[52] When Baumann counts mentions of directors in unit-reviews, for example, he reaches a longitudinal conclusion about the initially low profile of directors, which he concretizes with such remarks as: "In fact, *Time* magazine began to include the name of the director under the title of each film being reviewed only in the 1970s."[53] Given the ever-changing functions of film reviews, most everything Baumann sought fell outside the sample. Film connoisseurship and directorial style were topics worthy of their own articles much earlier in *Time*, including a 1934 cover story.[54] As early as the 1920s the *New York Times* readily discussed film as an art form equal to others even if it did so infrequently in judging individual releases.[55] The dissemination of television may have transformed the purpose of film reviews because audiences no longer treated an evening at the movies as a low-attention placebo.[56]

The assumption behind Baumann's conclusion that "mainstream" reviews relegated film to cheap fun until the 1960s is that films were produced and appreciated "all in the family." Whose? That of whites. From D. W. Griffin's *Birth of a Nation*, however, the middle-class African American press posed the critical and aesthetic questions about film that the mainstream white press could better afford to neglect.[57] In her book on black film criticism since 1909, *Returning the Gaze*, Anna Everett showed how periodicals such as *The Half-Century. A Coloured Monthly* pioneered in discussing the requirements for serious film that, in the words of its reviewers, "mastered the art in completeness."[58]

By critiquing Baumann's corpus, I aim less to "refute" him than to indicate how the significance of his collection as well as inquiry into refined versions of his hypotheses must both remain inside the interpretive domain of the humanist. Perhaps the question is not *whether* writers use technical vocabulary to affirm cinema as art but what they intend by placing an artifact under the umbrella of art, an essentially contested term.[59] Once we adopt the scientific framework, controversy about sampling falsely appears to concern bias correctable through better statistic-gathering. My thesis instead is that scientifically sampling "facts" is inapplicable to the relational quality of meaning and to explicating meaning's production. Only because researchers suppose they can prejudge the relevant sample do they create what Nassim Taleb has theorized as "Black Swans"—the stunning exceptions to our sense of conceivable occurrences.[60] My retrieval of Carl Sandburg and of film appreciation outside film reviews shows how we guarantee the centrality of exceptions because an objectivistic sample ignores the ecologies that create absences in a sample.

A LARGE-N SAMPLE DAMPENS CRITICAL DISCUSSION

To sum up the surprising implication: for any noteworthy purpose in cultural appreciation of textual evidence, the concept of the sample is unreservedly inapplicable. Perhaps then the function of the sampling and coding is to mobilize a scientific perspective for an extraneous purpose. The whole notion of generalizing from a sample rests on the assumption that the greater the number of instances of a phenomenon we gather, the less likely it is for additions to impact our cognitive framework. Putting everything into its place via coding effaces every potentially ramifying anomaly. The researcher using sampling and coding can acknowledge some coding "facts" were or are inaccurate, all the better to imply corrections would remain exiguous to the established trends.[61] The function of the large-N, opposite that of genuine sciences, seems to be shielding results from critical discussion via any texts in particular.

If cultural explanation is about establishing the conditions that activate some statements and derail others, then a single witness must potentially upend everything we had previously supposed about a culture or ourselves. For example, in Hannah Arendt's hands, the trial testimony of the SS-criminal Adolph Eichmann indicated he was empty not just of malice, but of forethought. Arendt's typifying of his words by her novel concept "the banality of evil" challenged what most everyone had previously assumed about responsibility, criminal law, and goal-governed human action.[62] As Giorgio Agamben, Michel Foucault, and many others have attempted to demonstrate, whether through research on "the state of political exception" or on the history of French psychiatry, if you equip an anecdotal episode with the power to upend a canonical generalization, this is not a nihilist denial of generalizing logic.[63] It is the path to finding the semiotic devices by which a culture takes shape, the real objects of investigation beyond the overt population averages.[64]

What are Codes "About"?

The scientific worldview has us conceive coding as a generalizing procedure in which the researcher simplifies the features given in the object, just as, say, the categories of computerized real estate listings for houses omit idiosyncratic detail but register prominent features in standard format. From this perspective, we can usefully trade off the generalizability of claims from a large sample against the verisimilar specificity of a single-case description. What makes items in the original text translatable into coding is that the codes "say" the same things more abstractly, as if there were spatial "levels" of meaning moving "up" from the specifics in the text, analogously to, say, baby blue, denim, and navy blue moving up into a shared code, blue.

To transfer this scientific perspective to the interpretation of texts looks suspiciously like a categorical error, because the measurement of "attributes" cannot leave intact the system-like relations that let us generate meaning from a text. Even automated mappings and translations, in Nelson Goodman's wording, "are as productive as reproductive."[65] For we refound our labels' characteristic referential ranges and intensional colorings according to the semantic contrasts in our own coding language and we excise other plays of meaning in the original (such as the independent military domain navy blue, Prussian blue, airforce blue versus camouflage green, rifle green, *Feldgrau*...).[66] The "ladder of abstraction" metaphor behind coding is impertinent to grasping the interworkings of culture.[67] For example, Griswold sets up a taxonomy when she codes separately for race, class, and colonialism as themes mentioned in book reviews, three distinct referents in the eyes of sociologists. The book reviews' mention of these themes, we have seen, can be glancingly brief. Griswold's assumption is that she can decide when a review mentions "colonialism" without carrying along race or class integrally. But to code in this fashion, we have to assume there were separate lexical systems among the original writers for race versus class versus colonialism and that colonialism did not activate the others. Or we have to assume that class really is a separate domain of reference and that *we* know when a review should be sorted as making a reference to class. From the scientific perspective, the output is apt to contain measurement error or noise.[68] From the interpretive perspective, there is no discernible reference taking place because one has looked past all that there is to a text, the interwoven distinctions that it invites us to ponder.[69] Griswold's reviewers from the West Indies warned that we are not entitled to compare references to race as the "same" thing across cultures.[70]

In the universe of interpretation, equivalence has to be based on elements' alignments in an overall system of contrasts, not on isolated predicates.[71] Since no one can legislate in advance what that entails, researchers have to display the original source in relation to the generalizing interpretation, case by case.[72] Even a meta-theorist such as Claude-Lévi Strauss went about showing singly *how* his myths fell under a single umbrella "structure."[73] But in professional sociology the very purpose of coding is to let the code *replace* texts economically across importantly different contexts. Since we cannot expediently seek out the differences between our measuring instruments and the source texts, we never appraise whether what we jettison is incidental or primary compared to what coding retains.[74] If we cannot assess the defects of a coding translation, we cannot imagine a net gain as if we "trade off" exactness of fit with individual cases for the benefit of making generalizations about a larger number of cases.[75] Once more, blurring genres garners the merits neither of stereotypical hard sciences nor of humanist interpretation.[76]

It is inevitable that coders suppress this problem of adequate translation by naturalizing their categories via spatial analogies. A category of meaning is imagined to be a "dimension," like a continuous variable "more" or "less" clearly present in a text.[77] That is why we seem to see spatial "degrees" of overall formal or substantive rationality in texts in *Playing God*, over/against any complete prototype (figure 3.3). Equally geometrically, in "Becoming a Nazi" a narrative tie is assumed to be a unitary "something," however vaguely it may be defined verbally, because it is diagrammatically similar to a line connecting two points.

Naturalizing a variable as a spatial, therefore universally applicable dimension makes it impertinent to ask whether it is a flexible container so vague you can code almost as you like. Political theorist Giovanni Sartori called this "degreeism":

> By this I mean the abuse (uncritical use) of the maxim that differences in kind are best conceived as differences of degree, and that the dichotomous treatments are invariably best replaced by continuous ones...This is wonderful, for the exceptions that might cripple a hypothesis generally lie in the vicinity of the cutting points. Thus, in the continuous treatment, the exception (disconfirmation) can simply be made to disappear by cutting a continuum at astutely doctored points.[78]

If such points are defined! One never learns what the cutoff is for verbally describing a text as "mostly" formally rational (*Playing God*), when a narrative sequence is not explicit enough to qualify as a linkage ("Becoming a Nazi") or when a reference is too oblique *not* to be a thematic reference ("The Fabrication of Meaning").

CODING AS RITUAL PRESUMES A TRANSCENDENT "SOCIETY"

Each of the three showcased studies contrasts its empirical and explanatory rigor as social science against more impressionistic and exegetical approaches to culture. Yet each invokes society as the key to stabilizing and decrypting "facts" just as the Azande summon omnipresent spirit forces. The researchers gravitate to the richness of texts, only to conjure a predestined function of writing that warrants reductive coding for core social meanings. In "Becoming a Nazi," stories are necessarily organized by relations in social networks; in *Playing God*, the purpose of writing is to expand one's intellectual jurisdiction to extract resources, with the effect of influencing "the beliefs and values of the public" [G 34]; in "The Fabrication of Meaning," the generic purpose of writing is to "grapple with present and pressing problems" defined by the social environment [1104].

Once a posited external function justifies decontextualizing the verbal compositions, it also intervenes to render the arrayed outputs legible. In "The Fabrication of Meaning," the generic social purpose given by the environment's tensions establishes a shared causal ecology "behind" the coding ciphers. That is necessary to suppose that patterns in thematic mentions across nations are not just tangential artifacts of the texts' own "variousness of purpose," as book critics say. In an autonomous literary culture, the essence of criticism is to explore hypothetical standards that surpass social functions. Similarly, in "Becoming a Nazi," reduction of auto-biographies to an evenly relevant social function, that of expressing social ties over real historical time, conjures a semiotically neutral space against which *change* in narrative ties register change in the social makeup of the self, not change inside the document in norms for composition. Otherwise, the exigencies of conveying to Nazi officials one's experience after the Nazi takeover might contaminate the reading of the "facts." Or, reversing the causal arrow, agents may organize their life trajectories to imitate the norms for a dramatic story, making social relations, in Goffman's phrasing, less of a foundation than "a laminated adumbration" of discursive models.[79]

In each primary study, summoning an external social power releases social "sci-entists" in a blurred genre from the standards of either the purely scientific or the humanistic perspectives. By the standards of either pure approach alone, moving so quickly outside the verbal nuances of texts incorrectly privileges external back-ground variables (the social) without ascertaining whether more immediate, pre-cisely delimitable factors (the textual system before us) explicate the patterns. In *Playing God*, sheer linguistic exigencies of democratic discussion may move inter-locutors toward abstracting goals and values to make them discussable outside par-ticularistic idioms. This autonomous verbal logic, not the extrinsic funding and prestige granted to writers as social players, may more immediately and parsimoni-ously explain formalized ethical expression [G 259 n. 75, 262 n. 126]. Without the concept of "society" as ultimate foundation, Zygmunt Bauman has proposed,

> imagination would spill all over the vast expanses…desperately seeking a common estuary yet unable to find it. Though imagination hovers above the level of daily expe-rience, it is the images made familiar through that experience which allow us to play the game of reading shapes into the clouds and constellations in the night sky.[80]

As with clouds and constellations, so with coding diagrams. When "society" pro-vides a ground for interpreting the results without attending to authors' autonomous literary energy, it is like reading the shape of clouds without studying the movement of moisture by winds. The purpose of the coding is to see *through* the texts to cap-ture an underlying social content.[81] Expressive complexity, what makes the evidence literary and voluble to researchers in the first place, is tidied out of the room.

RITUAL IN SOCIAL SCIENCE AT LARGE

The stylistic characteristics of social science as ritual include:

1. Pigeonholing text units into a coding system that affirms categories for social life worthy of perpetuation *sub specie aeternitatis*.
2. Naturalizing the coding process (not just the choice of categories) as a para-digm of human cognition.
3. Simplifying historical processes into ways of occupying transhistorical coding categories.
4. Institutionalizing coding to sustain a role for "us" as members of a research community that is revivified by redeploying the ritual format.

With these symptoms before us, let me recall other ritual performances that I suspect dizzyingly guarantee some of their results. A partial extension is *Models of Management*, a comparative study of organizational ideologies in business conducted by the sociologist Mauro Guillen. Guillen coded management journals for the components of practice they happened to prescribe in Europe and North America throughout the twentieth century. His coding scheme featured such benchmarks as the perceived motivations of employees or the prevailing conceptions of authority.[82] As a provisionally universal taxonomy, the coding system naturally generated provisionally universal results in the following sense: if one assumes as a researcher that the journals can be encrypted for how they "refer to the same menu" of challenges and solutions, one will indeed "find," by circular insurance, that the social agents, management intellectuals in Europe and North America, correlatively always "refer to the same menu." By Guillen's analysis, only the frequency of mentions oscillated through time, so this result supports the conclusion that intellectuals cyclically repeat themselves through history—another common "conclusion" in studies that use coding.[83] The problem of ascertaining *whether* in their own communicative practices agents are actually talking about the same things or organizing their distinctions in the same way is solved by the coding apparatus that fixes semantics. In consequence, we can consecrate the categories as cyclically recurring in history without limit.[84]

Critiquing these coding circles does not block professional audiences from supporting the whirling. As for any rite, the enactment projects outward from itself a community way of life. This imperviousness is the lesson of perhaps the most extraordinary coding circuit of all, one that has sustained appreciative elaboration over four decades. It is that of anthropologists Brent Berlin and Paul Kay in their book *Basic Color Terms*. Berlin and Kay encrypted the colorific vocabulary of a sample of the world's languages to show that there are basic semantic universals across cultures.[85] The color terms of modern English have the same elementary foci of hue as the rest of the world's languages at similar stages of development, they found.

The assumption permitting Berlin and Kay to code foreign colorific vocabulary is that color is naturally given as a separate lexical domain and that color is "about" what we moderns see, states of hue. Yet many if not most of the world's cultures fail to recognize color as a domain of descriptors separate from adjectives and verbs for evaluation, ripening, movement, causal explanation, or highly specific shapes and practices.[86] The adjectives for appearance in ancient Greece and medieval Europe blended texture, gleam, and brightness together with what we see on its own, hue.[87] Unclassifiable oddities therefore proliferate when we try to put radically foreign pegs into our own holes. Some cultures use the same terms for red and white, or have a term for yellow that also applies to full black.[88] How did Berlin and Kay code such color-like word usage? The performance depended on being able to pick out what was basic and fundamental versus what was contextual noise, all for "generalizing" across cultures.

It proved difficult for Berlin and Kay to justify retrospectively the procedures they had applied. But the stakes could not have been higher, for if the findings held up, the implication was that humankind's visual physiology—physical reality itself!—molded cultural criteria of discrimination. For as cultures multiplied the colors they recognized they appeared to follow similar sequences and pairings. As critics noted immediately, however, the researchers' encrypting of foreign vocabulary and referents seemed fluid, therefore impossible to replicate. The "reliability and validity," M. Durbin wrote with stunning examples in 1972, "are zero."[89] Nancy Hickerson showed that the coding was carried out inconsistently and that it outputted manipulated, preprocessed results. She advised that until the coding procedures were explained more precisely, further consideration of the data "should be held in abeyance."[90] No matter.

Three decades on, Berlin and Kay have continued to toy with the coding rules and with qualifying the principal results.[91] These coauthors anchor an expanding scholarly industry that would discern an underlying universal architecture for human communications about all things deemed colorific.[92] New generations of critics have repeated the puncturing of the circular madness in Berlin and Kay's ritual.[93] If we establish a system of pigeonholes based on our own system of "color," the rest of the globe's ways of viewing what we think of as color can be fit somehow into our system, or be seen to converge upon it. But the data one manufactures no longer maps or refers to meanings, they fabricate their own. For these "data" create their own semantic universe, or ritual arena, that lacks structural connection to the original usage or semantics of color-like phrases. Nonetheless, the search for improved coding rules to make Berlin and Kay's system work once and for good has been interminable. It was not a critic, only a staunch *advocate* for Berlin and Kay's research who remarked in 2005 on some of the ad hoc revisions Berlin and Kay had undertaken: "Mysteriously, the yellow-white composite category is no longer a permitted composite category, but this was a small price to pay for the much greater clarity and coherence of the framework."[94] The manipulation can be dismissed as the price of greater coherence so long as you already "know" that hue is obviously a self-standing core referent. Of course it is also easy to justify the coding as the Azande justify encoding dead chickens: with corroboratory evidence from context. Thus coding by our system of hues is backed up with "in-depth" lab data compiled about natural spectra or with records of the amazing facility with which the rest of the world picked up on these natural categories (ours) through the all-reaching commerce of colonialism.

Why then does repeated unmasking of such circularly self-fulfilling logic fail to disrupt the performance? Scientific rationality intervenes on the side of ritual. Once Berlin and Kay's data were considered from inside the worldview of sampling and coding, the objections looked like quibbles about noise, which Berlin and Kay could overshadow by their powerfully illuminating "central tendencies," just as we have seen happens in "large-N" samples in cultural sociology. Social scientists and others equip themselves with diverse vocabularies for expressing their conviction that whatever is true *preexists* the form in which it is able to be seen and pronounced true.[95] One can call this endorsing facts with "provisional positivism," as Wendy Griswold suggests, or discovering meaningful stories without "exogenous imputation," as Bearman and Stovel recommend. If one holds the premise that the truth is lent from without, then empirical discoveries that restate what was imported via one's own analytic definitions seem all the more compelling, not contrived, because their elegance suggests they tap into underlying realities.

As we have seen, the sociological investigators who trust that their categories touch upon a core meaning or who aver that expanding the sample size would just refine the original estimate of meaning are exactly those who blindly land in a circle of their own making.[96] These social "scientists" can lay hold of no voucher for their belief that their propositions correspond to things with a prior existence "out there" in the world. If they try to demonstrate that it is so, well, they beg the question of how the "out there" is known in the first place by presupposing the proposition about the world that is at issue.[97] Social "science" as ritual is *realist* in supposing that the concepts in a coding system grasp preexisting entities in the world, but it is fanciful in failing to document its application of those concepts for replication.[98]

This model of a coding circuit embraces other studies that categorize responses by an eternally reusable scale. Consider how Pierre Bourdieu, an inspiration for cultural sociology, famously applied his universal ladder of low versus high cultural dispositions in *Distinction*. Bourdieu elicited the test subjects' habitus by having them comment upon a photograph of an old woman's hands. The aesthetic disposition toward such an image, he posited, displays "a generalized capacity to neutralize ordinary urgencies and to bracket ends."[99] This know-how requires remoteness from the practical exigencies of the social world that only economic privilege can sustain.[100] But as Jacques Rancière noticed, Bourdieu's method for preprocessing the data resisted failures of fit.[101] Bourdieu gauged "distance from the world" among respondents' answers by ad hoc coding, as can be discerned from his extracts. The clerical worker who remarked in *Distinction* "It's as if it was a painting that had been photographed" seems no less aesthetically engrossed than the teacher who said "These two hands unquestionably evoke a poor and unhappy old age."[102] Yet Bourdieu coded the clerical worker's artsy response as lacking in cultural capital and aesthetic distance and in reverse he coded the teacher's social realism as high in aesthetic distancing.[103]

More generally, as with many abstract coding schemes, Bourdieu treats his scale of aesthetic distance as an instrument for pigeonholing responses across cultures, just as Berlin and Kay assume that all color-like speech and reference fit into European dimensions of hue. For Bourdieu, aesthetic distance based on cultural capital is the underlying dimension controlling the human reception of art, so it is in evidence whenever the *investigator* deems an artifact to be aesthetic. Bourdieu assumes without ado that unwillingness to activate one's aesthetic disposition with a particular stimulus—photography—betokens absence of such a formal disposition overall. As in every ritual process, Bourdieu's act of coding for class disposition iterates an eternal archetype:

> Those who classify themselves or others, by appropriating or classifying practices or properties that are classified and classifying cannot be unaware that...they classify themselves in the eyes of other classifying (but also classifiable) subjects, endowed with classificatory schemes analogous to those which enable them more or less adequately to anticipate their own classification.[104]

Through such incantations, Bourdieu casts his self-fulfilling preprocessing of data as an inbuilt mirror of the preprocessing already carried out by the human agents under study.[105] Finally, in the ritual phase of reintegration, Bourdieu delivers his primary timeless ritual message for social relations. He conveys to his audience of intellectuals their proper societal role by showing they must renounce "the illusion of the absence of limits." Instead they should honor the eternal repetition of Bourdieu's classificatory schemes, as in the usual ritual closure of historical time.[106]

You may glean from this analysis of Bourdieu that my critical conclusions about the self-confirming logic of sampling extends mutatis mutandis to cultural investigation of "hard" institutions. If we study complex business organizations, for example, and create a sample of comparable institutions via an organizational definition of sample items that we deem a priori equivalent, we circularly assume that our naive sense of morphology justifies the sample and a relevant causal environment inside of which social messages emerge and circulate. Just as Geertz suggested a cockfight was not really a sport event but a display of Balinese status structure, so a business organization may hum less by economic imperative than by the schemas of a sinecure, of a display of salvation by this-worldly asceticism, of family aggrandizement, of a dating playground, of a celebration of the reassuring powers of technology, or of a macho sports arena. We cannot via its morphological genus decide in advance the cultural "genre" to which it belongs. It would be naive to sample cockfights "as" cockfights across environments and to aggregate the results.[107] It appears better to defer decisions about what is comparable until after we have moved outside heretofore "natural" sample boundaries to establish afresh the relevant cultural models and analogies. If in the analysis of meanings what matters is case-by-potentially-relevant-case interpretation, why format our presentation as anything more?

SCOPE CONDITIONS OF MY CRITIQUE?

No matter how many studies I decompose, some investigators may prefer believing that sampling and coding are among the methods that may "produce findings that meet our criterion of sensitivity to the specific characteristics of cultural phenomena and our scientific desiderata of rigor and potential for generalization."[108] In principle, researchers could bypass the problems of coding but maintain sampling in some guise by using brute phrase counts from text corpora. These unmanipulated samples might provide approximate sketches and be conjoined with document-specific interpretation for illustration. Psychologists would call it "parallel play." This duplex of counting combined with intensive exegesis, widespread in France, has also enjoyed popularity among American historians.[109]

My thesis has been that the feasibility of combining perspectives can be assessed only in realized practice. If word counts are more transparent and reliable than qualitative coding, they are for that reason also impertinent. For instance, by mechanically registering words I once compared the units of time by which German versus British weavers calculated their average earnings at the start of the twentieth century. What did my sample results represent? It was necessary for me to invent the meaning of the quantitative profiles by hypothesizing how differing time units reflected differing worker cultures.[110] I ad-hoced but in truth, word frequencies never have a legible relation to cultural competencies, repertoires, or semiotic systems. Numbers do not sketch anything of verbal significance. If a new phrasing rises in frequency over the years, such as homages to "God" in American political tracts, we do not know if this is a synonym placeholder for a similar concept to be found in earlier tracts, a symptom of the tracts' migration across previously established genre positions rather than a genuine change in modes of thought, a decorative gloss orthogonal to political argument, an epiphenomenal reinstantiation of an older binary, part of an indifferent proliferation in God-references across multiple genres of publication, an artifact of a longitudinal redefinition of political tracts that fails to track the intended semiotic domain, or a negligible substitution of one word for another. If investigators accompany the numbers with an anecdote to assert what "typically" happens behind the raw occurrences, they lack a warrant unless they commit what they would prefer to deny. To make the anecdote stick, they must reinforce it by expounding on it as a sliver of a cultural universe, which is to return all over again to the thick description of artifacts as Clifford Geertz proposed.[111] In this circumstance, notice, building up independent leverage for the anecdote makes the quantitative counts logically superfluous. No one knows *to how many* occurrences in the sample the lesson of the anecdote applies actually and fully, not just plausibly.

A COUNTERETHIC IN THE SOCIOLOGICAL TRADITION

To adumbrate successful humanist inquiry more concretely, it is best to start with practices in its surprising affiliate, the "hard" natural sciences as rendered by Thomas Kuhn. A key sense of the term "paradigm" for Kuhn in *The Structure of Scientific Revolutions* is that of an operational exemplar whose suggestiveness sparks a search for analogues. The paradigmatic case tacitly directs elaboration of the original demonstration, not algorithmic generalization. Scientists access a prototype through a particular "wow" demonstration: Boyle's air pump, Newton's prisms, or the Leyden jar.[112] The Leyden jar's ability to store electrical shocks lent eighteenth-century observers an ideal case for rethinking electricity and for fooling around with the jar's transmission. The jar was recognized as a significant compound before anyone could codify what was going on with it to generalize in principle. Even after an exemplar inspires secure explanations, practitioners need agree only upon interesting new cases, not on the paradigm's explicit summary, to form a research community.[113] "Theory" and explicitly formalized "method" are overlays upon the real business: experimental or theatrical activities and the models they inspire.

A paradigm in agendas of natural science operates surprisingly like an "ideal type" in Max Weber's agenda for interpretive research. To identify the parallels, let me review neglected features of practice in hard sciences, based on Kuhn and other historians of sciences. Social "scientists" who blur genres sometimes invent a fairy-tale version of the "science" they wish to imitate.

1. *"A paradigm is a form of knowledge that is neither inductive nor deductive but analogical. It moves from singularity to singularity."* As Thomas Kuhn showed by reconstructing science in action, investigators we call hard scientists work neither by rules of induction toward universal principles nor by deduction.[114] These explorers work by case-to-case analogical reasoning, jumping off from a paradigm bound to a concrete test prototype and extending it to open-ended variants. There is seldom

any formula for what constitutes a proper elaboration of the prototype. Many natural sciences progress in this fashion by case-based, extemporaneous reasoning.[115]

Weber's concept of the ideal type similarly offers sociologists a concrete exemplar and possible rearticulations as "an invitation to case research."[116] No wonder his presentation of it is initially difficult:

> An ideal type is formed by the one-sided *accentuation* of one or more points of view and by the synthesis of a great many diffuse, discrete, more or less present and occasionally absent *concrete individual* phenomena, which are arranged according to those one-sidedly emphasized viewpoints into a unified *analytical* construct. In its conceptual purity, this mental construct cannot be found empirically anywhere in reality. It is a *utopia*...[w]e can make the characteristic features of this relationship [in historical evidence] pragmatically *clear* and *understandable* by reference to an *ideal* type.[117]

"Concrete individual phenomena" *and* "unified analytical construct"? Yes, as I endeavor to show. Synthesized from the phenomena in which it is intelligible *yet* also a one-sided, irreal "mental construct"? It helps to recall how Weber's most famous ideal type, that of "this-worldly ascetic Protestantism," assumes significance only because we find it profiled in the prototype of Calvinism. Our understanding of what this ideal type *means* is inseparable from Weber's demonstration in a particularly striking historical case of how it works. The same applies recursively to the very definition of ideal types, as Weber's awkward exposition betrayed. As more than one linguist has remarked, "the very notion of prototypicality is itself a prototype concept."[118]

Similar to cultural researchers working outward from an ideal type, natural scientists may be inspired by singular exemplars. According to Kuhn, Galileo's "theories" were analogies to the action of pendulums: "From the properties of the pendulum, for example, Galileo derived his only full and sound argument for the independence of weight and rate of fall," Kuhn concluded. The pendulum for Galileo was both a synthesized picture of empirical singularities and an idealized type: "Descriptively, the Aristotelian perception is just as accurate. When Galileo reported that the pendulum's period was independent of its amplitude for amplitudes as great as 90°, his view of the pendulum led him to see far more regularity than we can now discover there."[119] Concretized models that *shift* between the universal and the particular are productive because they are both captivating in their detail and conceptually suggestive.

How does the researcher following Weber's approach determine "in each individual case, the extent to which this ideal-construct approximates to or diverges from" the evidence?[120] If there is no standard for judging when an ideal type should be abandoned, this hopefully would spawn attention to the type's fragility rather than dogmatism.[121] But as the Weberian enthusiast Wilhelm Hennis conceded, "A Max Weber from whom a truly living body of research could come into being therefore does not exist."[122] Many natural sciences are equally lacking in impersonal rules for deciding whether a lab result departs from a theory, so relative conformity depends on interpretive techniques.[123] The key for Weber was to maintain the transparency of the process. "No sociologist, for instance, should think himself too good, even in his old age, to make tens of thousands of quite trivial computations in his head and perhaps for months at a time," Weber said in his most famous address on scholarship as a calling. "One cannot with impunity try to transfer this task entirely to mechanical assistants if one wishes to figure something... "[124] Even the workings of a machine calculator outside one's own mind might prove dangerously opaque.

For this ethic of transparency, the ideal type approach protects against the erroneous worship of intermediary technical instruments. It demands that the type's exaggerations be kept in mind by contrasting them to poignant original texts, as Weber ensured through his documentary notes in the *Protestant Ethic*. In the culture of coding, we have seen by contrast, the codes replace and speak *for* the texts. Readers never glimpsed "ambiguity" in a passage in "The Fabrication of Meaning." Meanwhile, when we subsume a body of meanings into tables of coding results, we scarcely notice how the formalization induces a way of thinking. The tables appear to summarize the gathered "facts" with simple "class" concepts, Weber's term for defining the meaning of a category criterially by checking off necessary and sufficient conditions, genus and differentia.[125] Whether coding "facts" were generated that way or not, such tables make class concepts appear constitutive of culture because they render the totality of relations as a classificatory grid.[126]

2. *"By neutralizing the dichotomy between the general and the particular, it [the paradigm] replaces a dichotomous logic with a bipolar analogical model."* There is a permanent challenge for anyone seeking generalizing principles that would comprise a "method" in cultural sociology: meanings in operation remain tied to concrete prototypes. As we know, Weber marshals Richard Baxter in *The Protestant Ethic* as a type that compacts the theological predicaments of Puritans' everyday life.[127] To suggest why such crystallizations are indispensable, look at how everyday thinking flows through prototypes rather than through criterially defined aggregates.[128] As psychologist Eleanor Rosch proposed, consider what transpires when we try to converge upon the characteristic significance of birds in our culture. We select prototypes such as sparrows or robins rather than offer a list of necessary and sufficient attributes for birds. A penguin or a clucking hen logically might satisfy the ascertainable criteria of birdness but remain somehow inapt for excavating focal meanings.[129] Our reliance on salient priming features and perceptual resemblance to the outstanding members of a family is partly what Max Weber was getting at when he insisted that significance in historical evidence is not retrievable from "simple class" concept. "[N]o class or generic concept," he insisted, "has a 'typical' [or typifying] character."[130] If meaning is inextricable from examples, we see again why cultural sociologists cannot in coding use broadened labels to trade away perfect exactitude for the advantage of standardizing meanings into unit "facts." A reportrayal of meaning has to retain some of the exemplifying qualities of the text if it is to stand for that text at all.[131]

If we sought to uncover the operative meanings of "bird" for a culture, there would be no extensional class of cultural happenings given in advance, which we should try to cover with an ideal type of a bird. Nor is the test of adequacy whether we can specify the denotational criteria of birdness or bird actions as class concepts for reliable coding. What then is the relevance of sampling? If agents discern meanings via concrete prototypes, the aim of cultural analysis cannot be that of reaching summaries of meanings "on average" nor to measure variation in outputted meanings across samples.[132] The aim is to reveal the semiotic *devices* of historical action across families of cases.[133] Following Weber's ideal type method, we can rethink the task of generalization as that of proposing characteristic constellations or iconic exemplars of how judgment and human conduct is organized.[134]

There is no way to warrant at a meta-level the necessity of prototypes for generalizing about cultural practices, because doing so would itself entail a resort to necessary and sufficient criteria for the communication of "meaning."[135] At best, in the manner of Wittgenstein, I can offer compelling prototypes of prototypes.[136] When a friend with ties to South America recently texted our family that he feared crossing into Arizona, due to Arizona's statutes for police to pick up suspected non-Americans by who-knows-what criteria, my friend happened not to describe his appearance via the predicate "nonwhite." Instead he expressed his anxiety by writing "I don't exactly look like Anderson Cooper," comparing himself to one impeccably pale Anglo news broadcaster. If we want to communicate about "whiteness" as a living category, we probably operate this way with exemplars, not with the more manageable criteria of a census.[137] The predicate "white" applies to Anderson Cooper, but Anderson Cooper exemplifies an innumerable array of white-ish characteristics, which we can endlessly unpack to approach the varying family resemblances of individuals belonging to the group we take as "white." Resorting to necessary and sufficient "class concepts," in Weber's terms, will not likely capture the constellational meaning of "white," especially since it remains open to historical revision by including new subtle cases.

If Weber was prescient for cultural analysis, he went amiss when he characterized the natural sciences as the preserve of "simple class" concepts. Weber imagined that "[t]he coming of age of science in fact always implies the transcendence of the ideal-type."[138] Yet many engineers and scientists get on with their business through a patchwork of purified images and rules of thumb for applying them.[139] Lack of a unified grid of definitions seems not to prevent natural scientists from evolving solutions to new puzzles.[140] Perhaps the theoretical sociologist Talcott Parsons, among others, should have read the historians who tracked natural sciences on the ground. Parsons concocted the charge of "type atomism" to claim that Weber's use of ideal types ran contrary to scientific, or if you prefer, "systematic," endeavors.[141]

3. *"The paradigmatic case becomes such by suspending and, at the same time, exposing its belonging to the [family] group, so that it is never possible to separate its exemplarity from its singularity."* The singularity of the paradigm or ideal typical exemplar keeps us moving in a productive uncertainty: we see a case *in terms of* a model without collapsing the case *into* the model, as would happen if the model were just a container of necessary and sufficient criteria for inclusion, a grid in which everything finds its place, even if that be as combinatorial "outlier."[142] The ideal type is not formulated to "correspond" to institutions or texts, only to clarify the foci of meaning in the evidence. An imaginative portrait remains patently that: few would suppose that Weber's stereotyped "ascetic Protestant ethic" is a natural entity rather than an iconic extreme. It has no warrant as a central case except that its singularity makes other cases of this-worldly discipline more intelligible.[143]

The paradigm assumes its role as a demonstration partly by activating its differences from real-life cases. If you want to convey what declension or what conjugation comprises in the linguistic sciences, you have to set up an artificial display of roots and variants, a paradigmatic table in which all the usual functioning of a verb, noun, or sentence as denotative or connotative is suspended for a reader.[144] Similarly, the artificial isolation of the experimental lab individualizes the paradigmatic case to establish both its intelligibility and, counterintuitively, its kinship to others. Likewise, when Weber calls upon the most widely circulated publication of English Puritanism, Bunyan's *Pilgrim's Progress*, it is as exceptional fiction:

> In the description of Christian's attitude after he had realized that he was living in the City of Destruction and he had received the call to take up the pilgrimage to the celestial city, wife and children cling to him, but stopping his ears with his fingers and crying "life, eternal life," he staggers forth across the fields...Only when he himself is safe does it occur to him that it would be nice to have his family with him.[145]

Weber detaches the canonical story from preaching and observed conduct, all the better to model the individual Puritan's spiritual isolation. In best practice, paradigms in the humanities and "hard" sciences set up "seeing as" by evident artifice, because the guiding exemplar, such as *Pilgrim's Progress*, functions by being set aside as exceptional. Unlike interpretation based on empathic understanding, the ideal type highlights the intervention of the investigator. It accentuates what is hypothetically *attributed to* authors or agents.

The knowledge we gain from Weber's ideal type agenda is paradoxically only self-knowledge of the relations we have constructed with the evidence. What we learn, Weber said, is "the adequacy of our *fantasy*."[146] For the concocted patterns in a type to initiate dialogue with the evidence, it is enough to suppose that the case evidence can resist the perspective in which the ideal type is suspended. In natural science, likewise, the key to identifying a revealing anomaly is attending to departures from the paradigm we invented for ourselves.[147] "An experimental system must be fluid enough to allow for unprecedented events," the scientist Hans-Jörg Rheinberger summed up, "but stable enough to allow them to be recognized."[148]

4. *"The paradigmatic group is never presupposed by the paradigms; rather, it is immanent in them."* When natural scientists took the Leyden jar as a prototype, they did not worry how representative the case was of a larger population. The paradigm called its own family members into focus, and how many relatives would be found was opened-ended, since the point of the operation was to generalize about mechanisms rather than about predefined populations. Likewise, in cultural inquiries, the average case may appear to have broader application, but this misses the point of how in practice we use demonstration cases. The whole or the population represented only *results from* the ideal exposition of the singularly intelligible, paradigmatic case (say, the robin for birds).

If this picture of analogical extension from the unique seems less satisfying than an aerial view of the attributes of a population, remember that the real object of a cultural analysis cannot be a catalog of empirical attributes or averages. The object, I have said, is what is potential or possible, the conditions that constrain or unleash action, whether you think of them as repertoires or linguistic rules.[149] In corpus-based research in linguistics, for example, no one is quite sure how to move from observed frequencies of a phenomenon (e.g., 90 percent consistency) to postulating whether the sample results are enough to support claims about the virtual grammar or the cognitive "rules" of a culture.[150] What we want to know is not the frequencies in culture that comprise the actual, but the mechanisms by which the culture manages both creativity and reproduction.[151] Our investigation of human cultures, Wittgenstein suggested, "is directed not towards phenomena, but as one might say, towards the 'possibilities' of phenomena."[152] Ought-of-sight ephemera that stretch or fail to meet the reigning conditions for making proper "sense" may trace those possibilities better than well-placed, acclaimed artifacts.

Therefore the foundation that quantitative sampling promises is specious. When cultural sociologists reach beyond what was enunciated in the sample to the more important premises of the saying, it seems almost inevitable that they choose unusual documents external to the sample.[153] For example, Shyon Baumann in *Hollywood Highbrow* illustrates the significance of his sample by shifting *outside* it to an unusual essay by Raymond Chandler in *The Atlantic*. Reading between the lines, Baumann extracts from Chandler the implicit assumptions for film appreciation.[154] The industrial character of Hollywood and what is most observable in film both work to conceal film's status, Chandler wrote, as "the only art at which we of this generation have any possible chance to greatly excel."[155] To test whether Chandler's words reveals the mechanisms stunting film reception, vocabulary counts from the sample are unhelpful. Only reading for remarks in individual reviews tests the scope of the interpretation derived from Chandler. Likewise, in the classic work *Deciphering Violence*, sociologist Karen Cerulo codes the lead sentences of news stories in a meticulous sample. But it seems the cases she uses to illustrate her coding method and to demarcate types of violence often do not originate in her sample at all.[156] She discerns mechanisms through handpicked exemplars.

CONVERGENCE ON PARADIGMS

Let me release the cat from the bag now: the four condensed principles of "paradigms" that I underscored in this chapter come neither from Kuhn nor from Weber. They derive verbatim from the philosophical historian Giorgio Agamben, whose fertile use of the ideal type method, like Foucault's invocation of the Panopticon, remains as vital today as it is open to questioning.[157] Agamben's presentation suggests how the ideal type registers locally a more telling convergence in the history of human inquiry. Agamben correlated features of Kuhn's and Foucault's reliance on the "paradigm" concept and its affiliations to Plato's usage of "paradigm" for ongoing dialogue.[158]

If I contrast the basic grammar of ideal-type ("paradigm") statements with those of "simple class" statements, you may observe that what is at stake are fundamentally incompatible ways of using symbols for making a human world. With "simple class" concepts, attributions in cultural research take the following forms.

1. *Cases "a," "b," and "c" are "realistic novels" (or "credit default swap practices," for example).* This sentence construes the case "a" as that which is to be classified.

It makes the predicates "novel" or of "credit default swaps" carry out their classifying by their definitions. The grammar appears unobjectionable if it is permissible to reapply the same classifying methods imposed on, say, dogs (mammalian canines constituted by biology) outward to texts and practices (historical conventions assembled by cultural meanings). But this transposition to matters of cultural significance is suspect because of the following reasons:

—The intensional definition of "dog" is historically closed, whereas newly discovered literary works and financial instruments stretch and revise the anterior category of "novel" or of "a hedge-fund practice." A previously unconsidered novel that stretches the distinctions between biography and fiction, for example, can remake the denotation of the label "novel."

—Our own definitional practices as social agents do not enter into the genesis of the dog, whereas our classifying helps constitute novels and hedge-fund practices themselves.

—Dogs are reproduced through and share recurrent genetic devices whereas novels and hedge-fund practices do not. The predicate "novel" does not tell us how a literary work functions or how it grew as the predicate "dog" so informs us.

—There are no hybrid dog-rabbits, whereas there are literary transcripts and hedging practices created by intersecting frames or by discordant financial instruments.[159] The trial of the Chicago Seven in 1969 was confined to the idioms neither of the solemn courtroom nor to those of waggish theater.[160]

—There are no "as if" dogs requiring depth interpretation of a specimen, whereas there are gimmicky financial instruments and tongue-in-cheek renderings that make inadequate the use of necessary and sufficient conditions for framing "what is going on here." Texts and practices are twinned with subversive look-alikes and stagings. The "credit default swaps market" in appearance and definition is a risk-minimizing insurance institution. Of what does this appliance consist as repainted by an expert *Financial Times* correspondent? "The ability to insure against the prospect of sovereign default, without being a stakeholder in that sovereign debt, and then to be able to short that country's debt, pushing it to the brink, is akin to allowing an arsonist to take out an insurance policy against every property he plans to set fire to." Regulators, Angus McDougall wrote, need to "identify rogue financial products masquerading as sophisticated milestones in the evolution of capital markets."[161]

—Texts and practices are not just artifacts, but include ways of presenting themselves by their own style and idiom. This historical style of expression constitutes the artifact as much as *what* it says or what it does.

Each of these considerations tells against subsuming cultural artifacts into a grid of predicate labels that will do the talking for the artifact. The ideal type heuristic correctly reverses the direction of ascription via the following grammar.

2. A "realistic novel" (or a "hedge-fund practice") is illustrated by case exemplars "a," "b," "c"....: In this statement 2 the ideal type cues us to patterns that we finally appreciate through the cases themselves. There is no strict definitional identity for the cases that can enter into the group we "see as" novels or as hedge-fund practices (or as "fascism" or as "total mental institutions" or as any of the meaning-saturated labels that make up social science).[162] The appreciated concrete cases help refine the implications of the ideal type and help activate the family resemblances that will decide the scope of the ideal type.[163] Inspecting concrete exemplars, not applying an intensional definition, decides what the ideal type means. Weber in the *Protestant Ethic* withholds "the conceptual formulation" of the spirit of capitalism for the end.[164]

Comparing statements 1 and 2 above shows how using ideal-type exemplars in interpretive social science reverses the direction of denotation. In statement 1, a definition of the "realistic novel" is used to denote the text-instances (including *The Gulag Archipelago*, let us say), whereas in statement 2, text-instances denote "realistic novel." As Erich Auerbach explained in *Mimesis*,

> The category of "realist works of serious style and character" has never been treated or even conceived as such. I have not seen fit to analyze it theoretically and to describe it systematically…The procedure I have employed—that of citing for every epoch a number of texts and using these as test cases for my ideas—takes the reader directly into the subject and makes him [or her] sense what is at issue long before he [or she] is expected to cope with anything theoretical.[165]

Investigators may attempt a working definition of "realism in novels" as narratives that mimic the representation of happenings in nonliterary texts of the same culture—"history as it might have happened."[166] But that parsing is an invitation, not a criterion, because cases "a," "b," and "c" exemplify realism in nonitemizable ways, modeled variously on letters of correspondence, diaries, autobiographies, and, in some epochs of cultural development, newspapers or email.[167] Artifacts preserve their own idioms through the research process.[168] That is why Weber said of the ideal type, "It is even less fitted to serve as a schema under which a real situation or action is to be subsumed as one *instance*."[169]

By elaborating the grammatical contrasts between the worlds of ideal-typical versus criterial statements, I conclude there is no conceptual ground on which to unify quantitative sampling and measuring with humanistic interpretation of texts. This volume has shown that humanist inquiry on its own better satisfies the "hard" scientific criteria of transparency, of retesting the validity of interpretations, of extrapolating from mechanisms, of appraising the scope of interpretations, of recognizing destabilizing anomalies, of displaying how we decide to "take" a case as meaning something, of forcing revision in interpretive decisions, of acknowledging the dilemmas of sampling, and of separating the evidence from the effects of instrumentation. Correlatively, ritual seems the best frame for understanding blurred social "science" because ritual process renders intelligible a constellation of logical oddities: fitting the world to a condensed map rather than examining the world to see if the map represents anything, declaring that what is missing in the ritual is missing from the world, using statistical measures to create truth from the form of expression as in liturgy, creating novel "facts" without concern for goodness of fit with referents, interpreting historical change via eternal codes, and using contextual interpretation to gloss bare "facts" when in an earlier moment such interpretation would undermine creation of those "facts." More fundamentally, only a processual model of ritual can account for the lengthy, contradictory circuits we have documented in which researchers radically decontextualize facts for the sake of selectively recontextualizing them.

Let me conclude therefore by surveying the advantages of a vibrant tradition of ideal-type research on which I hope cultural investigators can build. This tradition is prominent in every variety of inquiry reliant on texts, including comparative studies of selfhood, literary history, history of math, gender in political revolution, art criticism, and architecture. Historians in literary studies have been fascinated by the apparent ability of anecdotes to condense cognitive principles that are widely entrenched in a culture at large. In *Practicing New Historicism*, Catherine Gallagher and Stephen Greenblatt specify how Erich Auerbach in *Mimesis* generalizes about the apprehension of reality from brief excerpts:

> It is possible for Auerbach to unpack long works and even entire cultures out of a close encounter with a tiny fragment because he is less concerned with sequence and form than he is with "the representation of reality." Hence he does not need to say something about the origin and internal structure of a work so much as he needs to address and explicate its characteristic practice of referring to the world... The literary work is interesting to Auerbach not for its swerve away from reality... but rather for its claim on the world, its ability to give the reader access to the very condition for perception and action, along with the very condition for textuality, at a given place and time, in a given culture.[170]

In fewer than a dozen pages, Auerbach dramatizes but does not criterially theorize the differences between the Homeric versus the biblical styles of organizing human experience.[171] His examples of the mysteriously fraught decision-making in the Old Testament versus the pure enjoyment of physical being in Homer lets us discern for ourselves mechanisms of wide application in each of the two cultures.[172] After five decades of testing, the ideal types Auerbach adduced for each culture remain adequately representative and firm enough to inspire succeeding scholars to adapt them by analogy for new contexts. For example, literary specialists working from *Mimesis* address puzzling features of early modern narrative, in particular how protagonists are perturbed that they know their "self" only second-hand, by how it is represented via their own convention-laden actions.[173]

To clarify the use of evidence in the canon of ideal-type research, it is important to recall Erwin Panofsky's *Gothic Architecture and Scholasticism*, a work crucial to Bourdieu's theorizing about habitus. Panofsky by singular illustrations suggested that repertoires for presenting medieval scholastic reasoning in words were transferred to the design of Gothic churches in stone. He unearthed homologies between these two realms of practice by tracing in cathedrals "a gratuitous clarification of function through form just as it [scholasticism] accepted and insisted upon a gratuitous clarification of thought through language."[174] Panofsky had to adumbrate analogies between his specimens as *wholes* with such detail, he established highly restrictive conditions for observation that would confirms his hypothesis. The early Bourdieu wrote in homage that Panofsky "enables one to glimpse the added demands that are imposed by an increased demand for accuracy. Far from being able, like positivist interpretation, to hide behind an indefinite accumulation of minor true facts, structural interpretation involves all the acquired truth in each truth in order to attain its object..."[175] The historian Robert Marichal followed Panofsky's thesis to explain why the style of breaks in Gothic letters on parchment appeared simultaneously with the same breaks in stone, intersecting ribs in Gothic vaults.[176] Both shifts expressed an analysis of whole lines to cut them down and regroup them into clearer, hierarchically ordered parts of parts. Compare this depth of analysis to a quantitative argument about net trends in abstract codes. Such blurred social "science" is less stringent about the patterning required for confirmation and too indefinite to isolate productive anomalies. Again the humanist focus on precise designs draws it closer to the rigor of the "hard" sciences.[177]

The ideal-type heuristic shows us why generalizing about culture requires us to retain the minutia of the original evidence. The art historian Michael Baxandall illumed this methodological necessity with reference to a puzzle in the artist Piero della Francesca's Baptism of Christ. The riddle in this painting's composition is how Piero uncharacteristically (for him as an artist) designed a trio of angels so that the group was not too massive on the large vertical panel that Piero had been commissioned to decorate. A researcher could of course look for other art works with blatantly similar-looking angels, but this would make Piero look randomly passive. It would be nonexplanatory because it would not reveal "the actively transforming individuality" of Piero's own schemas that were on display elsewhere on the panel.

Baxandall shows why reductive coding for the sake of generalization is counterproductive. Mere resemblance, fatuously called "artistic influence," is a description without analytic purchase, Baxandall reasons. Resemblance or repetition by itself does not let us trace the semiotic mechanism of a doing nor the artist's making of an informed choice. Most specifically, Baxandall describes a paradox in how the researcher should seek a precedent from another artist to explicate how Piero came to model his trio so distinctively:

> What we want is not something that looks like Piero's Angels but something that, having been transformed by Piero, would look like Piero's Angels. What we would enjoy most all is something that looks very unlike Piero's Angels but reference to which, in the course of solving the larger problem of the picture, would have disturbed Piero's usual angel mode into something like the Angels here.[178]

Unless we exhibit an antecedent artwork that Piero could have manipulated, we reach no explanation at all, but what comprises this antecedent suitably is a matter of fine-grained judgment. It demands that an investigator recognize reconfigured echoes in difference, unamenable to the criterial similarity of coding. Baxandall lands upon angels in a frieze from Florence which Piero once studied as an apprentice. He shows how these angels share the same wreaths and off-the-shoulder drapery, but dance lightly. Baxandall concludes that "[t]he juxtaposition [to Piero's angels] is absurd in just the right critical way: it accounts for the oddities while being dissimilar enough to throw light on Piero's particularity," that is, Piero's transposition of signature schemas. As Baxandall lays it out for us, to explain culturally informed artifacts requires investigators to abandon a drive for similarities and averages. No researcher can surmise whether hypothesized schemas are lodged in the record unless the researcher documents how agents creatively reincorporate the schemas in *different* ways across *dramatically varying* contexts.[179]

The ideal-type tradition has to replace truisms with audacity to treat of anything. Lynn Hunt with her *Family Romance of the French Revolution* presents Freud's *Totem and Taboo* as a hypothetical model for illuminating struggles over political legitimacy in the French Revolution. Freud had fancifully condensed ethnographers' just-so stories according to his own magnetic archetypes of emotion: ambivalence toward patriarchal authority, parricide by brothers, and brutal internalization of the murdered father via a totemic meal.[180] As a model of authority relations in extremity, however, *Totem and Taboo* enables researchers to discern afresh the palette of emotions with which the beheading of Louis XVI was freighted.[181] More importantly, the ideal type helps specify a recurrent master problem: how to draw on well-known family roles to stabilize and naturalize governance in the revolution. Lynn Hunt had to present the exact phrasing by which French citizens described their thirst for the blood of Louis XVI, as well as the citizens' reticence to converse about the beheading, to explain the king's execution by a recurrently enacted schema of the ritual killing and eating of the father.[182]

The uncanny movement of similar schemas across diverse contexts unites contemporary ideal-type study. The historian of science Amir Alexander found parallels between dominant narratives of geographical exploration and the templates for mathematical discovery in the sixteenth century. The narratives comprised a kind of "how to" that intricately linked rarefied math to popular culture.[183] To this canon of research on schemas we must add Oleg Kharkhordin's book *The Collective and the Individual in Russia*. Kharkhordin obsessively circumstantiated the Orthodox Church's ceremonies of public penitence in pre-Soviet Russia to define it as a prototype for discipline and surveillance in the communist era.[184] Then he had to present unsuspected features of public penitence in notorious Soviet political trials to jolt readers into seeing, eerily reincarnated, Orthodox Church protocols for remaking sinners. Kharkhordin also lined up Soviet educational statutes with the monastic rules of Saint Joseph Volotsky (1503) to recover "curious" parallels in the conceptions of the righteous, of mutual surveillance, and of indoctrination.[185] Compulsive detail in these studies is congruent with generalizing. It is necessary to verify the transposition of schemas as constellations, and in turn these schemas integrate a culture or a process of change into an intelligible whole.[186] Blurred social "science" hinders the ability to recognize these general mechanisms, because it forces researchers to efface the telltale detail in favor of assigning general labels to atomized "facts." "We are 'unscientific' and have no method at all, at least not of the others," the legendary cultural historian Jacob Burckhardt wrote about his process of detecting patterns.[187]

I have mocked the pretensions of a cross-dressing social "science," not those of conventional natural science, whose clothing sociologists try to wear as their own by presenting "large-N" coding results. It may scandalize researchers in search of a recipe, but you will have noticed that Weber deprived an ideal type of any epistemic backup. Nor is there any underwriting for consentient samples. It is superior, by which I mean more transparent for progressive questioning and testing, to acknowledge the inevitable handpicking of sundry sources. Certainly it is more honest than reifying a mechanical en masse choice as natural. Preferring "the wariest of wary reasonings" may be as close as we should venture toward anything so beguiling as method.[188] As the engineer-novelist Robert Musil once wrote, every case on which thoughtful investigators land "has the ability to overturn everything that people had up to then believed."[189]

NOTES

1   INSIDE THE RITUALS OF SOCIAL SCIENCE

1. On recent expansion of qualitative coding into the humanities as well, see Franco Moretti, *Graphs, Maps, Trees* (London: Verso: 2005), pp. 31–33, 76–77.
2. Harry Frankfurt, *On Bullshit* (Princeton: Princeton University Press, 2005), p. 51.
3. Historians have criticized Poovey's anecdotes, but her scaffolding remains invaluable. Mary Poovey, *A History of the Modern Fact. Problems of Knowledge in the Sciences of Wealth and Society* (Chicago: University of Chicago Press, 1998), pp. 8–9.
4. Ibid., p. 98.
5. Michèle Lamont, *How Professors Think* (Cambridge, MA: Harvard University Press, 2009), pp. 174, 184; David Herman, *Story Logic; Problems and Possibilities of Narrative* (Lincoln: University of Nebraska Press, 2002), pp. 243, 353; Christopher Grasso, *A Speaking Aristocracy. Transforming Public Discourse in Eighteenth-Century Connecticut* (Chapel Hill: University of North Carolina Press, 1999), p. 490. To maintain the analogy between the natural scientists' retrieval of facts from "experience" and the coders' retrieval of facts from texts, I will in the main exclude research that merely tracks the frequency of words. I focus on research that qualitatively sorts meanings.
6. François Rastier, *Arts et sciences du texte* (Paris: Presses Universitaires, 2001), p. 224.
7. For an example of the dissemination of coding into the humanities, see R. Alberich, J. Miro-Julia, and F. Rossello, "Marvel Universe Looks Almost Like a Real Social Network," February 11, 2002, Cornell University Library. Abstract at http://arxiv.org.
8. "Wonder" is perception that exceeds classificatory cultures. Mary Baine Campbell, *Wonder and Science* (Ithaca: Cornell University Press, 1999), pp. 4, 19.
9. Illustratively, Catherine Gallagher and Stephen Greenblatt, *Practicing New Historicism* (Chicago: University of Chicago Press, 2000). See chapter five in this volume.
10. Eric Donald Hirsch, Jr., *Validity in Interpretation* (New Haven: Yale University Press, 1967); Hans Ulrich Gumbrecht, *The Powers of Philology* (Urbana: University of Illinois Press, 2003), pp. 4, 42.
11. Lars Furuland, "The Rise of Literacy: From Rote Reading to Cultural Literacy," *The Nordic Roundtable Papers* 3 (1989): 9; Lars Sandberg, "The Case of the Impoverished Sophisticate: Human Capital and Swedish Economic Growth Before World War I," *The Tasks of Economic History* 39 (1979): 230.
12. Karen Dovring, "Quantitative Semantics in 18th Century Sweden," *The Public Opinion Quarterly* 18 (1954–1955): 392–394.
13. Karin Dovring, "Communication, Dissenters and Popular Culture in Eighteenth Century Europe," *Journal of Popular Culture* 7 (1973): 565.

14. On the adminstrative gaze, Francis Earle Barcus, "Communications Content: Analysis of the Research, 1900–1958. A Content Analysis of Content Analysis," PhD dissertation, University of Illinois, 1959, p. 25.

15. For historical appreciation of how "single-point perspective" was a condition of modern governance, see John Ruggie, "Territoriality and Beyond: Problematizing Modernity in International Relations," *International Organization* 47 (1993): 159. Cataloguing collective representations as "facts" emerged in modern projects to manage "society" from above. Zygmunt Bauman, "Durkheim's Society Revisited," in *The Cambridge Companion to Durkheim*, ed. Jeffrey Alexander and Philip Smith (Cambridge: Cambridge University Press, 2005), p. 367.

16. Richard Biernacki, *The Fabrication of Labor: Germany and Britain, 1640–1914* (Berkeley: University of California Press, 1995), pp. 179–185.

17. For example, in nineteenth-century Britain, a married woman could not enter into a labor contract in her own name. If a husband not employed at the factory complained about a male overlooker's ambiguously consensual encounters with his wife, was this a complaint about workplace harassment or about male sex rights? On the inseparability of agents' renderings of their action from what that action *is*, see Peter Winch, *The Idea of a Social Science* (London: Routledge and Kegan Paul, 1958), pp. 123–128.

18. Diary examples in "Back to Sociology's Origins: Contracts in the Protestant Ethic" at http://www.havenscenter.org/vsp/richard_biernacki.

19. Borges likewise had to rely on counterfactual reasoning about a body of literature to establish the meaning of a frequency: "If there were any doubt as to the authenticity of the Koran, this absence of camels would be sufficient to prove it is an Arabian work." Only a faker would insert camels repetitively for local color. Jorge Luis Borges, *Labyrinths. Selected Stories and Other Writings* (New York: New Directions, 1964), p. 181. The Koran, like the Bible, contains only a handful of camels.

20. For example, potlatchs are not usefully classified by our sense of "economic" function, nor do genealogical relations establish kinship as a generic object. David M. Schneider, *A Critique of the Study of Kinship* (Ann Arbor: University of Michigan Press, 1984), p. 183.

21. Erving Goffman, *Frame Analysis* (Boston: Northeastern University Press, 1986), p. 8.

22. Clifford Geertz, *Local Knowledge* (New York: Basic Books, 1983), p. 21.

23. Wendy Griswold, "A Methodological Framework for the Sociology of Culture," *Sociological Methodology* 17 (1987): 4.

24. Bernard Berleson, *Content Analysis in Communication Research* (New York: Hafner Press, 1952), p. 17. I followed Berleson in reasoning that approximate counting underlies aggregate coding conclusions in Richard Biernacki, "After Quantitative Cultural Sociology: Interpretive Science as a Calling," in *Meaning and Method*, ed. Isaac Reed and Jeffrey Alexander (Boulder: Paradigm Press, 2009), p. 166.

25. Gilbert Shapiro and John Markoff, *Revolutionary Demands* (Stanford: Stanford University Press, 1998), p. 18. For qualitative content analysis, see David Winter, "Content Analysis of Archival Materials," in *Motivation and Personality: Handbook of Thematic Content Analysis*, ed. Charles Smith (Cambridge University Press, 1992), pp. 110–125; "Content Analysis: An important form of qualitative coding," in *Dictionary of Modern Sociology* (Totowa, NJ: Littlefield Adams, 1969), p. 83. For "content analysis" without counts, see Steven Philip Barker, "Fame: A Content Analysis Study of the American Film Biography," PhD dissertation, Ohio State University, 1983.

26. Biernacki, "After Quantitative Cultural Sociology," p. 164.

27. Matthew Miles and A. Michael Huberman, *Qualitative Data Analysis. An Expanded Sourcebook* (Thousand Oaks: SAGE, 1994). On "clear operational definitions," see

ibid., p. 63; on logs of "decision rules" for assembling data, see p. 242; on the term "content analysis" as the commonsense processing of qualitative coding, see p. 253.

28. Gilbert Shapiro and John Markoff, "A Matter of Definition," in *Culture, Code and Content Analysis*, ed. Thelma McCormack (Greenwich, CT: JAI Press, 1982), pp. 9–31, esp. pp. 29–30.

29. Roger Sanjek, "The Secret Life of Fieldnotes," in *Fieldnotes. The Makings of Anthropology*, ed. Roger Sanjek (Ithaca: Cornell University Press, 1990), pp. 187–270.

30. Deborah Winslow, NSF, "Field Notes…What Will Happen to Yours?" *Anthropology News*, September 2009, p. 36; Jean Jackson, "*Déjà entendu*. The Liminal Qualities of Anthropological Fieldnotes," in *Representation in Ethnography*, ed. John Van Maanen (Thousand Oaks: SAGE, 1995), pp. 36–78, esp. p. 66; Nancy Luktkehaus, "Refractions of Reality: On the Use of Other Ethnographers' Fieldnotes," in *Fieldnotes. The Makings of Anthropology* (Ithaca: Cornell University Press, 1990), pp. 303–323.

31. Martin Orans, *Not Even Wrong: Margaret Mead, David Freeman, and the Samoans* (Novato, Calif.: Chandler & Sharp, 1996); American Educational Research Association, "Standards for Reporting on Humanities-Oriented Research in AERA Publications," *Educational Researcher* 38 (2009): 481–486.

32. Harvey Molotch and Marilyn Lester, "Accidental News: The Great Oil Spill as Local Occurrence and National Event," *American Journal of Sociology* 81 (1975): 240.

33. Michael Frede, "Plato's *Sophist* on False Statements," in Richard Kraut, editor, *The Cambridge Companion to Plato* (Cambridge University Press, 1992), pp. 397–424.

34. Allen Grimshaw, "Happy Auguries of the Decline of an Emergent Specialty," *Contemporary Sociology* 10 (1981): 25.

35. Geertz, *Local Knowledge*, p. 23.

36. Ibid., pp. 23–34, 35.

37. Ibid., p. 23.

38. Alenka Zupancic, *The Odd One In. On Comedy* (Cambridge, MA: MIT Press, 2008), pp. 89–90, 114. Bernard Traimond saw pranks arising in anthropology from the dilemmas of translating indigenous idioms into authoritative discourse of social science. Bernard Traimond, *Vérités en quête d'auteurs* (Bourdeaux: William Blake, 2000), pp. 12–13. When Stuart Macdonald and Jacqueline Kam found that social researchers and economists displayed "dizzying circularity" in their conduct, publishing to get articles cited as the indicator for quality rather than publishing quality articles, they concluded that laughter "is the appropriate reaction to such farce." See "Quality Journals and Gamesmanship in Management Studies," *Management Research News* 31 (2008): 595, online abstract, DOI:10.1108/01409170810892154.

39. Analogously, Goffman, *Frame Analysis*, p. 181. As Garfinkel intimated, agreement in coding results—"reliability"—can result from extraneous but shared social framings that run contrary to the actuarial definitions of necessary and sufficient conditions for categorizing text features. *Studies in Ethnomethodology* (Cambridge: Polity Press, 1984), p. 20.

40. J. Zvi Namenwirth and Robert Philip Weber, *Dynamics of Culture* (London: Allen & Unwin, 1987), p. 196.

41. C. Picart, "Scientific Controversy as Farce: The Benveniste-Maddox Counter Trials," *Social Studies of Science* 24 (1994): 7–37; Brian Martin, "Suppressing Research Data," *Accountability in Research* 6.4 (1999): 340–341.

42. Max Weber, *The Methodology of the Social Sciences* (Glencoe: The Free Press, 1949), p. 92.

43. Goffman, *Frame Analysis*, p. 251.

44. Geertz, *Local Knowledge*, p. 24.

45. Harrison White, "Can Mathematics Be Social? Flexible Representations for Interaction Process and Its Sociocultural Constructions," *Sociological Forum* 12 (1997): 58.

46. Greimas suggests that crossing quantitative measurement with qualitative distinction mobilizes the face of rationality for mythical ends. Algirda Julien Greimas, *Du sens. Essais sémiotiques* (Paris: éditions du Seuil, 1983), vol. 2, p. 128. As Wittgenstein put it without apology, "My aim is: to teach you to pass from a piece of disguised nonsense to something that is patent nonsense." Ludwig Wittgenstein, *Philosophical Investigations* (Oxford: Blackwell, 1997), p. 133e.

47. Gustave Flaubert, *Dictionary of Accepted Ideas* (New York: New Directions, 1968), p. 25; Sidney Tarrow, "Bridging the Quantitative-Qualitative Divide," in *Rethinking Social Inquiry. Diverse Tools, Shared Standards*, ed. Henry Brady and David Collier (Lanham, MD: Rowman and Littlefield, 2010), pp. 101–110.

48. David Henige, *Historical Evidence and Argument* (Madison: University of Wisconsin Press, 2005), pp. 210, 223.

49. An art historian on interpretive experiments: "the point is that an experiment must be repeatable and open to testing by other people." Michael Baxandall, *Patterns of Intention. On the Historical Explanation of Pictures* (New Have: Yale University Press, 1985), p. 136.

50. Robert Bergman, "Irreproducibility in the Scientific Literature: How Often Do Scientists Tell the Whole Truth and nothing But the Truth?" *Perspectives on the Professions* 9 (1989): 2–3; Frederick Grinnell, *The Scientific Attitude* (New York: Guilford Press, 1992), p. 123.

51. Jon Wiener, *Historians in Trouble. Plagiarism, Fraud, and Politics in the Ivory Tower* (New York: The New Press, 2005), pp. 37, 49.

52. A rare discussion of reanalysis of other researchers' qualitative data is Shulamit Reinharz, "Empty Explanations for Empty Wombs: An Illustration of Secondary Analysis of Qualitative Data," in *Qualitative Voices in Educational Research*, ed. Michael Schratz (London: The Falmer Press, 1993), pp. 157–178. On the rarity with which alternative methods of coding are tried out on the same texts, see J. Zvi Namenwirth and Robert Philip Weber, *Dynamics of Culture* (London: Allen & Unwin, 1987), p. 196.

53. Robert Franzosi, *From Words to Numbers* (Cambridge: Cambridge University Press, 2004), p. 281.

54. See the Durkheim extract from *Année sociologique* featured in Anthony Giddens, *Émile Durkheim. Selected Writings* (Cambridge: Cambridge University Press, 1972), pp. 248–249.

55. Ideologies, unlike rituals, saturate their keynote messages with historical diagnosis. Karl Mannheim, *Ideology and Utopia* (London: Routledge & Kegan Paul, 1936), pp. 60 ff.

56. On the use of ritual to regenerate secular cosmologies, see Stanley Jeyaraja Tambiah, *Culture, Thought, and Social Action* (Cambridge, MA: Harvard University Press, 1985), p. 130.

57. Experiencing an enactment as authentic poses a distinctive problem for contemporary performances. Jeffrey Alexander, "Cultural Pragmatics: Social Performance Between Ritual and Strategy," *Sociological Theory* 22 (2004): 527–573.

58. Ian Hacking, *Representing and Intervening. Introductory Topics in the Philosophy of Natural Science* (Cambridge: Cambridge University Press, 1983).

59. Michael Lynch, *Scientific Practice and Ordinary Action* (Cambridge University Press, 1997), p. 270.

60. Ronald Giere, *Understanding Scientific Reasoning* (New York: Holt, Rinehart and Winston, 1984), pp. 60, 165.

61. Marcello Pera, *The Discourses of Science* (Chicago: University of Chicago Press, 1994), pp. 105–107; Thomas Kuhn, *The Structure of Scientific Revolutions* (Chicago: University of Chicago Press, 1970), p. 11.

62. Ludwig Wittgenstein, "Bemerkungen über Frazers 'The Golden Bough," *Synthese* 17 (1967): 233–253.

63. Benedict Anderson, *Imagined Communities* (London: Verso, 1991), p. 35.

64. Stephen Greenblatt, *Shakespearean Negotiations. The Circulation of Social Energy in Renaissance England* (Berkeley: University of California Press, 1988), p. 9.

65. Wendy Griswold, "The Fabrication of Meaning: Literary Interpretation in the United States, Great Britain, and the West Indies," *American Journal of Sociology* 92 (1987): 1077–1117.

66. See chapter four. Griswold's footnotes and charts confirm the same operationalization created one variable that reappeared across tables with significations that appear discrepant.

67. "Later, of course, logic and grounding are important, but to be able to 'see' what is in the data, you must be able to think creatively." Juliet Corbin and Anselm Strauss, *Basics of Qualitative Research* (Newbury Park: SAGE, 1990), p. 200.

68. Bruno Bachimont, "Formal Signs and Numerical Computation," in *Instruments in Art and Science*, ed. Helmar Schramm, Ludger Schwarte, and Jan Lazardig (Berlin: Walter de Gruyter, 2008), p. 372.

69. Arnold van Gennep, *Les rites de passage* (Paris: Emile Nourry, 1909), p. 14; Nicole Belmont, *Arnold Van Gennep. The Creator of French Ethnography* (Chicago: University of Chicago, 1979), p. 69.

70. Mary Douglass, *Purity and Danger* (London: Routledge & Kegan Paul, 1966), pp. 62–63.

71. Victor Turner, "Variations on a Theme of Liminality," in *Secular Ritual*, ed. Sally Moore, Barbara Myerhoff (Assen: Van Gorcum, 1977), p. 37.

72. Robert K. Merton, "Social Structure and Anomie," *American Sociological Review* 3 (1938): 672–682.

73. René Girard, *Violence and the Sacred* (Baltimore: Johns Hopkins University Press, 1977).

74. Mircea Eliade, *The Myth of the Eternal Return* (Princeton: Princeton University Press, 1971), p. 27.

75. Van Gennep, *Rites de passage*, p. 275; Victor Turner, *From Ritual to Theatre* (New York: PAJ Publications, 1982), p. 27.

76. W. J. T. Mitchell, *Picture Theory* (Chicago: University of Chicago Press, 1994), p. 48.

77. Rodney Needham, *Exemplars* (Berkeley: University of California Press, 1985), pp. 11–12.

78. The production of data inscriptions supports the ritual circuit by "calling up a deficit of intelligibility," which explorers fill in during the liminal phase. Bruno Bachimont, "Formal Signs and Numerical Computation," in *Instruments in Art and Science*, ed. Helmar Schramm, Ludger Schwarte, and Jan Lazardig (Berlin: Walter de Gruyter, 2008), p. 377.

79. In such a ritual phase, the genuine philosophical problem cannot arise, namely, whether the gist unexpectedly escapes us or is in fact simply not "there" to be witnessed. Vincent Descombes, *Objects of All Sorts. A Philosophical Grammar* (Oxford: Basil Blackwell, 1986), p. 18.

80. Breiger cites Otis Dudley Duncan as opining that "a model-rich environment" is not a comfortable one for the statistician hoping that results have obvious interpretations.

R. L. Brieger, "Writing (and Quantifying) Sociology," in *Writing and Revising the Disciplines*, ed. Jonathan Monroe (Ithaca: Cornell University Press, 2002), p. 108.

81. "Given a complex mechanism put at your disposal by a previous modeler, likely from another discipline, look for corners within his room of valid solutions that he disdained to sweep up." White, "Can Mathematics Be Social?" p. 55.

82. Miles and Huberman, *Qualitative Data Analysis*, p. 56.

83. Moshe Halbertal and Avishai Margalit, *Idolatry* (Cambridge, MA: Harvard University Press, 1992), pp. 45, 48.

84. John Mohr, "Measuring Meaning Structures," *Annual Review of Sociology* 24 (1998): 354.

85. K. Carley, "Content Analysis," in *The Encyclopedia of Language and Linguistics*, ed. R. E. Asher (Oxford: Pergamon Press, 1994), vol. 2, p. 730.

86. John Evans, *Playing God? Human Genetic Engineering and the Rationalization of Public Bioethical Debate* (Chicago: University of Chicago Press, 2002), p. 209; my emphasis. As in chapter three, I abbreviate this exemplar by "G."

87. Nelson Goodman, *Problems and Projects* (Indianapolis: Bobbs-Merrill, 1972), p. 445; Peter Gärdenfors, *Conceptual Spaces: The Geometry of Thought* (Cambridge, MA: MIT Press, 2000), pp. 109–112.

88. Paul Lazarsfeld and A. H. Barton, "Qualitative Measurement in the Social Sciences: Classifications, Typologies, and Indices," in *The Policy Sciences*, ed. D. Lerner and H. D. Lasswell (Stanford: Stanford University Press, 1951), p. 155; Giovanni Sartori, "The Tower of Babel," in *Tower of Bable. On the Definition and Analysis of Concepts in Social Science*, ed. Giovanni Sartori, Fred Riggs, and Henry Teune (Pittsburgh: University Center for International Studies, 1975), p. 25.

89. Mohr, "Measuring Meaning Structures," p. 367; emphasis added.

90. "If you take any random collection and data and squint hard enough, you'll see a pattern of some sort." Charles Seife, *Proofiness. The Dark Arts of Mathematical Deception* (Viking Penguin, 2010), p. 56; also p. 64.

91. Cognitive scientists notice that most of us are programmed to find pattern in random numbers. Leonard Mlodinow, *The Drunkard's Walk. How Randomness Rules Our Lives* (New York: Vintage, 2009), pp. 175, 179, 183,

92. Mohr, "Measuring Meaning Structures," p. 353.

93. "Azande observe the action of the poison oracle as we observe it, but their observations are always subordinated to their beliefs and are incorporated into their beliefs and made to explain them and justify them... For their mystical notions are eminently coherent, being interrelated by a network of logical ties..." E. E. Evans-Pritchard, *Witchcraft, Oracles, and Magic Among the Azande* (Oxford: Clarendon Press, 1976), p. 150.

94. Richard Shweder, *Thinking through Cultures* (Cambridge, MA: Harvard University Press, 1991), p. 116. Magical thinking is as efficient as scientific idioms "from the perspective of explanatory power" in placing events into causal chains. Henri Atlan, *Enlightenment to Enlightenment. Intercritique of Science and Myth* (Albany: State University of New York Press, 1993), p. 192.

95. John Creswell and Vicki L. Plano Clark, *Designing and Conducting Mixed Methods Research* (Thousand Oaks: SAGE, 2007); or Tarrow, "Bridging the Quantitatve-Qualitative Divide," pp. 101–110.

96. Peter Wagner, "'An Entirely New Object of Consciousness of Volition, of Thought.' The Coming Into Being and (Almost) Passing Away of 'Society' as a Scientific Object," in *Biographies of Scientific Objects*, ed. Lorraine Daston (Chicago: University of Chicago Press, 2000), p. 142.

97. "[T]he British indicated their preoccupation with colonialism by avoiding the subject so persistently…" Griswold, "The Fabrication of Meaning," p. 1102.

98. Charles Seife, *Proofiness. The Dark Arts of Mathematical Deception* (Viking Penguin, 2010), pp. 53–54.

99. For a critique of the confirmation of projected social functions, see Susan Sculten, "The Perils of Reading National Geographic," *Reviews in American History* 23 (1995): 524.

100. Originally from I. de S. Pool, *Trends in Content Analysis* (Urbana: University of Illinois Press, 1959), quoted in Ole Holsti, *Content Analysis for the Social Sciences and Humanities* (Reading, MA: Addison-Wesley, 1969), p. 11; my emphasis.

101. On the semantics of baggage in discussing linguistic or referential "similarity," see Goodman, *Problems and Prospects*, p. 445.

102. This paragraph draws on John Lucy, "The Linguistics of 'Color,'" in *Color Categories in Thought and Language*, ed. C. L. Hardin and Luisa Maffi (Cambridge: Cambridge University Press, 1997), pp. 320–346.

103. Max Weber, *The Protestant Ethic and the Spirit of Capitalism* (New York: Charles Scribner's Sons, 1958), p. 155, and notes, pp. 258–268.

104. Will Wright, *Six Guns and Society. A Structural Study of the Western* (Berkeley: University of California Press, 1975), pp. 38–49.

105. So preoccupied was Bentham with how fiction shaped reality, it is fitting that his blueprints for a Panopticon were never executed in stone. Robin Evans, *The Fabrication of Virtue. English Prison Architecture, 1750–1840* (Cambridge: Cambridge University Press, 1982), p. 228.

106. Weber crystallized Baxter's reasoning by its divergence from pure Calvinism. *The Protestant Ethic and the Spirit of Capitalism* (New York: Charles Scribner's Sons, 1958), pp. 258–259, n. 1,

107. Weber said that correlating elementary relations among decontextualized units— variables—caused "malignant confusion…for obviously there is a priori not the slightest probability that exactly what is *meaningful* and essential to concrete patterns would be captured by the generic concepts in correlations." *Gesammelte Aufsätze zur Wissenschaftslehre* (Tübingen: J.C.B. Mohr, 1968), p. 14; emphasis in the original.

108. In particular Weber rejected as misleading reification the attempt to explain historical patterns as outcomes of countervailing, mutually clashing, or interacting variables— merely "a spatial and physical image." Max Weber, *On the Methodology of the Social Sciences* (Glencoe, IL: The Free Press, 1949), p. 187.

109. Steven Shapin, *Never Pure. Historical Studies of Science as if It Was Produced by People with Bodies, Situated in Time, Space, Culture, and Society, and Struggling for Credibility and Authority* (Baltimore: Johns Hopkins Press, 2010), pp. 354–368.

110. Derek Phillips, *Knowledge From What?* (Chicago: Rand McNally, 1971), p. 3.

111. On texts as "the primary element (basic unit) of culture," see B. A. Upenskij, V. V. Ivanov, V. N. Toporov, A. M. Pjatigorski, and J. M. Lotman, "Theses on the Semiotic Study of Cultures," in *Structure of Texts and Semiotics of Culture*, ed. Jan van der Eng and Grygar Mojmir (The Hague: Mouton, 1973), p. 6. An acute synopsis of the switch from culture in the individual head to culture in public symbols: Ann Swidler, "Cultural Power and Social Movements," in *Social Movements and Culture*, ed. Hank Johnston and Bert Klandermans (Minneapolis: University of Minnesota Press, 1995), p. 28. For an exacting discussion of "the mental" as belonging to the order of material representations, see Vincent Descombes, *The Mind's Provisions* (Princeton University Press, 2001), pp. 3–29; 65.

112. Clifford Geertz, *The Interpretation of Cultures* (New York: Basic Books, 1983), p. 83.

113. Michel Foucault, *Maurice Blanchot. The Thought from Outside* (New York: Zone Books, 1987).

114. Geertz, *The Interpretation of Cultures*, p. 83. For the literary exteriority of affect, see Rei Terada, *Feeling in Theory. Emotion after the "Death of the Subject"* (Cambridge, MA: Harvard University Press, 2001).

115. Kimberly Neuendorf, *The Content Analysis Guidebook* (Thousand Oaks: Sage, 2002), p. 30.

116. John Evans, "Two Worlds of Cultural Sociology," in *Meaning and Method*, ed. Reed and Alexander (Boulder: Paradigm 2009), p. 212.

117. Wendy Griswold, *Bearing Witness. Readers, Writers, and the Novel in Nigeria* (Princeton: Princeton University Press, 2000), Appendix C; Irwin Hoffman and Merton Gill, "A Scheme for Coding the Patient's Experience of the Relationship to the Therapist," in *Psychoanalytic Process and Research Strategies*, ed. Harvig Dahl, Horst Kächele, and Helmut Thomä (Berlin: Springer, 1988), pp. 67–98; Shyon Baumann, *Hollywood Highbrow* (Princeton: Princeton University Press, 2007); Carol Mueller, "Claim 'Radicalization?' The 1989 Protest Cycle in the GDR," *Social Problems* 46 (1999): 528–547; Denna Harmon and Scot Boeringer, "A Content Analysis of Internet-Accessible Written Pornographic Depictions," in *Approaches to Qualitative Research*, ed. Sharlene Hesse-Biber and Patricia Leavy (Oxford: Oxford University Press, 2004), pp. 402–407.

118. Benedict Carey, "Does a Nation's Mood Lurk in Its Songs and Blogs?" *New York Times*, August 4, 2009, p. D5.

119. For one of the few attempts to reconnoiter the inferable relations between text evidence and social meanings, see Aaron Cicourel, "Three Models of Discourse Analysis: The Role of Social Structure," *Discourse Processes* 3 (1980): 101–131.

120. "Content Analysis," in R. E. Asher, ed., *The Encyclopedia of language and linguistics* (Oxford: Pergamon Press, 1994), vol. 2, p. 730; emphasis added.

121. Kathleen Carley and Michael Palmquest, "Extracting, Representing, and Analyzing Mental Models," *Social Forces* 70.3 (March 1992): 601–636.

122. Harold D. Lasswell, Daniel Lerner, and Ithiel de Sola Pool, *The Comparative Study of Symbols* (Stanford: Stanford University Press, 1952), Hoover Institute Series C, Symbols, No. 1, p. 9.

123. Ibid., pp. 10–11. To be sure, links between signifier and signified were defined as "short" (p. 10).

124. Michael Stubbs, "Computer-Assisted Text and Corpus Analysis: Lexical Cohesion and Communicative Competence," in *The Handbook of Discourse Analysis*, ed. Deborah Shiffrin, Deborah Tannen, and Heidi Hamilton (Oxford: Blackwell Publishers, 2001), p. 315.

125. See Lasswell, Lerner, and de Sola Pool's references to classics such as C. K. Ogeden and I. A. Richards's *The Meaning of Meaning* in *The Comparative Study of Symbols*, p. 84, n. 19.

126. Brandon Alszewski, Deborah Macey, and Lauren Lindstrom, "The Practical Work of <Coding>; "An Ethnomethodological Inquiry," *Human Studies* 29 (2007): 364.

127. David Altheide, "Ethnographic Content Analysis," *Qualitative Sociology* 10 (Spring 1987): 68. In World War II, American coders of German media were expected to bring their own sensitive competencies to bear on the raw sources. In this setting, a methodologist remarked, it seems "counterproductive to demand that different scientists must attain the same results." Gunnar Andrèn, "Reliability and Content Analysis," in

Advances in Content Analysis, ed. Karl Erik Rosengren (Beverly Hills: SAGE, 1981), p. 60.

128. Traimond, *Vérités en quête d'auteurs*, p. 13.

129. Pera, *The Discourses of Science*, pp. 54–55.

130. Harold Garfinkel, *Studies in Ethnomethodology* (Cambridge: Polity Press, 1984), p. 22.

131. Franzosi, *From Words to Numbers*, p. 288.

132. John Evans, "Playing God," *Journal of the Society of Christian Ethic* 24 (2004): 206.

133. *A Dictionary of Sociology*, Gordon Marshall, ed. (Oxford: Oxford University Press, 1998), p. 81.

134. John Evans, *Playing God?*, p. 144.

135. Jean-Baptiste Michel, Juan Kui Shen, Erez Lieberman Aiden, Adrian Veres, Matthew Gray, Joseph Pickett, Dale Holberg, Dan Clancy, Peter Norvig, Jon Orwant, Steven Pinker, and Martin Novak, "Quantitative Analysis of Culture Using Millions of Digitized Books," *Science* 331.6014 (2010): 176–182.

136. G. William Domhoff, *The Scientific Study of Dreams. Neural Networks, Cognitive Development, and Content Analysis* (Washington, DC: American Psychological Association, 2003), p. 170; Rebcecca Lemov, "Towards a Data Base of Dreams: Assembling an Archive of Elusive Materials, c. 1947–1961," *History Workshop Journal* 67 (2009): 44–68.

137. Stubbs, "Computer-Assisted Text and Corpus Analysis,," p. 317.

138. Michael Silverstein, "Language Structure and Linguistic Ideology," in *The Elements: A Parasession on Linguistic Units and Levels*, ed. P. Clyne, W. F. Hanks, and C. F. Hofbauer (Chicago: Chicago Linguistics Society, 1979), pp. 193–247.

139. Anatol Stefanowitsch, "Corpus-Based Approaches to Metaphor and Metonymy," in *Corpus-Based Approaches to Metaphor and Metonymy*, ed. Anatol Stefanowitsch and Stefan Gries (Berlin: Mouton de Gruyter, 2006), pp. 1–16.

140. "Obama's Words," *USA Today*, January 22, 2009; Matthew Ericson, "The Words They Used," *New York Times*, September 5, 2008, p. A24; Katherine Seelye, "The Past As a Guide for an Inaugural Address that Frames the Moment," with graph entitled "A Look Back in History," *New York Times*, January 18, 2009, p. A26.

141. On classical precedents for reading texts as aggregations of bits, see Tim Martin, "No Jacket Required," *Financial Times*, February 27, 2010, p. 12. On how Internet formats alter text comprehension, see Thomas Theil, "Ist unser Gehirn in Gefahr, Mrs. Wolf?" *Frankfurter Allgemeine Zeitung*, Gespräch, June 2010.

142. Stanley Fish, "Barack Obama's Prose Style," *New York Times*, January 22, 2009.

143. Nicholas Carr, *The Shallows: What the Internet Is Doing to Our Brains* (New York: W.W. Norton, 2010).

144. See also the Literary Laboratory at http://litlab.stanford.edu.

145. Italics in original except for the concluding seven words. I excerpt broadly from Franco Moretti, "Network Theory, Plot Analysis," *New Left Review* 68 (March–April 2011): 81, 94, 102.

146. Rastier, *Arts et sciences du texte*, pp. 203–220.

147. Peter Bearman and Katherine Stovel, "Becoming a Nazi," *Poetics* 27 (2000): 69–90.

148. Evans, *Playing God?* (Chicago: University of Chicago Press, 2002).

149. Gordon Marshall, *In Search of the Spirit of Capitalism* (London: Hutchinson, 1982), p. 113.

150. Richard Biernacki, "The Action Turn? From Goals to Schemas in the Explanation of Action," in *Remaking Modernity*, ed. J. Adams , E. S. Clemens, and A. S. Orloff (Chapel Hill: Duke University Press, 2005), pp. 75–91.

151. When writers discuss human genetic engineering within a framework, treating, say, biotechnology within the US laws protecting individual rights, it is uncertain whether the coding distinguishes between use of a framework versus ethical endorsement of a framework. Evans, *Playing God?* pp. 22, 159–160.

152. Wendy Griswold, "The Fabrication of Meaning: Literary Interpretation in the United States, Great Britain, and the West Indies," *The American Journal of Sociology* 92 (1987): 1077–1117.

153. Bearman and Stovel, "Becoming a Nazi," p. 72.

154. Ibid., pp. 70, 88.

155. Evans, *Playing God?*, p. 211.

156. Griswold, "Fabrication of Meaning," p. 1096.

157. Bearman and Stovel, "Becoming a Nazi," p. 72, n. 4; Evans, *Playing God?*, p. 43; Griswold, "Fabrication of Meaning," p. 1080. See also Wendy Griswold, "A Methodological Framework for the Sociology of Culture," *Sociological Methodology* 17 (1987): 2, 26.

158. For an example of a research team disagreeing over codes, see Susan Walzer and Thomas P. Oles, "Accounting for Divorce: Gender and Uncoupling Narratives," *Qualitative Sociology* 26 (2003): 338.

159. Traimond, *Vérités en quête d'auteurs*, p. 159.

160. On ethnographic analyses of "scientific" texts, see Alan Gross, *The Rhetoric of Science* (Cambridge, MA: Harvard University Press, 1996), pp. xv–xvi.

161. Revisiting the minutia of primary cases helps avoid the fallacy of assuming a priori that problems are correctable. Phil Hutchinson, Rupert J. Read, and W. W. Sharrock, *There Is No Such Thing as a Social Science: In Defence of Peter Winch* (Aldershot, England: Ashgate, 2008); Creswell and Clark, *Designing and Conducting Mixed Methods Research*, pp. 173–174.

162. Steven Shapin, "Pump and Circumstance: Robert Boyle's Literary Technology," *Social Studies of Science* 14 (1984): 481–520.

163. Emily Grosholz and Roald Hoffmann, "How Symbolic and Iconic Languages Bridge the Two Worlds of the Chemist. A Case Study from Contemporary Bioorganic Chemistry," in *Of Minds and Molecules. New Philosophical Perspectives on Chemistry*, ed. Nalini Bhushan and Stuart Rosenfeld (Oxford: Oxford University Press, 2000), pp. 230–247.

164. Algirda Julien Greimas, *The Social Sciences: A Semiotic View* (Minneapolis: University of Minnesota Press, 1990), pp. 11–36.

165. Robert Bannister, "Sociology," in *The Cambridge History of Science. The Modern Social Sciences*, ed. Theodore Porter and Dorothy Ross (Cambridge University Press, 2003), pp. 352–353; Geertz, *Local Knowledge*, pp. 34–35.

166. Michael Lynch, "Pictures of Nothing? Visual Construals in Social Theory," *Sociological Theory* 9 (1991): 11. On fashionable matings between mathematical metaphors and cultural analysis, see Bernice Pescosolido and Beth Rubin, "The Web of Group Affiliations Revisited:Social Life, Postmodernism, and Sociology," *American Sociological Review* 65 (2000): 52–76. More broadly, see Jan Fuhse, *Relationale Soziologie: Zur kulturellen Wende der Netzwerkforschung* (Wiesbaden: VS Verlag, 2010).

167. Natural scientists label their field and laboratory categorizations "qualitative" and their notes "interpretation" while such evidence is transparent and shared. Lawrence Prelli, *A Rhetoric of Science. Inventing Scientific Discourse* (Columbia, SC: University of South Carolina, 1989), pp. 149–158 and accompanying notes.

168. Baudrillard's axiom that "the simulacrum is true" operates in unsuspected locations. See Jean Baudrillar, *The Perfect Crime* (London: Verso, 1996), p. 21.

169. Ian Rutherford, "Theoria and Darsan: Pilgrimage and Vision in Greece and India," *Classical Quarterly* 50 (2000): 133–142.

170. Ian Rutherford, "Theoric Crisis: The Dangers of Pilgrimage in Greek Religion and Society," *Studi e materiali di Storia delle Religioni* 61 (1994): 282.

171. Andrea Wilson Nightingale, *Spectacles of Truth in Classical Greek Philosophy* (Cambridge: Cambridge University Press, 2004), pp. 69–70.

172. Steven Shapin, "The House of Experiment in Seventeenth-Century England," *Isis* (1988): 378, 384, 400.

173. On the ritual abolition of linear time, see Mircea Eliade, *The Myth of the Eternal Return* (Princeton: Princeton University Press, 1971).

174. Pascal saw liturgical ritual and experimental science as closely related forms of collective passage to a realm of action in which eternal truths are revealed to worshippers. See Michael Kerze, "Science and Ritual. A Study of Pascal," University of California Los Angeles PhD dissertation, 1983, pp. 268–269.

175. Nancy Cartwright, "Where do the Laws of Nature Come From?," *Dialectica* 51 (1997): 65–78.

176. James Boyd White, *How Should We Talk about Religion? Inwardness, Particularity, and Translation* (University of Notre Dame: Erasmus Institute, 2001), p. 5; Caroline A. Jones and Peter Galison, *Picturing Science. Producing Art* (New York: Routledge, 1998).

177. I draw on John Roche, "The Semantics of Graphics," in *Non-Verbal Communication in Science Prior to 1900*, ed. Renato Mazzolini (Florence: Olschki, 1993), p. 233.

178. "Einstein's great work had sprung from physical intuition and when Einstein stopped creating it was because he stopped thinking in concrete physical images and became a manipulator of equations." Richard Feynman, as quoted in J. Gleick, *Genius. The Life and Science of Richard Feynman* (New York: Pantheon, 1992), p. 244.

179. Algirda Julien Greimas, *The Social Sciences: A Semiotic View* (Minneapolis: University of Minnesota Press, 1990).

180. On knowledge via performance, see Karen Feldman, *Binding Words. Conscience and Rhetoric in Hobbes, Hegel, and Heidegger* (Evanston: Northwestern University Press, 2006). On performatives petrifying into constatives, see Paul de Man, *Allegories of Reading* (New Haven: Yale University Press, 1982), pp. 120, 124,131.

181. Gumbrecht, *The Powers of Philology*, pp. 64–65.

182. Benedict Anderson, *Imagined Communities* (London: Verso, 1991), p. 35. The remainder of this paragraph paraphrases Anderson.

183. Poovey, *A History of the Modern Fact*, pp. xvii, xxv.

184. Bruno Latour and Steve Woolgar, *Laboratory Life* (Princeton: Princeton University Press, 1986); for the relative absence of multistabile diagrams in the natural sciences, consider John D. Barrow, *Cosmic Imagery. Key Images in the History of Science* (London: Bodley Head, 2008), pp. 500–505.

185. Van Gennep, *Les rites de passage*, p. 267.

186. Victor Turner, *The Drums of Affliction* (Oxford: Oxford University Press, 1968), p. 270; Victor Turner, "Hidalgo: History as Social Drama," in *Dramas, Fields, and Metaphors. Symbolic Action in Human Society* (Ithaca: Cornell University Press, 1974), pp. 98–155; Jeffrey Alexander, *The Civil Sphere* (Oxford: Oxford University Press, 2006), pp. 318 ff.

187. Natural science accessorily affirms social identities as well. James Jacob and Margaret Jacob, "The Anglican Origins of Modern Science: The Metaphysical Foundations of the Whig Constitution," *Isis* 71.2 (1980): 251–267; John Zammito, *A Nice Derangement of Epistemes* (Chicago: University of Chicago Press, 2004), p. 176.

2 "THE ENTIRE STORY"

1. Thomas Childress, "Introduction" to Theodore Abel, *Why Hitler Came into Power* (Cambridge, MA: Harvard University Press, 1986), p. xviii.
2. Jan Fuhse, *Relationale Soziologie: Zur kulturellen Wende der Netzwerkforschung* (Wiesbaden: VS Verlag, 2010), pp. 16, 29.
3. Robert Smith, *Cumulative Social Inquiry. Transforming Novelty into Innovation* (New York: Guilford Press, 2008), pp. 94–95, 111. Pachucki and Breiger highlight how Bearman and Stovel avoided "researcher imputation of motive." Mark Pachucki and Ronald Breiger, "Cultural Holes: Beyond Relationality in Social Networks and Culture," *Annual Review of Sociology* 36 (2010): 210. See also John Mohr, "Introduction: Structures, Institutions, and Cultural Analysis," *Poetics* 27 (2000): 62.
4. At the Humboldt University in Berlin, "Becoming a Nazi" has been assigned to PhD students for imparting nothing less than "the narrative constitution of reality." Research Unit Comparative Structural Analysis, Institute for Social Sciences, Humboldt University, Berlin, "From Words to Structures," Winter 2004/2005.
5. Life Story Number 286 uses stationary. My reference "life story" indexes the Theodore Fred Abel papers, Hoover Institution Archives, Stanford, inventoried at http://cdn .calisphere.org/data/13030/vz/tf3489n5vz/files/tf3489n5vz.pdf.
6. Life Story 61. Life Story 296 opens like a sociology exam.
7. Life Stories Number 56, 264, 270, 271, and 290. On Nazis concretizing the Christian ethic of "love thy neighbor" through Hitler, see Life Story 163, p. 3.
8. See first page, Life Story 267.
9. Bracketed numbers in main text indicate pages in Peter Bearman and Katherine Stovel, "Becoming a Nazi: A Model for Narrative Networks," *Poetics* 27 (2000): pp. 69–90. "D" refers to the manuscript of Herr D., Theodore Fred Abel Collection, Story 267.
10. For earlier reductions of stories to arcs and nodes, see Arthur C. Graesser, *Prose Comprehension beyond the Word* (Berlin: Springer Verlag, 1981), pp. 138–148; and Peter Abell, *The Syntax of Social Life. The Theory and Method of Comparative Narratives* (Oxford: Clarendon Press, 1987), pp. 54–55.
11. Bearman and Stovel remark that the same data could be displayed variously. On changing network maps with constant data, see Jacques Bertin, *Semiologie graphique* (Paris: Mouton, 1973), p. 271.
12. Hannah Arendt, *The Origins of Totalitarianism*, new edition (New York: Harcourt Brace & Company, 1973), pp. 323–324.
13. "The Story of a Middle-Class Youth," in Abel, *Why Hitler Came into Power*, pp. 262–274. The clinching detail is that Bearman and Stovel cite an incident that occurs (due to mistranslation) only in the abridgment. Bearman and Stovel, "Becoming a Nazi," p. 87, note 21. The real story is Abel File 267.
14. Bearman and Stovel extend "a special debt to Connie Witte for her able translations of many life stories." Bearman and Stovel, "Becoming a Nazi," p. 69.
15. Bearman and Stovel reconfirmed use of the abridgment.
16. Ibid., p. 75; emphasis added. Bearman et al. emphasized that autobiographers "select from an endless sea of events just those events he or she sees as important (on the basis of a theory) for the story to be revealed." Peter Bearman, Robert Faris, and James Moody, "Blocking the Future: New Solutions for Old Problems in Historical Social Science," *Social Science History* 23.4 (Winter 1999): 511.
17. In some autobiographies the content supports Bearman and Stovel's conception of a Nazi: "He who swears on the flag to Hitler has nothing anymore that belongs to

himself" (Life Story 88). But the "data" should retain the narrative connectives and social complexities for idealists fulfilling the ideology.

18. Herr D. articulates the independence of other militants. Thomas Childers, "The Limits of Nationalist Socialist Mobilisation: The Elections of 6 November 1932 and the Fragmentation of the Nazi Constituency," in *The Formation of the Nazi Constituency 1919–1935*, ed. Thomas Childers (London: Croom Helm, 1986), p. 255.

19. In her important book about the moral structure of news stories, Karen Cerulo coded 126 newspaper articles but never listed this easily condensed sample. *Deciphering Violence* (New York: Routledge, 1998). Cerulo wrote that revealing sources per my request would be overly "time consuming."

20. Victor Turner, *The Anthropology of Performance* (New York: PAJ Publications, 1986), p. 25.

21. Franco Moretti, *Graphs, Maps, Trees. Abstract Models for a Literary History* (London: Verso, 2005), p. 92.

22. Arnold van Gennep, *The Rites of Passage* (University of Chicago Press, 1960), p. 21.

23. Edmund Morris, *Dutch: A Memoir of Ronald Reagan* (New York: Random House, 1999). The University of California Libraries catalog this work under "Fiction" and "Biography."

24. Victor Turner, "Variations on a Theme of Liminality," in *Secular Ritual*, ed. Sally Folk Moore and Barbara Meyerhoff (Assen: Van Gorcum, 1977), pp. 37, 47.

25. Bearman and Stovel's source on subordinating kin ties: James Peacock and Ruel Tyson, "Pentecostal and Primitive Baptist: Comparative Life Histories," *Social Science* 71 (1986): 52.

26. J. Huizinga, *Homo Ludens* (Boston: Beacon, 1950), p. 10.

27. Robert Jay Lifton, *The Nazi Doctors; Medical Killing and the Psychology of Genocide* (New York: Basic Books, 1986).

28. As quoted in Stephan and Norbert Lebert, *My Father's Keeper* (Boston: Little, Brown and Company, 2001), p. 183.

29. Ibid., p. 181.

30. Juan Linz, "Some Notes toward a Comparative Study of Fascism in Sociological Historical Perspective," in *Fascism: A Reader's Guide: Analyses, Interpretations, Bibliographies*, ed. Walter Laquer (Berkeley: University of California Press, 1976), p. 42; my emphasis.

31. Rudy Koshar, "From Stammtisch to Party: Nazi Joiners and the Contradictions of Grass Roots Fascism in Weimar Germany," *Journal of Modern History* 59 (1987): 7; Bernt Hagtvet, "The Theory of Mass Society and the Collapse of the Weimar Republic: A Re-Examination," in *Who Were the Fascists*, ed. Stein Larsen et al. (Bergen, Norway: Universitetsforlaget, 1980), pp. 95, 104; Michael Stephen Steinberg, *Sabers and Brown Shirts. The German Students' Path to National Socialism, 1918–1935* (Chicago: University of Chicago Press, 1973), pp. 71, 81.

32. Peter Merkl, *Political Violence under the Swastika. 581 Early Nazis* (Princeton: Princeton University Press, 1975), p. 237. For associational ties, Life Stories 10, pp. 2–3; 62, pp. 7–8; 69, p. 3; 97, pp. 1–2; 101, pp. 1–6; 103, pp. 1–3; 114, pp. 4–5; 173, pp. 1–2; 181, p. 3; 264, p. 8; 265, p. 3; 292, p. 4; 296, pp. 3, 5–6; 316, p. 2; 321, p. 3; 389, p. 1; 394, p. 1; 395, p. 2; and 398, pp. 2–3.

33. Trabasso and Linda Sperry, "Causal Relatedness and Importance of Story Events," *Journal of Memory and Cognition* 24 (1985): 596–598.

34. Linguists remark that Labov's procedure looks feasible only by "special pleading." Richard Biernacki, "After Quantitative Cultural Sociology," in *Meaning and Method*,

ed. Jeffrey Alexander and Isaac Reed (Boulder: Paradigm, 2009), p. 200, notes 136–140.

35. Richard Gerrig, *Experiencing Narrative Worlds. On the Psychological Activities of Reading* (New Haven: Yale University Press, 1993), pp. 49–53.

36. Harvey Sacks, "On the Analyzability of Stories by Children," republished in John Gumperz and Dell Hymes, eds., *Directions in Sociolinguistics. The Ethnography of Communication* (Oxford: Basil Blackwell, 1986), pp. 330–331; Catherine Emmott, "Constructing Social Space: Sociocognitive Factors in the Interpretation of Character Relations," in *Narrative Theory and the Cognitive Sciences*, ed. David Herman (Stanford: Center for the Study of Language and Information, 2003), p. 310.

37. Jerome Bruner, *Actual Minds, Possible Worlds* (Cambridge, MA: Harvard University Press, 1986), p. 5; Gérard Genette, *Figures of Literary Discourse* (New York: Columbia University Press, 1982), p. 143.

38. Francesca Polletta, *It Was Like a Fever. Storytelling in Protest and Politics* (Chicago: University of Chicago Press, 2006), p. 10.

39. David Rumelhart, "Notes on a Schema for Stories," in *Representation and Understanding. Studies in Cognitive Science*, ed. Daneil Bobrow and Allan Collins (New York: Academic Press, 1975), pp. 226–232; Charlotte Linde, *Life Stories. The Creation of Coherence* (Oxford: Oxford University Press, 1993).

40. Marisa Bortolussi and Peter Dixon, *Psychonarratology. Foundations for the Empirical Study of Literary Response* (Cambridge: Cambridge University Press, 2003), pp. 121–123; A. Michotte, *The Perception of Causality* (New York: Basic Books, 1963), pp. 359, 368; Isabelle Tapiero, *Situation Models and Levels of Coherence. Toward a Definition of Comprehension* (Mahwah, NJ: Lawrence Erlbaum, 2007), p. 162.

41. "Lead to" bridges between clauses may be evaluative or metaphorical, not quasi-causal or temporal. Livia Polanyi, *Telling the American Story* (Norwood, NJ: Ablex, 1985), p. 63; Murray Singer and Eric Richards, "Representing Complex Narrative Goal Structures," *Discourse Processes* 39 (2005): 201; Murray Singer, Arthur Graesser, and Tom Trabasso, "Minimal or Global Inference during Reading," *Journal of Memory and Language* 33 (1994): 438.

42. Livia Polanyi Bowditch, "Why the Whats are When: Mutually Contextualizing Realms of Narrative," *Proceedings of the Second Annual Meeting of the Berkeley Linguistics Society* 2 (1976): 64, 68.

43. Charlotte Linde, *Life Stories. The Creation of Coherence* (Oxford: Oxford University Press, 1993), pp. 128, 135.

44. David Herman, *Story Logic* (Lincoln: University of Nebraska Press, 2004), p. 83.

45. Wiliam Labov, *Language in the Inner City* (Philadelphia: University of Pennsylvania Press, 1972), pp. 363, 366, 392–396.

46. Jerome Bruner, *Making Stories. Law, Literature, Life* (New York: Farrar Straus and Giroux, 2002), p. 20. For immaturely abrupt closing, Abel File 97.

47. Victor Turner, *From Ritual to Theatre* (New York: PAJ, 1982), p. 27.

48. The Abel autobiographies I noticed that are lacking in feeling for family ties display this style from beginning to end due to the author's understanding of the assignment. See, illustratively, Stories 163 and 397.

49. The party veterans who wrote in a 1936/1937 contest said "very little about the motivations that led them into the Nazi movement." Christoph Schmidt, "Zu den Motiven 'alter Kämpfer' in den NSDAP," in *Die Reihen fast geschlossen. Beiträge zur Geschichte des Alltags unterm Nationalsozialismus*, ed. Detlev Peukert and Jürgen Reulecke (Wuppertal: Peter Hammer, 1981), p. 32.

50. Bortolussi and Dixon, *Psychonarratology*, p. 116.

51. Anselm Faust, *Der Nationalsozialistische Deutsche Studentenbund* (Düsseldorf: Pädagogischer Verlag, 1973), vol. 1, pp. 132–133; Enzo Traverso, *The Origins of Nazi Violence* (New York: The New Press, 2003), pp. 143, 146; Daniel Goldhagen, *Hitler's Willing Executioners* (New York: Vintage, 1997). Nazi autobiographers also emphasized the "biological superiority" of Aryans without mentioning Jews: Life Story 69, p. 3.

52. Richard Bessel, "The Nazi Capture of Power," *Journal of Contemporary History* 39 (2004): 176.

53. Life Stories 35, p. 2; 349, p. 2; and 383, p. 2.

54. Life Stories 100A, p. 1; 163, 296, p. 3; 272, pp. 4, 6; 302, p. 2; 311, p. 2; 386, p. 6 and 416. Jews are also thematically central via indirect quotes: Life Stories 181, p. 2 and 296, p. 3.

55. On differences between focal importance in plots versus causal linking, see Bortolussi and Dixon, *Psychonarratology*, p. 116. "The reason I hate the Jews is because I have experienced so much about them, that I must say this kind of human does not qualify to be included in a state such as Germany" (Life Story 163, p. 9).

56. See "The Legend of Hitler's Childhood," in *Childhood and Society*, second edition, ed. Erik Erickson (New York: W.W. Norton, 1963), p. 327.

57. Adolf Hitler, *Mein Kampf* (Munich: Zentralverlag der NSDAP, 1940), p. 54. Nazi propaganda and the autobiographies see Marxism, cosmopolitanism, pacifism, and capitalism as ultimately Jewish, making it difficult to code anti-Semitism as absent. Life Stories 25, 114, 280, and 296.

58. Balthasar Brandmayer, *Meldegänger Hitler* (Überlingen am Bodensee: Franz Walter, undated sixth printing), p. 92.

59. Life Story 291, p. 1.

60. Life Story 88, p. 2. Analogously, Stories 386, 416

61. Abel considered *Volksgemeinschaft* a key to the autobiographies: see his *Why Hitler Came into Power*, pp. 137–143.

62. George Mosse, *The Nationalization of the Masses. Political Symbolism and Mass Movements in Germany from the Napoleonic Wars through the Third Reich* (Ithaca: Cornell University Press, 1975), p. 131; Michael Wildt, *Volksgemeinschaft als Selstermächtigung* (Hamburg: Hamburger Edition, 2007), p. 64.

63. Roger Chank, "The Structure of Episodes in Memory," in *Representation and Understanding*, p. 260.

64. On recreated father-son relations in the Nazi party, see Schmidt, "Zu den Motiven 'alter Kämpfer in den NSDAP," p. 31.

65. It is typical but contrary to Bearman and Stovel's model that if one family member advised against devoting time to party work [D 10], this built up relations to other kin in the party.

66. Adolf Wehler, *Bild-Chronik. Trier in der Besatzungszeit 1918–1930* (Trier: Petermännchen-Verlag, 1992), pp. 126–127.

67. Dilemmas in coding family as elided or united: Life Story 79, in which an ill wife commands her husband to separate by working for the party (p. 2); Story 392, in which joining the Nazis leads a worker to be fired and to return home to angry parents as well as to the embrace of a supportive aunt (pp. 2–3).

68. Hayden White, *Figural Realism. Studies in the Mimesis Effect* (Baltimore: Johns Hopkins University Press, 1999), p. 89.

69. Catherine Emmott, *Narrative Comprehension. A Discourse Perspective* (Oxford: Clarendon Press, 1997), p. 239; Blain Mullins and Peter Dixon, "Narratorial Implicatures: Readers Look to the Narrator to Know What is Important," *Poetics* 35 (2007): 263.

70. Jenna Baddeley and Jefferson Singer, "Charting the Life Story's Path: Narrative Identity Across the Life Span," in *Handbook of Narrative Inquiry. Mapping a Methodology*, ed. Jean Clandinin (Thousand Oaks: SAGE, 2007), p. 183; White, *Figural Realism*, p. 99

71. I crib the sentences from Michael Toolan, *Narrative. A Critical Linguistic Introduction* (London: Routledge, 1988), p. 148.

72. Ibid.

73. Bearman and Stovel promise that the advantage of having a single model of intelligibility is that they can compare and classify at a deeper level the structures in narratives of "diverse scope" and social content [72]. Obviously there are an unlimited number of quantitative measurements whose form can equally well be calculated across narrative compositions of diverse substance, but most such measuring would be horseplay.

74. Turner, *From Ritual to Theatre*, p. 27.

75. Luc Herman and Bart Vervaeck, *Handbook of Narrative Analysis* (Lincoln; University of Nebraska Press, 2005), p. 101; Bruner, *Actual Minds, Possible Worlds*, pp. 33–35.

76. Michel Foucault, *The Order of Things. An Archaeology of the Human Sciences* (New York: Vintage Books, 1973), p. 19.

77. "Just like theories, life stories organize facts (elements, states, events etc) into interpretable sequences and patterns…" [76].

78. Tzvetan Todorov, *Poétique de la Prose* (Paris: Éditions du Seuil, 1971), p. 230; Algirdas Julien *Greimas, Du Sens. Essais sémiotiques* (Paris: Éditions du Seuil), p. 181.

79. "The cosmos becomes a complex weave of 'correspondences' based on analogy, metaphor, and metonymy." Turner, *From Ritual to Theatre*, p. 29.

80. Richard Biernacki, "After Quantitative Cultural Sociology," in *Meaning and Method*, ed. Jeffrey Alexander and Isaac Reed (Boulder: Paradigm, 2009), p. 134.

81. Mohr, "Introduction; Structures, Institutions, and Cultural Analysis," p. 62; emphasis added.

82. René Girard, *Violence and the Sacred* (Baltimore: Johns Hopkins University Press, 1977), p. 271.

83. I draw on Roy A. Rappaport, *Ritual and Religion in the Making of Humanity* (Cambridge: Cambridge University Press, 1999), p. 345.

84. Algirdas Julien Greimas, *The Social Sciences: A Semiotic View* (Minneapolis: University of Minnesota Press, 1990), p. 51.

3   "METHODOLOGICAL CANONS IN MY FIELD"

1. Evans presents his codes as warranting his conclusions: John Evans, "Playing God?" *Journal of the Society of Christian Ethics* 24 (2004): 206, 208. Remainder from John Evans, *Playing God? Human Genetic Engineering and the Rationalization of Public Bioethical Debate* (Chicago: University of Chicago Press, 2002), p. 211. Evans coded all passages in the most influential works, except for "chapters of large books that seemed to contain no ethical claims. These were by and large chapters designed to give the reader the requisite technical background in genetics" ("Playing God," PhD dissertation, Princeton University, 1998, p. 59). For coded sources, only a few of which would have avoided dissection, see Evans, *Playing God?*, pp. 217–226. [G] abbreviates the book *Playing God*.

2. Mary Poovey captures this theory-neutral cover for modern facts with the term "deracinated" particulars. Poovey, *A History of the Modern Fact* (Chicago: University of Chicago Press, 1998), p. 273.

3. An unmistakable category ought not require a pooling of coders' opinions. William Schulz, "On Categorizing Qualitative Data in Content Analysis," *Public Opinion Quarterly* 22.4 (1958–1959), p. 512.

4. Graham Harman, *Prince of Networks: Bruno Latour and Metaphysics* (Melbourne: "re. press," 2009), pp. 37–44.

5. Max Weber, *The Protestant Ethic and the Spirit of Capitalism* (New York: Charles Scribner's Sons, 1958), p. 51.

6. Ibid., pp. 52–53.

7. Jere Cohen, *Protestantism and Capitalism. The Mechanisms of Influence* (New York: Aldine de Gruyter, 2002), p. 74.

8. Gordon Marshall, *In Search of the Spirit of Capitalism* (London: Hutchinson, 1982), p. 120.

9. Margaret Somers, "The Narrative Constitution of Identity," *Theory and Society* 23 (1994): 628.

10. Gregor Schöllgen, *Handlungsfreiheit und Zweckrationalität* (Tübingen: J.C.B. Mohr, 1984), pp. 97–98; Susan Hekman, *Weber, The Ideal Type, and Contemporary Social Theory* (Notre Dame: University of Notre Dame Press, 1983), pp. 48–49; Zenonas Norkus, *Max Weber und Rational Choice* (Marburg: Metropolis Verlag, 2001), pp. 300–301; Hartmann Tyrell, "Antagonismus der Werte—ethisch," in *Max Webers "Religionssystematik,"* ed. Hans Kippenberg and Martin Riesebrodt (Tübingen: Mohr Siebeck, 2001), pp. 322–323; Richard Biernacki, "After Quantitative Cultural Sociology," in *Meaning and Method*, ed. Jeffrey Alexander and Isaac Reed (Boulder: Paradigm, 2009), pp. 153–164.

11. Gordon Marshall, *In Search of the Spirit of Capitalism* (London: Hutchinson, 1982).

12. Evans, *Playing God*, pp. 217-226.

13. Donald Nielsen, "The Protestant Ethic and the Spirit of Capitalism as Grand Narrative," in *The Protestant Ethic Turns 100. Essays on the Centenary of the Weber Thesis*, ed. William Swatos and Lutz Kaelber (Boulder: Paradigm Publishers, 2005), pp. 65–66.

14. Gianfranco Poggi, "Historical Viability, Sociological Significance, and Personal Judgment," in *Weber's Protestant Ethic. Origins, Evidence, Contexts*, ed. Hartmut Lehmann and Guenther Roth (Cambridge: Cambridge University Press, 1993), p. 298.

15. Perry Anderson, "The River of Time," *New Left Review* Issue 26 (2004): 74.

16. Roger Cotterrell, *Living Law. Studies in Legal and Social Theory* (Aldershot: Dartmouth, 2008), p. 175. On Weber's fusion of instrumental/formal and value/substantive rationality in practice, see Jürgen Habermas, *Theorie des kommunikativen Handelns* (Frankfurt am Main: Suhrkamp Verlage, 1985), vol. 1, pp. 245–246.

17. C. Cohen, J. Vianna, L. Battistella, E. Massad, "Time Variation of Some Selected Topics in Bioethical Publications," *Journal of Medical Ethics* 34 (2008): 81–84.

18. S. I. Been, "Abortion, Infanticide, and Respect for Persons," in *The Problem of Abortion*, ed. Joel Feinberg (Belmont, CA: Wadsworth, 1973), p. 103.

19. Evans, "Playing God," *Journal of the Society of Christian Ethics*, p. 210. As a reviewer of *Playing God* remarked, "For those who, like me, are surprised to learn that there is an official form of professional bioethical argumentation, it turns out to be principlism…" Robert Baker, "On Being a Bioethicist," *American Journal of Bioethics* 2 (2002): 67.

20. Also Daniel Kevles, *In the Name of Eugenics* (Cambridge, MA: Harvard University Press, 1995), pp. 286–289.

21. A book reviewer claimed, "Evans defines anyone who does not argue formal rationality as not a bioethicist." See Paul Wolpe, review in *American Journal of Sociology* 109 (2003): 216. As Evans wrote, deviants who use case-based moral reasoning "would then not be bioethicists by my definition." Evans, "Playing God," *Journal of the Society of Christian Ethics*, p. 210.

22. The "form of argumentation of the bioethics profession was created to be useful for unelected government policy makers" [G 157]; "the bioethicists *created* the focused frame *to be able* to obtain resources from the state." Evans, "Playing God?" PhD dissertation, p. 404; my emphasis.

23. Joseph Fletcher, *Morals and Medicine. The Patient's Right to Know the Truth. Contraception. Artifical Inseminiation. Sterilization. Euthenasia* (Princeton: Princeton University Press, 1954).

24. Paul Wolpe, review of *Playing God?* in *American Journal of Sociology* 109 (2003): 216.

25. Warren Reich, "Shaping and Mirroring the Field: The 'Encyclopedia of Bioethics,'" in *The Story of Bioethics*, ed. Jennifer Walter and Eran Klein (Washington, DC: Georgetown University Press, 2003), pp. 166–167.

26. President's Council on Bioethics, *Human Dignity and Bioethics*, March 2008.

27. NSF File Location 97-01966.

28. Thomas Kuhn, *The Structure of Scientific Revolutions* (Chicago: University of Chicago Press, 1962), pp. 43–48.

29. Wolfgang Iser, *The Range of Interpretation* (New York: Columbia University, 2000), p. 156.

30. James Sorenson, ed., *Social and Psychological Aspects of Applied Human Genetics: A Bibliography. Fogarty International Center* (Washington, DC: DHEW Publication No. (NIH) 73-412), pp. 73–78.

31. The keyword "cloning" was less likely to occur in arguments tending toward formal rationality [G 268, n. 12].

32. Arthur Caplan, "Moral Experts and Moral Expertise. Does Either Exist?" in *If I Were a Rich Man Could I Buy a Pancreas?*, ed. Arthur Caplan (Bloomington: Indiana University Press, 1991), pp. 18–39. Arthur Caplan qualified as statistically influential about HGE in "Playing God" the 1998 dissertation.

33. Robert Baker, review of *Playing God?*, "On Being a Bioehicist, "*American Journal of Bioethics* 2 (2002): 67.

34. A Biothicsline search for texts with HGE as "primary topic" logically would autogenerate the "finding" that formally rational texts tend not to discuss "abortion and in-vitro fertilization" [G 20]. Fishing for texts that use the same HGE terms as keywords may reverse this result. John Fletcher, "Abortion Politics, Science, and Research Ethics: Take Down the Wall of Separation," *Journal of Contemporary Health Law and Policy* 8 (1992): 95–121.

35. Evans, "Playing God?" PhD dissertation, p. 403.

36. Evans, "Playing God," *Journal of the Society of Christian Ethics*, p. 206.

37. Evans's protocol repeated at Biernacki, "After Quantitative Cultural Sociology," p. 142.

38. Evans, "Playing God," *Journal of the Society of Christian Ethics*, p. 206.

39. Ibid., p. 201.

40. The community is labeled as that of bioethicists, and it totals six individual and corporate authors in the 1985–1991 period, as specified at G 144, line 21 and G 138, figure 4.

41. Evans, "Playing God?" PhD dissertation, p. 390.

42. Peter Singer and Deane Wells, "Genetic Engineering," in *Ethical Issues in Scientific Research: An Anthology*, ed. Edward Erwin et al. (New York: Garland, 1994), pp. 307–320. Cites of this work would be credited to Singer.

43. Stanley Hauerwas, symposium on *Playing God* in *Journal of the Society of Christian Ethics* 24 (2004): 185.

44. Evans, "Playing God," *Journal of the Society of Christian Ethics*, p. 212.

45. For an illustrative string, see G 67, notes 97, 98, 99, and 100.

46. Biernacki, "After Quantitative Cultural Sociology," pp. 148–151 and p. 260.

47. Evans, "Playing God," *Journal of the Society of Christian Ethics*, p. 209.

48. Struan Jacobs, "Scientific Community: Formulations and Critique of a Sociological Motif," *The British Journal of Sociology* 38 (1987): 266–276.

49. W. French Anderson, "Human Gene Therapy: Why Draw a Line?," *The Journal of Medicine and Philosophy* 14 (1989): 686; W. French Anderson, "A Cure That May Cost Us Ourselves," *Newsweek Magazine*, January 1, 2000.

50. Roy Rapport, *Ritual and Religion in the Making of Humanity* (Cambridge: Cambridge University Press, 1999), pp. 344–346.

51. In the early period of substantively rational discussion "the intended consumer of their texts" is "the educated public." Evans, "Playing God," PhD dissertation, p. 169.

52. Evans indicated that classifying authors' "intended audience" was a central research task. NSF File 97-01966.

53. For replication, see Biernacki, "After Quantitative Cultural Sociology," p. 142. Evans seems to maintain in "Playing God" the dissertation that letters to the editor signal healthy debate (p. 431).

54. Bernard Davis, "Cells and Souls," *New York Times*, June 28, 1983; Alexander Capron and Morris Abram, "On the Control of Human Genetic Engineering," *New York Times*, January 6, 1983. See the very sophisticated article by Leon Kass, "A Caveat on Transplants," *Washington Post*, January 14, 1968, which considers a Lederberg column and an article by Joseph Fletcher for *Harpers*.

55. "Guests on Television Talk Shows Sunday," *Washington Post*, October 21, 1972; Robin Herman, "Tinkering with the Essence of Humanity," *Washington Post*, October 8, 1991; W. French Anderson, "A Cure That May Cost Us Ourselves" *Newsweek Magazine*, January 1, 2000; Robin Marantz Henig, "Dr. Anderson's Gene Machine," *New York Times Magazine*, March 31, 1991: 30–35, 50.

56. As a reviewer of *Playing God* noted, "In public talks, on radio and television, and in op-ed pieces, bioethicists publicly discuss the most fundamental issues of human strivings and ultimate goals." Paul Wolpe, review of *Playing God?*, *American Journal of Sociology* 109 (2003): 216.

57. *Washington Post*, July 24, 1966, to September 12, 1971. Also see www.nlm.nih.gov/hmd/lederberg/public.html.

58. "Even a democratic society, however, may be entrapped by its short-term goals into a commitment, as we have made to nuclear weaponry and may be doing to biological weaponry." Joshua Lederberg, "Curbs on Human Engineering," *Washington Post*, October 21, 1967.

59. Joshua Lederberg, "Man May Program Progeny Before He's Morally Ready," *Washington Post*, October 14, 1967.

60. Robin Herman, "Tinkering with the Essence of Humanity," *Washington Post*, October 8, 1991.

61. Robin Mrantz Henig, *Pandora's Baby* (New York: Houghton Mifflin Harcourt, 2004), p. 280.

62. Nowadays: MSNBC's Arthur Caplan, "Breaking Bioethics," archived at www.msnbc.msn.com.

63. Troy Duster, *Backdoor to Eugenics* (New York: Routledge, 1990), pp. 35, 75, 128–129; Evans, "Playing God," *Journal of the Society of Christian Ethics*, p. 213.

64. Evans, "Playing God," PhD dissertation, p. 353.

65. The five citations derived from the coauthored book with Ted Howard would exceed *Declaration of a Heretic* and be signaled at G 225. Cf. "Playing God" PhD dissertation, p. 479.

66. Compare G 138 to "Playing God," PhD dissertation, p. 304.

67. G 279, n. 23; Evans, "Playing God," PhD dissertation, p. 451. In the dissertation "Playing God," cites of the coauthored book were not credited to Rifkin: see p. 332, n. 34.

68. Mark Aldenderfer and Roger Blashfield, *Cluster Analysis* (Newbury Park: SAGE, 1984), p. 16. "The concept of 'no structure' in a data set (one possible null hypothesis) is far from clear, and it is not obvious what types of tests could be devised to determine if structure is or is not present" (p. 53).

69. Evans, "Playing God," PhD dissertation, p. 56, n. 6.

70. Ibid., pp. 61, 137, 304, 353.

71. Sheldon Krimsky, "Human Gene Therapy: Must we Know Where to Stop Before We Start?," *Human Gene Therapy* 1 (1990): 173.

72. Sheldon Krimsky, *Biotechnics and Society. The Rise of Industrial Genetics*, cited at Evans, "Playing God," PhD dissertation, p. 479.

73. David T. Suzuki and Peter Knudtson, *Genethics* (Cambridge, MA: Harvard University Press, 1989), pp. 344–345, 348.

74. David Suzuki was professor of zoology at the University of British Columbia. For David Suzuki's honorary degrees and CV, see http://www.davidsuzuki.org/About_us /Dr_David_Suzuki. Peter Knudtson was a biologist and a writer who received a Canada Council grant, for example.

75. Evans, "Playing God," PhD dissertation, p. 353.

76. Brian Martinson, Melissa Anderson, and Raymond de Vries, "Scientists Behaving Badly," *Nature* 435 (June 2005): 737.

77. Barrington Moore, Jr., *Political Power and Social Theory* (Cambridge, MA: Harvard University Press, 1958), pp. 107–108.

78. "But when you average the citations of hundreds of texts, idiosyncratic reasons to cite someone become noise, with the reason that we thought a text was important to our writing remaining as signal." Evans, "Playing God," *Journal of the Society of Christian Ethics*, p. 207.

79. Pierre Bourdieu, "The Market of Symbolic Goods," *Poetics* 14 (1985): 41.

80. Harold Varmus, *The Art and Politics of Science* (New York: W.W. Norton, 2009), p. 250.

81. Evans, "Playing God," PhD dissertation, p. 331.

82. Ibid.

83. Evans, "Playing God," *Journal of the Society of Christian Ethics*, p. 212.

84. Biernacki, "After Quantitative Cultural Sociology," p. 172.

85. Brian Johnstone, "The Human Genome Project. Catholic Theological Perspective," in *The Interaction of Catholic Bioethics and Secular Society*, ed. Russell Smith (The Pope John Center, 1992), p. 275. See my parallel cite from Anderson at Biernacki, "After Quantitative Cultural Sociology," p. 172.

86. Charles Bazerman, *Shaping Written Knowledge* (Madison: University of Wisconsin Press, 1988), p. 203.

87. Pierre Bourdieu, "The Market of Symbolic Goods," *Poetics* 14 (1985): 41.

88. Were Evans to make his NSF-funded data set available, we could pursue questions about the meaning of the citations systematically.

89. Ted Howard and Jeremy Rifkin, *Who Should Play God?* (New York: Delacorte Press, 1977), p. 227, cited at G 222.

90. On variation across genres in purpose and frequency of citation, see Lowell L. Hargens, "Using the Literature: Reference Networks, Reference Contexts, and the Social Structure of Scholarship," *American Sociological Review* 65 (2000): 859–860.

91. Laura Jane Bishop and Marry Carrington Coutts, "Religious Perspectives on Bioethics. Part Two," *Kennedy Institute of Ethics Journal* 4 (1994): 357–386.

92. Aaron Cicourel, *Method and Measurement in Sociology* (New York: The Free Press, 1964), p. 15.

93. Nelson Goodman, *Ways of Worldmaking* (Indianapolis: Hackett, 1978).

94. Bioethicsline cannot be used for longitudinal measurement because texts in the 1959–1974 period and some into the 1980s lack keywords. Nor do keywords indicate styles of rationality.

95. Evans, "Playing God," *Journal of the Society for Christian Ethics*, p. 206; my emphasis.

96. Ibid., p. 208.

97. Ibid., p. 210; my emphasis.

98. "Coding all 1,465 texts would have been too time-consuming." Ibid., p. 206.

99. Ibid., p. 205.

100. Ibid., p. 209.

101. Matthew Miles and Michael Huberman, *Qualitative Data Analysis* (Thousand Oaks: Sage, 1994), pp. 56–57; my emphasis. Evans quotes from this same passage in Evans, "Two Worlds of Cultural Sociology," in Alexander and Reed, *Meaning and Method*, p. 212.

102. The "established approach" in qualitative coding is to create a means for retrieving "marked data segments." Amanda Coffey and Paul Atkinson, *Making Sense of Qualitative Data* (Thousand Oaks: SAGE, 1996), p. 52.

103. Matthew Miles and Michael Huberman, *Qualitative Data Analysis* (Thousand Oaks: SAGE, 1994), p. 63.

104. Evans, "Two Worlds of Cultural Sociology," p. 229.

105. NSF File 97-01966.

106. Evans, "Two Worlds of Cultural Sociology," p. 236.

107. Hermann Muller, "The Guidance of Human Evolution," *Perspectives in Biology and Medicine* 3 (1959): 24–25. Muller confirmed that the key faculties for happiness "count the most for everyone," the quintessence of formal universalism (p. 25).

108. Hermann Muller, "Means and Ends in Human Genetic Betterment," in *The Control of Human Heredity and Evolution*, ed. T. M. Sonneborn (New York: Macmillan, 1965), pp. 100, 119.

109. Evans, "Playing God," PhD dissertation, p. 40.

110. Muller, "The Guidance of Human Evolution," pp. 20–21; emphasis added.

111. Ibid., p. 22.

112. Ibid.

113. Ibid., p. 32.

114. Muller, "Means and Aims," p. 117.

115. Ibid., p. 116.

116. Muller, "The Guidance of Human Evolution," p. 32.

117. Ibid., p. 37.

118. Muller, "Means and Aims," p. 100.

119. Ibid, p. 121.

120. Muller, "The Guidance of Human Evolution," p. 19.

121. Ibid.

122. Ibid., p. 23.

123. Muller, "Means and Aims," p. 112.

124. Weber, *The Protestant Ethic and the Spirit of Capitalism* (New York: Charles Scribners' Sons, 1958), p. 261.

125. "I am definitely following the mainstream sociological interpretation of Weber and rationalization..." Evans, "Playing God," *Journal of the Society of Christian Ethics*, p. 212.

126. Jonathan Glover, *What Sort of People Should There Be?* (Harmondsworth, England: Penguin Books, 1984).

127. Ibid., p. 32. My quote combines Glover's main text with its accompanying footnote about Muller.

128. Ibid., p. 33.

129. Ibid., p. 179.

130. Ibid., p. 132.

131. Jonathan Glover, *Ethics of New Reproductive Technologies. The Glover Report to the European Commission* (DeKalb: Northern Illinois University Press, 1989), pp. 138–144.

132. Glover, *What Sort of People*, p. 47.

133. Ibid., pp. 49–51.

134. Ibid., p. 51.

135. Glover's stance in *What Sort of People Should There Be?* reads similarly to that in *The Glover Report to the European Commission*, a corroboratory source. Glover et al., *Ethics of New Reproductive Technologies*, p. 140.

136. Glover, *What Sort of People*, p. 161.

137. Ibid., p. 136; emphasis in original.

138. Biernacki, "After Quantitative Cultural Sociology," p. 154.

139. Glover, *What Sort of People*, p. 18.

140. Ibid.

141. Ibid., pp. 51, 184.

142. Ibid., p. 49.

143. Ibid., p. 51.

144. Ibid.

145. Evans, "Playing God?" PhD dissertation, p. 392.

146. Ibid., p. 393; emphasis in the original.

147. Glover, *What Sort of People*, p. 51.

148. Paul Wolpe, review of *Playing God?* in *American Journal of Sociology* 109 (2003): 216.

149. Biernacki, "After Quantitative Cultural Sociology," pp. 166–167.

150. Table 1.1, "Playing God," PhD dissertation, p. 39.

151. Evans's typification in the dissertation of substantive value rationality as potentially focused on one end conforms to Weber. Zenonas Norkus, *Max Weber und Rational Choice* (Marburg: Metropolis Verlag, 2001), p. 291.

152. Evans, "Playing God," PhD dissertation, pp. 76, 83. My quote aligns two sentences from separate pages.

153. Evans reiterates agreement upon "the *end*"; see ibid., p. 97, line 7 and p. 98, lines 3 and 7.

154. Ibid., p. 71; emphasis in the original.

155. Biernacki, "After Quantitative Cultural Sociology," p. 187, note 27.

156. Evans, "Playing God," PhD dissertation, p. 79; my emphasis.

157. NSF File 97-01966, which produces additional qualitative coding enumerations: "'perception of mandate' (3 codes) marks discussions regarding what an actor thinks the commission is supposed to be doing."

158. Biernacki, "The Banality of Misrepresentation," in Alexander and Reed, *Meaning and Method*, p. 258.

159. Evans, "Two Worlds of Cultural Sociology," p. 273. For a sociologist who (a) coded for styles of reasoning and (b) used Miles and Huberman as a template for qualitative coding, but (c) adduced counts of classifications, see Michèle Lamont, *How Professors Think* (Cambridge, MA: Harvard University Press, 2009), pp. 177, 288.

160. Evans, "Playing God," PhD dissertation, p. 88.

161. Ibid., p. 90 line 17 regarding ends and p. 91 lines 5, 14, 15.

162. NSF File 97-01966.

163. Evans, "Two Worlds in Cultural Sociology," pp. 211, 214–216, 218–220.

164. Ibid., pp. 218–219.

165. Supposing no univocal code were assigned to a text as a whole, it was still characterized at the individual level, as Evans assures us: "This text is generally formally rational…" Ibid., p. 229.

166. Ibid., p. 218.

167. Evans, "Playing God," *Journal of the Society of Christian Ethics*, p. 212.

168. "Coding" is "a research procedure in which the data collected…are prepared for counting and tabulation by classification and codification." George A. Theodorson and Achilles G. Theodorson, *A Modern Dictionary of Sociology* (New York: Thomas Crowell, 1969), p. 54.

169. Miles and Huberman, *Qualitative Data Analysis*, p. 253. When I once used the term "content analysis" I followed Evans's preferred handbook, whereas Evans asserts I write of it "unlike everyone else in sociology" ("Two Worlds in Cultural Sociology," p. 272). For a survey of usage, see Gilbert Shapiro and John Markoff, "A Matter of Definition," in *Text Analysis For the Social Sciences*, ed. Carl Roberts (Mahwah, NJ: Lawrence Erlbaum, 1997), pp. 13, 28. Frequency counts are seen as requisite even for nominal-level codes: Ian Dey, *Qualitative Data Analysis. A User-Friendly Guide for Social Scientists* (London: Routledge, 1993), p. 179.

170. Evans, "Two Worlds in Cultural Sociology," p. 218; my emphasis. Sociologists insist that qualitative conclusions about "dominant or leading ideas" in a text sample represent quantitative claims: Gilbert Shapiro and John Markoff, *Revolutionary Demands* (Stanford: Stanford University Press, 1998), p. 27.

171. Evans, "Two Worlds in Cultural Sociology," pp. 218, 220; emphasis in original.

172. Ibid., pp. 219–220; emphasis in original.

173. Evans, *Journal of the Society of Christian Ethics*, p. 210.

174. Ibid., p. 207.

175. Evans, "Two Worlds of Cultural Sociology," p. 219.

176. Ibid., p. 229; emphasis in original.

177. It is the "reduction in the number of ends that is critical for the case at hand" [G 16].

178. Evans, "Playing God," *Journal of the Society of Christian Ethics*, p. 212.

179. For a review, see Biernacki, "After Quantitative Cultural Sociology," pp. 155–157.

180. Evans once declared it is adequate for the frame of substantive rationality that "not *all* ends are commensurable." See his "Playing God," PhD dissertation, p. 40; emphasis added.

181. Jeffrey Stout, "Playing God," *Journal of the Society of Christian Ethics*, p. 189.

182. James Childress, "Playing God," *Journal of the Society of Christian Ethics*, p. 199.

183. Evans, "Playing God," *Journal of the Society of Christian Ethics*, p. 205.

184. Ibid., p. 213.

185. Michael Walzer, *Thick and Thin. Moral Argument at Home and Abroad* (Notre Dame: University of Notre Dame Press, 1994), pp. 32, 39.

186. Ibid., pp. 6, 33.

187. J. Daryl Charles, "The 'Right to Die' in the Light of Contemporary Rights-Rhetoric," in *Bioethics and the Future of Medicine. A Christian Appraisal*, ed. John Kilner and D. C. Thomasma (Grand Rapids, MI: William Eerdmans, 1995), p. 266; Michela Marzano, *Je consens, donc je suis… Éthique de l'autonomie* (Paris: Presses Universitaires de France, 2006), pp. 50, 68, 128.

188. Roberta M. Berry, *The Ethics of Genetic Engineering* (London: Routledge, 2007), p. 167.

189. Albert Jonsen, *The Birth of Bioethics* (Oxford University Press, 1998), pp. 150, 153.

190. Joseph Fletcher's curiously unclassifiable *Situation Ethics* [G 86] subordinates all means to one end, Christian Love, while it insists such love lacks fixed meaning across situations. One end therefore—or many? Fletcher expresses distaste for formal reduction and of consequential, "in order to's" (therefore substantively rational), yet consequences define the meaning of one's acts (formal rationality?). Joseph Fletcher, *Situation Ethics. The New Morality* (Philadelphia: Westminster Press, 1966), pp. 129, 157, 163.

191. For the apparent incompatibility of Weber's perspective with Evans's application, see Biernacki, "After Quantitative Cultural Sociology," pp. 151–153, 158, 163–164.

192. Victor Turner, *The Forest of Symbols* (Ithaca: Cornell University Press, 1967), p. 106.

193. Michel Foucault, "Of Other Spaces," *Diacritics* 16 (1986): 22–27.

194. Biernacki, "After Quantitative Cultural Sociology," p. 173.

195. Andrew Abbott, "For Humanist Sociology," in *Public Sociology*, ed. Dan Clawson, Joya Misra, Naomi Gerstel, and Randall Stokes (Berkeley: University of California Press, 2007), p. 205.

196. "Studies reveal that papers are published to be counted rather than read." Stuart Macdonald, "Gamemanship in the Hands of Academic Peers," *Financial Times*, March 2, 2010.

197. Harold Varmus, *The Art and Politics of Science* (W.W. Norton, 2009), p. 250.

198. Jon Wiener, *Historians in Trouble. Plagiarism, Fraud, and Politics in the Ivory Tower* (New York: The New Press, 2005), p. 209.

199. Evans, "Playing God," *Journal of the Society of Christian Ethics*, p. 209.

200. John Berkman, "Playing God," *Journal of the Society of Christian Ethics*, p. 183.

201. "We desire something concretely either 'for its own sake' or as a means of achieving something else which is more highly desired." Max Weber, *Methodology of the Social Sciences* (Glencoe: The Free Press, 1949), p. 52. Weber dogmatically supposed the means-end schema was exceptional in establishing a "rational" link between concept and reality. Alan Sica, *Weber, Irrationality, and Social Order* (Berkeley: University of California Press, 1988), pp. 132–133, 152.

202. Niklas Luhmann, *Essays on Self-Reference* (New York: Columbia University Press, 1990), p. 42; Stephen Turner and Regis Factor, *Max Weber and the Dispute Over Reason and Value* (London: Routledge & Kegan Paul, 1984); Mustafa Emirbayer, "Beyond Weberian Action Theory," in *Max Weber's Economy and Society*, ed. Charles Camic, Philip Gorski, and David Trubek (Stanford: Stanford University Press, 2005), pp. 185–203.

203. Jesus P. Zamora Bonilla, "Economists: Truth-Seekers or Rent-Seekers?" in *Fact and Fiction in Economics*, ed. Usakli Maki (Cambridge: Cambridge University Press, 2002), pp. 356–357.

204. Stanley Tambiah, "A Performative Approach to Ritual," in *Proceedings of the British Academy*, vol. 65, 1979 (London: Oxford University Press, 1981).

4 "A Quantifiable Indicator of a Fabricated Meaning Element"

The chapter title has been taken from Wendy Griswold, "Provisional, Provincial Positivism. Reply to Denzin," *American Journal of Sociology* 95 (1990): 1582.

1. On the divergence between occurrence of what is mentioned versus significance, see François Rantier, *Arts et sciences du texte* (Paris: Presses Universitaires, 2001), pp. 220–225.
2. James Gleick, *The Information. A History. A Theory. A Flood* (New York: Pantheon Books, 2011), p. 348.
3. On cultural environments for defining Pi, see L. Berggren, J. M. Borwein, and P. B. Borwein, *Pi. A Source Book* (New York: Springer, 1997).
4. Dionysis Goutsos and Georgia Fragaki, "Lexical Choices of Gender Identity in Greek Genres: The View From Corpora," *Pragmatics* 19 (2009), pp. 317–340.
5. Wendy Griswold, "The Fabrication of Meaning: Literary Interpretation in the Unites States, Great Britain, and the West Indies," *American Journal of Sociology* 92 (1987): 1077–1117.
6. "One example of an empirical study...that uses quantitative content analysis is Griswold's study of book reviewers' reviews of novels." Robert Wuthnow and Marsha Witten, "New Directions in the Study of Culture," *Annual Review of Sociology* 14 (1988): 54.
7. Victoria D. Alexander, *Sociology of the Arts. Exploring Fine and Popular Forms* (Oxford: Blackwell Publishing, 2003), p. 281; Stefano Putoni et al., "Polysemy in Advertising," *ERIM Report Series Research in Management* no. 43 (August 2006): 20.
8. Jeffrey Alexander, Ronald Jacobs, and Philip Smith, "Introduction: Cultural Sociology Today," *Oxford Handbook of Cultural Sociology* (Oxford: Oxford University Press, 2011), p. 7.
9. Wendy Griswold, "A Methodological Framework for the Sociology of Culture," *Sociological Methodology* 17 (1987): 4.
10. Numbers in brackets in this chapter reference pages in "The Fabrication of Meaning."
11. Rogers Brubaker and Margit Feischmidt, "1848 in 1998: The Politics of Commemoration in Hungary, Romania, and Slovakia," *Comparative Studies in Society and History* (2002): 700.
12. Yuko Ogasawara, *Office Ladies and Salaried Men: Power, Gender, and Work in Japanese Companies* (Berkeley: University of California Press, 1998), pp. 107, 196.
13. Alan Bryman, "Global Disney," in *The American Century: Consensus and Coercion in the Projection of American Power*, ed. David Slater and Peter J. Taylor (Oxford: Blackwell, 1999), p. 269; "Cultural Power," in *Sacred Companies: Organizational Aspects of Religion and Religious Aspects of Organizations*, ed. N. J. Demerath III, P. D. Hall, T. Schmitt, and R. H. Williams (New York: Oxford University Press, 1998), p. 374; Fred Kniss, "Ideas and Symbols as Resources in Intrareligious Conflict: The Case of the American Mennonites," *Sociology of Religion* 57 (1996): 9–10; Elizabeth Armstrong and Suzanna Crage, "Movements and Memory; The Making of the Stonewall Myth," *American Sociological Review* 71 (October 2006): 727; Virag Molnar, "Cultural Politics and Modernist Architecture in Hungary," *American Sociological Review* 70 (2005): 115.
14. Amin Ghaziani and Marc Ventresca, "Keywords and Cultural Change: Frame Analysis of 'Business Model' Public Talk, 1975–2000," *Sociological Forum* 20 (2005): 533, 535.

15. John Mohr, "Measuring Meaning Structures," *Annual Review of Sociology* 24 (1998): 347–348.

16. The sample list is indispensable for Griswold to communicate results.

17. William Epson, *Seven Types of Ambiguity* (London: Chatto and Windus, 1956), pp. 5–6.

18. Israel Scheffler, "Ambiguity: An Inscriptional" Approach," in *Logic and Art. Essays in Honor of Nelson Goodman*, ed. R. Rudner and I. Scheffler (Indianapolis: Bobbs-Merrill, 1972), pp. 251 ff.

19. "'Cultural power' refers to the capacity of certain works to linger in the mind and, over and above the individual effect, to enter the canon..." [1105].

20. Paul Theroux, "Versions of Exile," *Encounter*, May 1972, vol. 38, p. 69. Douglas Dunn, *New Statesman*, January 28, 1972, p. 119.

21. Michael Cooke, "A West Indian Novelist," *Yale Review*, vol. 62, 1973, pp. 623–624.

22. Ibid., pp. 621, 624.

23. Review of *Water with Berries*,Victor Questel, "Caliban's Circle of Death," *Tapia*, Trinidad, December 17, 1972.

24. *Times Literary Supplement*, February 11, 1972, p. 145.

25. Chalmer St. Hill, *Bim*, July–December 1972, pp. 190–191.

26. Griswold commits the ecology fallacy by reporting a positive correlation between ambiguity and praise in the aggregate for each novel whereas at the level of individual reviews for each novel it is logically possible and I think probable that there is an inverse relation between ambiguity and praise.

27. Earl Cash, "Water with Berries," *College Language Association Journal* 17 (March 1974): 441.

28. George Lamming, *Water with Berries* (Trinidad and Jamaica: Longman Caribbean, 1971), p. 200.

29. *The Commonweal*, vol. 98, June 1, 1973, pp. 317–318.

30. "San Cristobal Unreached: George Lamming's Two Latest Novels," *World Literature in English*, 1973, p. 112.

31. *The Library Journal*, vol. 97, August 1972, p. 2645.

32. *Times Literary Supplement*, March 27, 1953, p. 206.

33. Greig Henderson, "A Rhetoric of Form," in *Unending Conversations. New Writings By and About Kenneth Burke*, ed. Greig Henderson and David Williams (Carbondale: Southern Illinois University Press, 2001), pp. 132–133; James Gleick, *The Information* (New York: Pantheon Books, 2011), p. 354.

34. *Manchester Guardian*, April 24, 1953.

35. *Virginia Kirkus' Bookshop Service*, August 15, 1953, p. 545.

36. *Library Journal*, vol. 78, September 15, 1953, p. 1531.

37. *London Magazine*, vol. 1, no. 6, July 1954, p. 97.

38. *The Gleaner* (Kingston, Jamaica), February 8, 1976.

39. G. Lewis Chandler, "At the Edge of Two Worlds," *Phylon* 14.4 (1953): p. 438.

40. *San Francisco Chronicle*, November 17, 1953, p. 25.

41. Gertrude Rivers, "In the Castle of My Skin," *The Journal of Negro Education* 23 (1954): 155.

42. Wilfred Cartey, "The Realities of Four Negro Writers," *Columbia University Forum*, Summer 1966, p. 40.

43. *Harvey Curtis Webster*, "The Halls of Color," Saturday Review, December 5, 1953, p. 36.

44. Crosstabulating Griswold's data at pages 1090 n. 18, 1099, and 1109 confirms she applied the same data on ambiguity for different purposes.

45. John Caputo, *More Radical Hermeneutics. On Not Knowing Who We Are* (Bloomington: Indiana University Press, 2000), p. 211.

46. *Times Literary Supplement*, March 27, 1953, p. 206.

47. *Kyk-over-Al*, vol. 9, 1961, pp. 192–193; "Versatile Writers from the West Indies," *Times British Colonies Review*, Summer 1953.

48. Jürgen Habermas, *Religion and Rationality* (Cambridge, MA: MIT Press, 2002), p. 65.

49. Marvin Anderson, "Martin Tyndale: A Martyr for All Seasons," *The Sixteenth Century Journal* 17 (1986): 347.

50. Exception: Roberto Franzosi, *From Words to Numbers* (Cambridge: Cambridge University Press, 2004).

51. Griswold, "The Fabrication of Meaning," p. 1079.

52. Norman Denzin, "Reading Cultural Texts, Comment on Griswold," *American Journal of Sociology* 95 (1990): 1577–1580.

53. Wendy Griswold, "Provisional, Provincial Positivism. Reply to Denzin," *American Journal of Sociology* 95 (1990): 1581.

54. Griswold, "The Fabrication of Meaning," p. 1090.

55. The prescriptions of a genre "vary in content and in severity." Jacques Dubois and Pascal Durand, "Literary Field and Classes of Texts," in *Literature and Social Practice*, ed. Philippe Desan, Priscilla Parkhurst Ferguson, and Wendy Griswold Chicago: University of Chicago Press, 1989), p. 143.

56. For an example of a critic of Lamming explicitly invoking a literary schema, see Rosalind Wade, *Contemporary Review Literary Supplemen* 220 (April 1972): 215–216.

57. Griswold tabulates names of literary figures, not their functions [1095].

58. Joseph Henry Jackson, "Bookman's Notebook. A Novel of Barbados," *San Francisco Chronicle*, November 17, 1953.

59. Another review indicating how difficult it is to code for "mention" of race if race is subordinate: *Times British Colonies Review*, Summer 1953, p. 45.

60. *The Journal of Negro Education* 23.2 (Spring 1954): 155.

61. O. R. Dawthorne, "Caribbean Narrative," in *Consequences of Class and Color. West Indian Perspectives*, ed. David Lowenthal and Lambros Comitas (Garden City: Anchor Books, 1973), p. 278.

62. W. I. Carr, "The West Indian Novelist," in *Consequences of Class and Color. West Indian Perspectives*, ed. David Lowenthal and Lambros Comitas (Garden City: Anchor Books, 1973), p. 286.

63. "As Lamming's work goes forward, we come to understand that the title of that first book is not a signature of colour, but a symbol of personal isolation." L. E. Braithwaite, "The New West Indian Novelists—Part II," *Bim* 8.32 (1961): 273.

64. Jeanne Fahnestock, *Rhetorical Figures in Science* (Oxford: Oxford University Press, 1999), p. 42.

65. Measures of dispersion depend artificially on the length of reviews. David Hoover, "Another Measure of Vocabulary Richness," *Computers and the Humanities* 37 (2003): 154, 173.

66. Nancy Cartwright, *The Dappled World. A Study of the Boundaries of Science* (Cambridge: Cambridge University Press, 1999), p. 137.

67. "[T]hree different groups of recipients *regularly* construed different meanings from George Lamming's *In the Castle of My Skin...*" Wendy Griswold, "A Methodological Framework for the Study of Culture," p. 13. Emphasis added.

68. James B. Rule, *Theory and Progress in Social Science* (Cambridge: Cambridge University Press, 1997), p. 210.

69. *Manchester Guardian*, April 24, 1953.

70. *London Observer*, Issue 9, 454, October 8, 1972.

71. *London Magazine*, July 1954, vol. 1, p. 92.

72. Peter Worsley, "Colonial Culture," *Guardian*, July 29, 1960.

73. *The Spectator*, October 28, 1960, p. 664.

74. Of 37 American reviews, not a single one by Griswold's coding mentioned "humor" [1093]. Yet choose an American review of *In the Castle of My Skin*: "The background is the poverty and the almost insurmountable obstacles in the way of survival, the poetry and the laughter, and the series of anecdotes, from the bawdy to the infinitely sad..." *Kirkus*, p. 545, October 27, 1953. Coding for "humor" turns on whether Rablesian jest qualifies.

75. *The Spectator*, November 14, 1958, p. 65.

76. *Punch*, June 24, 1953, p. 753. *New Statesman*, April 18, 1953.

77. From the relatively low rate of mentions of "class" in the British reviews, Griswold concludes the British were not referring to race surreptitiously [1097]. But this inference from aggregate numbers does not reveal meaningful interdependencies inside individual reviews.

78. Wendy Griswold, "Reply to Denzin," *American Journal of Sociology* 95 (1990): 1583.

79. Alfred Kazin, "Criticism and Isolation," *Virginia Quarterly Review* 17 (1941): 450.

80. Nassim Taleb, *The Bed of Procrustes* (New York: Random House, 2010), p. 77.

81. For the potential of idiosyncratic contexts to impact reviews, see "Dog Nibbles Dog," *The Spectator*, September 30, 1963, p. 340.

82. Aaron Cicourel, "Three Models of Discourse Analysis: The Role of Social Structure," *Discourse Processes* 3 (1980): 123; emphasis in original. Analogously, Ronnie Steinberg Ratner and Paul Burstein, "Ideology, Specificity, and the Coding of Legal Documents," *American Sociological Review* 45 (1980): 523.

83. For an example of the influence of Lamming as a person on reviews, see Wilfred Cartey, "Lamming and the Search for Freedom," *New World. Barbados Independence Issue* 3.1/2 (1967): 121–128.

84. Jorge Luis Borges, *Labyrinths. Selected Stories and Other Writings* (New York: New Directions, 1964), pp. 180–181.

85. V. S. Pritchett, "A Barbadous Village," *New Statesman*, April 18, 1953, p. 460; David Paul, "Surfaces and Depths," *The Observer*, March 15, 1953, p. 9.

86. *London Magazine*, vol. 2, May 1955, p. 110.

87. Michael Swan, *London Magazine*, vol. 1, July 1954, p. 97.

88. I found the Stern and Swan book reviews via a beginner's guide that mentioned a Library of Congress listing of reviews.

89. *The Times British Colonies Review*, Summer 1953, p. 45.

90. Joseph Henry Jackson, "Bookman's Notebook. A Novel of Barbados," *San Francisco Chronicle*, November 17, 1953, p. 25.

91. Robert Bellah, "Durkheim and Ritual," in *Cambridge Companion to Durkheim*, ed. Jeffrey Alexander and Philip Smith (Cambridge: Cambridge University Press, 2005), p. 205.

92. Aaron Cicourel, "Three Models of Discourse Analysis: The Role of Social Structure," *Discourse Processes* 3 (1980): 127.

93. George Lamming, "An Introduction," *Bim* 6.22 (June 1955): 66.

94. Paul de Man, "Literary History and Literary Modernity," in *Time and the Literary*, ed. Karen Newman, Jay Clayton, and Marianne Hirsch New York: Routledge, 2002), p. 165.

95. Stuart M. Hall, "Lamming, Selvon, and Some Trends in the W.I. Novel," *Bim* 6.23 (December 1955): 178.

96. Robert Holub, *Reception Theory. A Critical Introduction* (London: Methuen, 1984), p. 142.

97. Geroge Lamming, "An Introduction," *Bim* 6.22 (June 1955): 66.

98. In the "Guyana Independence Issue" of *New World*, edited by Lamming, L. E. Brathwaite ("Kyk-Over-Al and the Radicals"), p. 55.

99. John Mohr, "Measuring Meaning Structures," *Annual Review of Sociology* 24 (1998): 353.

100. "Society" since the nineteenth century has gradually "inherited, or rather burgled" the powers of religion. Roberto Calasso, *Literature and the Gods* (New York: Alfred A. Knopf, 2001), p. 173.

101. It is unclear how "society" interacts with the cultural artifact if readers choose which literary schemas to apply. Given diffusion among English-speaking intellectuals, it is difficult to claim a schema was unavailable or unworkable for a reviewer.

102. The problem of identifying the semantic stimulus disables reader reception experiments. Holub, *Reception Theory*, p. 150.

103. Marisa Bortolussi and Peter Dixon, *Psychonarratology* (Cambridge: Cambridge University Press, 2003), p. 119.

104. Jonathan Culler, "Defining Narrative Units," in *Style and Structure in Literature*, ed. Roger Fowler (Oxford: Basic Blackwell, 1975), pp. 123–142.

105. Richard Wright, "Introduction" to *In the Castle of My Skin* (New York: McGraw-Hill, 1953), p. vii.

106. Greig Henderson, "A Rhetoric of Form: The Early Burke and Reader-Response Criticism," in *Unending Conversations, New Writings By and About Kenneth Burke*, ed. Greig Henderson and David Cratic Williams (Carbondale: Southern Illinois University Press, 2001), pp. 127–142.

107. Kenneth Burke, *Counter-Statement* (Berkeley: University of California Press, 1968). Similarly, Marisa Bortolussi and Peter Dixon, *Psychonarratology. Foundations for the Empirical Study of Literary Response* (Cambridge: Cambridge University Press, 2003), pp. 239–240.

108. Society can be affected by history, but as is fitting for a rite, the definition of society itself is not historicized. Judith Butler, "Reanimating the Social," in *The Future of Social Theory*, ed. Nicholas Gane (London: Continuum, 2004), pp. 52–53.

109. Alasdair MacIntyre, "Is a Science of Comparative Politics Possible?" in *The Philosophy of Social Explanation*, ed. Alan Ryan (Oxford: Oxford University Press, 1973), p. 178.

110. Wilfred Sellars, "Toward a Theory of the Categories," in *Experience and Theory*, ed. Lawrence Foster and J. W. Strawson (University of Massachusetts Press, 1970), pp. 55–78.

111. Hans Robert Jauss, *Toward an Aesthetic of Reception* (Minneapolis: University of Minnesota, 1982), p. 161; Wolfgang Iser, *The Act of Reading. A Theory of Aesthetic Response* (Baltimore: Johns Hopkins University Press, 1978), p. 72; Alan Liu, "The Future Literary: Literature and the Culture of Information," in *Time and the Literary*, ed. Karen Newman, Jay Clayton, and Marianne Hirsch (New York: Routledge, 2002), pp. 71, 96 n. 37; Holub, *Reception Theory*, pp. 89, 150.

112. Alexander Star, "A Man of Good Reading," *New York Times*, August 23, 2009.

113. Pierre Bourdieu, "The Market of Symbolic Goods," *Poetics* 14 (1985): 22.

114. Valerio Valeri, *Fragments from Forests and Libraries* (Durham, NC: Carolina Academic Press, 2001), p. 48.

115. I draw here on Ian McNeely and Lisa Wolverton, *Reinventing Knowledge* (W.W. Norton, 2008), p. 271.

116. Michael Oakeshott, *Rationalism in Politics and Other Essays* (London: Methuen, 1962), p. 93.

117. Wendy Griswold, "Number Magic in Nigeria," *Book History* 5 (2002): 281.

118. Frank Kermode, *The Genesis of Secrecy* (Cambridge, MA: Harvard University Press, 1979), p. 123.

119. When reviewers dissect Lamming's novels for sociopolitical topics, they stray from the literary experience Griswold sought to probe. Susan Craig, review of *Natives of My Person*, in *Race Today*, January 1975, pp. 21–22.

120. John Caputo, "In Praise of Ambiguity," in *Ambiguity in the Western Mind*, ed. Craig J. N. de Paulo, Patrick Messina, and Marc Stier (New York: Peter Lang, 2005), p. 25.

121. Max Weber, *Gesammelte Aufsätze zur Wissenschaftslehre* (Tübingen: J.C.B. Mohr, 1968), p. 14.

122. Peter Galison, "Image of Self," in *Things that Talk. Object Lessons From Art and Science*, ed. Lorraine Daston (New York: Zone Books, 2004), p. 276.

123. On the difference between an originally opaque sense (as in a joke whose humor escapes us) versus an absence of sense, see Emil Angehrn, "Hermeneutik und Kritik," in *Was ist Kritik?*, ed. Rathel Jaeggi and Tilo Wesche (Frankfurt am Main: Suhrkamp, 2009), pp. 330–331.

124. Kenneth Ranchand, "The Theatre of Politics," *20th-Century Studies*, December 1973, no. 10, p. 21.

125. Stuart M. Hall, "Lamming, Selvon, and Some Trends in the W.I. Novel," *Bim* 6.23 (December 1955): 172–178.

126. Hall's piece probably made its way into Griswold's sample, since Zola and Woolf occur adjacent in Griswold's table [1095].

127. Gloria Yarde, "George Lamming—the Historical Imagination," *The Literary Half-Yearly* 11 (1970): pp. 35–45; Charlotte Bruner, "The Meaning of Caliban in Black Literature Today," *Comparative Literature Studies* 13 (1976): 240–253.

5   WARY REASONING

1. Mary Poovey, *A History of the Modern Fact* (Chicago: University of Chicago Press, 1998), pp. 327–328; Clifford Geertz, *After the Fact* (Cambridge, MA: Harvard University Press, 1995).

2. T. Lewens, "Realism and the Strong Program," *British Journal for the Philosophy of Science* 56 (2005): 573.

3. Giorgio Agamben, *The End of the Poem. Studies in Poetics* (Stanford: Stanford University Press, 1999), p. 30; Cleanth Brooks, *Historical Evidence and the Reading of Seventeenth-Century Poetry* (Columbia: University of Missouri Press, 1991), pp. 156–159; Paul de Man, *The Rhetoric of Romanticism* (Columbia: Columbia University Press, 1984), pp. 313–314.

4. Anthony Grafton, *The Footnote. A Curious History* (Cambridge, MA: Harvard University Press, 1997), pp. 19–22, 234.

5. Paul de Man, *Allegories of Reading* (New Haven: Yale University Press, 1979); Cleanth Brooks, *The Well Wrought Urn: Studies in the Structure of Poetry* (London: Dobson, 1968).

6. John Evans, "Two Worlds in Cultural Sociology," in *Meaning and Method*, ed. Jeffrey Alexander and Isaac Reed (Boulder: Paradigm, 2009), p. 209.

7. "Playing God?" NSF Proposal 9701966; "would not then be bioethicists by my definition," John Evans, "Playing God," *Journal of the Society of Christian Ethics* 24 (2004): 210.

8. Ronald Grimes, "Victor Turner's Definition, Theory, and Sense of Ritual," in *Victor Turner and the Construction of Cultural Criticism*, ed. Kathleen Ashley (Bloomington:

Indiana University Press, 1990), p. 142; Max Scharnberg, *The Non-Authentic Nature of Freud's Observations* (Uppsala: Uppsala University, 1993), vol. 2, p. 203.

9. Roy Sorensen, *Vagueness and Contradiction* (Oxford: Clarendon Press, 2001), p. 138.

10. Lorraine Daston and Peter Galison, *Objectivity* (New York: Zone Books, 2007), pp. 290–293, 301–302.

11. Norman Denzin, "Reading Cultural Texts: Comment on Griswold," *American Journal of Sociology* 95 (1990): 1577–1580.

12. For a twin reference to "the meaning of the cultural object as constituted by the object itself," see Wendy Griswold, "A Methodological Framework for the Sociology of Culture," *Sociological Methodology* 17 (1987): 5.

13. Claude Lévi-Strauss, *The Savage Mind* (Chicago: University of Chicago Press, 1966), pp. 18–19, 204–210, 268.

14. Claude Lévi-Strauss, *The Way of Masks* (Seattle: University of Washington Press, 1979), pp. 8, 219–220.

15. Roy Rappaport, *Ritual and Religion in the Making of Humanity* (Cambridge: Cambridge University Press, 1999), p. 71.

16. Chip Heath, http://connectedthebook.com/pages/reviews.html; my emphasis. Nicholas Christakis and James Fowler, *Connected: The Surprising Power of Our Social Networks and How They Shape Our Lives* (Little, Brown and Co., 2009).

17. Paul de Man, *Allegories of Reading* (New Haven: Yale University Press, 1979), p. 11.

18. Maurice Georges Barrier, *L'art du récit dans l'étranger d'Albert Camus* (Paris: A.G. Nizet, 1962), p. 54.

19. Derek Phillips, *Knowledge From What? Theories and Methods in Social Research* (Chicago: Rand McNally and Co., 1971), pp. 18–19.

20. Abraham Kaplan, *The Conduct of Inquiry. Methodology for Behavioral Science* (New York: Crowell, 1964), p. 75.

21. David Altheide and John M. Johnson, "Criteria for Assessing Interpretive Validity in Qualitative Research," in *Handbook of Qualitative Research*, ed. Norman Denzin and Yvonna Lincoln (Thousand Oaks: SAGE, 1994), p. 496.

22. Franco Moretti, *Graphs, Maps, Trees* (London: Verso, 2005), p. 53.

23. In discussing the validity of coding categories, Irving Janis elucidated primarily the criterion of "productivity," namely, interesting correlations of codes with codes. Irving Janis, "The Problem of Validating Content Analysis," in *Language of Politics*, ed. Harold Lasswell and Nathan Leiter (New York: George Stewart, 1949), pp. 60–81.

24. Wendy Griswold, "Provisional, Provincial Positivism: Reply to Denzin," *American Journal of Sociology* 95 (1990): 1582.

25. Doug Arnold, Louisa Sadler, and Aline Villavicencio, "Portuguese: Corpora, Coordination, and Agreement," in *Roots. Linguistics in Search of Its Evidential Base*, ed. Sam Featherston and Wolfgang Sternefeld (Berlin: Mouton de Gruyter, 2007), pp. 25, 27; Richard Biernacki, "The Banality of Misrepresentation," in Reed and Alexander, *Meaning and Method*, p. 260.

26. Mark Rowlands, "Situated Representation," in *The Cambridge Handbook of Situated Cognition*, ed. Phillip Robbins and Murat Aydede (Cambridge: Cambridge University Press, 2009), pp. 117–133.

27. Paul Roth, *Meaning and Method in the Social Sciences* (Ithaca: Cornel University Press, 1987), p. 143.

28. Max Black, "Some Puzzles About Meaning," in *Human Communication: Theoretical Explorations*, ed. Albert Silverstein (Hillsdale, NJ: Lawrence Erlbaum, 1974), pp. 87–93.

29. James Bohman, *New Philosophy of Social Science* (Cambridge, MA; MIT Press, 1993), p. 123.

30. Evans, "Playing God," *Journal of the Society of Christian Ethics* 24 (2004): 209.

31. Ibid., 210; my emphasis.

32. Pierre Bourdieu, "The Market of Symbolic Goods," *Poetics* 14 (1985): 41.

33. Griswold, "Provisional, Provincial Positivism," p. 1582.

34. Cosma Shalizi, "Graphs, Trees, Materialism, Fishing," in *Reading Graphs, Maps, Trees*, ed. Jonathan Goodwin and John Holbo (Anderson, SC: Parlor Press, 2011), p. 121; Barrington Moore, Jr., *Political Power and Social Theory* (Cambridge, MA: Harvard University Press, 1958), p. 132.

35. Roberto Calasso, *Literature and the Gods* (New York: Alfred A. Knopf, 2001), pp. 176–180.

36. Andrew Bowie, *From Romanticism to Critical Theory* (London: Routledge, 1996), p. 71.

37. E. D. Hirsch, *The Aims of Interpretation* (Chicago: University of Chicago Press, 1976), p. 134.

38. R.C. North, *Content Analysis. A Handbook With Applications for the Study of International Crisis* (Northwestern University Press, 1963), p. 33.

39. The tweed example follows Nelson Goodman, *Languages of Art* (Indianapolis: Hackett, 1976).

40. Roger Chartier, "Text, Symbols, and Frenchness," *Journal of Modern History* 57 (1985): 682–695.

41. Thomas Kuhn, *The Structure of Scientific Revolutions* (Chicago: University of Chicago Press, 1996), pp. 141–143; Paul de Man, *Allegories of Reading* (New Haven: Yale University Press, 1979), pp. 11–13.

42. Geoffrey Hawthorn, *Plausible Worlds* (Cambridge University Press, 1991), p. 124. On earnest philosophy switched into comedy, see Olga Russel, *Humor in Pascal* (North Quincy: Christopher Publishing, 1977), pp. 161–162.

43. Opposing but seemingly equally adequate interpretations of objects create incompatible universes. Nelson Goodman, *Ways of Worldmaking* (Indianapolis: Hackett, 1978), pp. 114–116.

44. Harold Sampson and Joseph Weiss, "Our Research Approach," in *The Psychoanalytic Approach. Theory, Clinical Observations, and Empirical Research*, ed. Joseph Weiss, Harold Sampson, and the Mount Zion Psychotherapy Research Group (New York: The Guilford Press, 1986), p. 151.

45. Additionally, consider the excisions by Markoff and Shapiro of irregular, potentially revelatory documents. Gilbert Shapiro and John Markoff, *Revolutionary Demands* (Stanford: Stanford University Press, 1998), pp. 224–230.

46. The interdependencies between text-like artifacts run across media (literature versus film) and may be governed by relations between subordinate and among dominant social groups. William Sewell, Jr., "The Concept(s) of Culture," in *Beyond the Cultural Turn*, ed. Victoria Bonnell and Lynn Hunt (Berkeley: University of California Press, 1999), pp. 35–61.

47. Shyon Baumann, *Hollywood Highbrow. From Entertainment to Art* (Princeton: Princeton University Press, 2007).

48. Ibid., p. 113.

49. Arnie Berstein, *"The Movies Are." Carl Sandburg's Film Reviews and Essays, 1920–1928* (Chicago: Lake Claremont Press, 2000), p. 1; my emphasis.

50. On Sandburg treating directors as "main star" and "creative artist," see ibid., pp. 8, 345. Compare Baumann, *Hollywood Highbrow*, p. 115.

51. Berstein, *"The Movies Are,"* p. 9.

52. On nonexistence of cultural "units," see Catherine Gallagher and Stephen Greenblatt, *Practicing New Historicism* (Chicago: University of Chicago Press, 2000), p. 14.

53. Baumann, *Hollywood Highbrow*, p. 127.

54. *Time*'s cover, August 27, 1934; or *Time*, August 10, 1931: "Ten best cinema directors of 1930–1931."

55. Benjamin de Casseres, "Seven Months in the Movies," *New York Times*, June 26, 1921, p. 45; "Seeks Votes of 10,000 on Movie as Fine Art," *New York Times*, June 8, 1928, p. 10.

56. Full disclosure: In *The Fabrication of Labor* I admitted worker grievances into the cross-national sample only if they appeared in complaint columns that made them "comparable." This excluded unique headline stories that may have better accessed workers' construal of their experience.

57. Anna Everett, "Inside the Dark Museum; A Genealogy of Black Film Criticism. 1909–1949," PhD dissertation, University of Southern California, 1996, vol. 1, pp. 311–312.

58. My quote from *Half Century*, May 1919, p. 11. Anna Everett, *Returning the Gaze. A Genealogy of Black Film Criticism, 1909–1949* (Durham: Duke University Press, 2007), pp. 107–178. African American commentators precociously judged film comparable to "all efforts of a literary nature." Howe Alexander, "Colored Motion Picture Drama," *The Half-Century Magazine*, March 1919, p. 9.

59. Pascal Manuel Heu, '*Le Temps*' *du cinéma. Émile Vuillermoz. Père de la critique cinéma. 1910–1930* (Paris: L'Harmattan, 2003), pp. 93–104.

60. Nassim Nicholas Taleb, *The Black Swan. The Impact of the Highly Improbable* (New York: Random House, 2007).

61. Eric Slauter, *The State as a Work of Art* (Chicago: University of Chicago Press, 2009), p. 350.

62. Susan Neiman, *Evil in Modern Thought. An Alternative History of Philosophy* (Princeton: Princeton University Press, 2002), pp. 271–277; Hannah Arendt, *Eichmann in Jerusalem. A Report on the Banality of Evil* (New York: Penguin Books, 1994), p. 252; Timothy Clark, *The Poetics of Singularity* (Edinburgh: Edinburgh University Press, 2005), p. 34.

63. Giorgio Agamben, *Homo Sacer. Sovereign Power and Bare Life* (Stanford: Stanford University Press, 1998), p. 166; Michel Foucault, ed., *I, Pierre Rivière, Having Slaughtered My Mother, My Sister, and My Brother…: A Case of Parricide in the 19th Century* (New York: Pantheon Books, 1975); and the masters discussed in Gallagher and Greenblatt, *Practicing New Historicism*, pp. 49–74.

64. At the extreme, Jacques Derrida, *Of Grammatology* (Baltimore: Johns Hopkins Press, 1976), p. 168. Or, from an author less suspect: Moore, *Political Power and Social Theory*, p. 141.

65. Goodman, *Ways of Worldmaking*, p. 101.

66. Douglas Medin and Robert Goldstone, "The Predicates of Similarity," in *Similarity in Language, Thought, and Perception*, ed. Christina Cacciari (Turnhout: Brepols, 1995), pp. 83–110.

67. Giovanni Sartori, *Concepts and Method in Social Science* (New York: Routledge, 2009), pp. 97–150; Moore, *Political Power and Social Theory*, p. 151.

68. Shapiro and Markoff, *Revolutionary Demands*, pp. 212, 216.

69. Edith Grossman, *Why Translation Matters* (New Haven: Yale University Press, 2010), p. 76.

70. W. I. Carr, "The West Indian Novelist," in *Consequences of Class and Color*, ed. David Lowenthal and Lambros Comitas (Garden City, NY: Anchor, 1973), p. 286.

71. Dedre Gentner and Arthur Markman, "Similarity is Like Analogy: Structural Alignment in Comparison," in *Similarity in Language, Thought, and Perception*, ed. Christina Cacciari (Turnhout: Brepols, 1995), pp. 111–137.

72. Cleanth Brooks, *The Well Wrought Urn* (London: Dennis Dobson, 1968), p. 159.

73. Claude Lévi-Strauss, *Structural Anthropology* (Chicago: University of Chicago Press, 1976), vol. 2, pp. 242–256; Claude Lévi-Strauss, *The Jealous Potter* (Chicago: The University of Chicago Press, 1988), pp. 25–29, 184.

74. Lawrence Prelli, *A Rhetoric of Science: Inventing Scientific Discourse* (Columbia, SC: University of South Carolina Press, 1989), p. 149.

75. "A literary work, then, is not the compliance-class of a text but the text or script itself..." Goodman, *Languages of Art*, p. 209.

76. Marcello Pera, *The Discourses of Science* (Chicago: University of Chicago Press, 1994), pp. 131–132.

77. Richard Biernacki, "Rationalization Processes Inside Cultural Sociology," in *The Oxford Handbook of Cultural Sociology*, ed. Jeffrey Alexander, Ronald Jacobs, and Philip Smith (New York: Oxford University Press, 2012), pp. 46–69.

78. Sartori, *Concepts and Method in Social Science*, p. 155.

79. Erving Goffman, *Frame Analysis* (Boston: Northeastern University Press, 1986), p. 562.

80. Zygmunt Baumann, *Society under Siege* (Cambridge: Polity Press, 2002), p. 44; Zygmunt Baumann, "Durkheim's Society Revisited," in *The Cambridge Companion to Durkheim*, ed. Jeffrey Alexander and Philip Smith (Cambridge: Cambridge University Press, 2005), pp. 360–382.

81. Ulrich Beck, "The Cosmopolitan Turn," in *The Future of Social Theory*, ed. Nicholas Gane (London; Continuum, 2004), pp. 154–155.

82. Mauro Guillen, *Models of Management. Work, Authority and Organization in a Comparative Perspective* (Chicago: University of Chicago Press, 1994), p. 306. Guillen shines by listing each sample source.

83. Ibid., pp. 288–291.

84. Roy Rappaport, *Ritual and Religion in the Making of Humanity* (Cambridge University Press, 1999), p. 230.

85. Brent Berlin and Paul Kay, *Basic Color Terms. Their Universality and Evolution* (Berkeley: University of California Press, 1969).

86. Rolf Kuschel and Torben Monberg, "'We Don't Talk Much About Colour Here': A Study of Color Semantics on Bellona Island," *Man* 9 (1974): 218, 221, 229.

87. Nigel Barley, "Old English Color Classification: Where do Matters Stand?" in *Anglo-Saxon England 3*, ed. Peter Clemoes (Cambridge: Cambridge University Press, 1974), p. 21; J. D. Burnley, "Middle English Lexical Terminology and Lexical Structure," *Linguistische Berichte* 41 (1976): 42, 44; Klaus Ostheeren, "Toposforschung und Bedeutungslehre," *Anglia* 89 (1971): 47; C. P. Biggam, "Aspects of Chaucer's Adjectives of Hue," *The Chaucer Review* 28 (1993): 51; Eleanor Irwin, *Colour Terms in Greek Poetry* (Toronto: Hakkert, 1974), p. 202; B. A. C. Saunders and J. van Brakel, "Are There Non-Trivial Constraints on Colour Categorization?," *Behavioral and Brain Sciences* 20 (1997): 176.

88. J. Van Brakel, "The Plasticity of Categories: The Case of Colour," *British Journal for the Philosophy of Science* 44 (1993): 103–135. Some speakers use the same word for black as for white: Barbara Saunders and J. Van Brakel, "Rewriting Color," *Philosophy of the Social Sciences* 31 (2001): 542; Barbara Saunders, "Revisiting Basic Color Terms," *Journal of the Royal Anthropological Institute* 6 (2000): 81–99.

89. M. Durbin, "Basic Terms Off-Color?" *Semiotica* 6 (1972): 259.

90. Nancy Hickerson, review in *International Journal of American Linguistics* 19 (1971): 265–267, 270.

91. Paul Kay, Brent Berlin, Luisa Maffi, and William Merrifield, "Color Naming Across Languages," in *Color Categories in Thought and Language*, ed. C. L. Hardin and Luisa Maffi (Cambridge: Cambridge University Press, 1997), pp. 21–58.

92. Robert MacLaury, "From Brightness to Hue: An Explanatory Model of Color-Category Evolution," *Current Anthropology* 33 (1992): 137–186.

93. Barbara Saunders, "Toward a New Topology of Color," in *Anthropology of Color* (Amsterdam: J. Benjamins, 2007); John A. Lucy, "The Linguistics of 'Color,'" in Hardin and Maffi, *Color Categories*, pp. 320–346.

94. James Boster, "Categories and Cognitive Anthropology," in *Handbook of Categorization in Cognitive Science*, ed. Henri Cohen and Claire Lefebvre (Amsterdam: Elsevier, 2005), p. 109.

95. Paul Feyerabend, *Against Method* (London: Verso, 1978), pp. 45, 75.

96. Evans, "Playing God," *Journal of the Society of Christian Ethics*, p. 210.

97. Bowie, *From Romanticism to Critical Theory*, p 17; Bruno Latour and Steve Woolgar, *Laboratory Life* (Beverly Hills: Sage, 1979), p. 180.

98. Christopher Norris, *Truth Matters* (Edinburgh: Edinburgh University Press, 2002), p. 194.

99. Pierre Bourdieu, *Distinction* (Cambridge, MA: Harvard University Press, 1984), p. 54.

100. Ibid.

101. Jacques Rancière, *The Philosopher and His Poor* (Durham, NC: Duke University Press, 2003), pp, 165–202.

102. Bourdieu, *Distinction*, pp. 44–45.

103. Tony Bennett, "Habitus Clivé. Aesthetics and Politics in the Work of Pierre Bourdieu," in *New Directions in American Reception Study*, ed. Philip Goldstein and Jaes Machor (Oxford: Oxford University Press, 2008), pp. 57–86.

104. Bourdieu, *Distinction*, p. 482.

105. On Bourdieu's categories as mythic "megadistinctions," see Stephan Fuchs, *Against Essentialism* (Cambridge, MA: Harvard University Press, 2001), p. 159.

106. Bourdieu, *Distinction*, p. 484.

107. Jeffrey Alexander, "Clifford Geertz and the Strong Program," in *Interpreting Clifford Geertz* (New York: Palgrave MacMillan, 2011), p. 57.

108. Griswold, "A Methodological Framework for the Sociology of Culture," p. 26.

109. Eric Slauter, "Revolutions in the Meaning and Study of Politics," *American Literary History* 22: 1–16; John Loeschen, *The Divine Community: Trinity, Church and Ethics in Reformation Theologies* (Kirksville, MS: Northeast Missouri State University Press, 1981), p. 222. Thomas Tanselle, "Some Statistics on American Printing, 1764–1783," in *The Press and the American Revolution*, ed. Bernard Bailyn and John Hench (Worcester: America Antiquarian Society, 1980), pp. 315–363.

110. Richard Biernacki, "Time Cents: The Monetization of the Workday in Comparative Perspective," in *Now Here. Space, Time, and Modernity*, ed. Roger Friedland and Deirdre Boden (Berkeley: University of California Press, 1994).

111. Clifford Geertz, *The Interpretation of Cultures* (New York: Basic Books, 1977), pp. 412–453.

112. The air pump as in Steven Shapin and Simon Schaffter, *Leviathan and the Air Pump. Hobbes, Boyle, and the Experimental Life* (Princeton: Princeton University Press, 1989).

113. Joseph Rouse, "Kuhn's Philosophy of Scientific Practice," in *Thomas Kuhn*, ed. Thomas Nickles (Cambridge: Cambridge University Press, 2003), pp. 101–121.

114. Thomas Kuhn, *Structure of Scientific Revolutions* (Chicago: University of Chicago Press, Third Edition, 1996), pp. 44, 192.

115. Thomas Nickles, "Kuhn, Historical Philosophy of Science, and Case-Based Reasoning," *Configurations* 6 (1998): 72–73.

116. The phrase was Reinhard Bendix's classroom definition of an ideal type at University of California, Berkeley.

117. Max Weber, *Max Weber on The Methodology of the Social Sciences* (Glencoe: The Free Press, 1949), p. 90; emphases in the original. My quote inverts the original order of sentences.

118. John Taylor, *Linguistic Categorization. Prototypes in Linguistic Theory* (Oxford: Clarendon Press, 1995), p. 258.

119. Kuhn, *Structure of Scientific Revolutions*, p. 119.

120. Weber, *Methodology of the Social Sciences*, p. 90.

121. Tzvetan Todorov, *The Fantastic* (Case Western Reserve University Press, 1973), p. 22.

122. Wilhelm Hennis, *Max Weber. Essays in Reconstruction* (London: Allen & Unwin, 1988), p. 47.

123. Ronald Bontekoe, *Dimensions of the Hermeneutic Circle* (New Jersey: Humanities Press, 1996), p. 185.

124. Max Weber, *From Max Weber* (New York: Oxford University Press, 1946), p. 135.

125. Weber, *Methodology of the Social Sciences*, pp. 100–104.

126. Bruno Bachimont, "Formal Signs and Numerical Computation," in *Instruments in Art and Science*, ed. Helmar Schramm, Ludger Schwarte, and Jan Lazardig (Berlin: Walter de Gruyter, 2008), p. 372.

127. Max Weber, *The Protestant Ethic and the Spirit of Capitalism* (New York: Charles Scribner's Sons, 1958), pp. 155–161.

128. Zoltán Kövecses, *Metaphor and Emotion* (Cambridge: Cambridge University Press, 2000), p. 176.

129. Eleanor H. Rosch, "On the Internal Structure of Perceptual and Semantic Categories," in *Cognitive Development and the Acquisition of Language*, ed. Timothy Moore (New York: Academic Press, 1973), pp. 138, 142.; John Taylor, *Linguistic Categorization. Prototypes in Linguistic Theory* (Oxford: Clarendon Press, 1995).

130. Weber, *Methodology of the Social Sciences*, p. 101.

131. Goodman, *Languages of Art*, p. 60; James Boyd White, *Heracles' Bow. Essays on the Rhetoric and Poetics of the Law* (Madison: University of Wisconsin Press, 1985), pp. 122–124.

132. Larry Hedges, "The Role of Construct Validity in Generalization," in *Causality in Crisis? Statistical Methods and the Search for Causal Knowledge in the Social Sciences*, ed. Vaugn McKim and Stephen P. Turner (University of Notre Dame Press, 1997), pp. 325–342.

133. Roy D'Andrade, *The Development of Cognitive Anthropology* (Cambridge: Cambridge University Press, 1995), p. 247.

134. William F. Hanks, *Language and Communicative Practices* (Westview Press, 1996), pp. 295–305.

135. Ernst Tugendhat, *Philosophische Aufsätze* (Frankfurt am Main: Suhrkamp, 1992), pp. 267–272.

136. Richard Robinson, *Definition* (Oxford: Clarendon Press), pp. 111–113.

137. Peter Barker, Xiang Chen, and Hanne Andersen, "Kuhn on Concepts and Categorization," in *Thomas Kuhn*, ed. Thomas Nickels (Cambridge: Cambridge University Press, 2003), pp. 218–219.

138. Weber, *Methodology of the Social Sciences*, p. 104.

139. Henry Petroski, *Design Paradigms. Case Histories of Error and Judgment in Engineering* (Cambridge: Cambridge University Press, 1994), p. 166; John Warrall, "Normal Science and Dogmatism, Paradigms and Progress; Kuhn 'versus' Popper and Lakatos," in Nickels, *Thomas Kuhn*, pp. 79–80.

140. Arthur Miller, "Metaphor and Scientific Creativity," in *Metaphor and Analogy in the Sciences*, ed. Frenand Hallyn (Dordrecht: Kluwer, 2000), pp. 147–163; Hanne

Andersen, Peter Barker, and Xiang Chen, *The Cognitive Structure of Scientific Revolutions* (Cambridge: Cambridge University Press, 2006).

141. Talcott Parsons, introduction to Max Weber, *The Theory of Social and Economic Organization* (New York: The Free Press, 1997), p. 15.

142. J. Zvi Namenwirth and Robert Philip Weber, *The Dynamics of Culture* (Boston: Allen & Unwin, 1987), p. 238. Where translation fails, the hermeneuticist Hans-Georg Gadamer wrote of classification, "there thinking breaks through."

143. Weber, *The Protestant Ethic and the Spirit of Capitalism*, p. 98.

144. Giorgio Agamben, *The Signature of All Things* (New York: Zone Books, 2009), p. 24.

145. Weber, *The Protestant Ethic and the Spirit of Capitalism*, p. 107.

146. Max Weber, *Gesammelte Aufsätze zur Wissenschaftslehre* (Tübingen: J.C.B. Mohr, 1968), p. 192.

147. Paul Jorion, *Comment la vérité et la réalité furent inventées* (Paris: Gallimard, 2009), p. 250.

148. As cited in Avital Ronell, *The Test Drive* (Urbana: University of Illinois Press, 2005), p. 47.

149. Robert Stenvenson, "In Praise of Dumb Clerks," in *Theory, Method, and Practice in Computer Content Analysis*, ed. Mark West (Westport, CT: Ablex, 2001), p. 17.

150. Doug Arnold, Louisa Sadler, and Aline Villavicencio, "Portuguese: Corpora, Coordination, and Agreement," in *Roots. Linguistics in Search of Its Evidential Base*, ed. Sam Featherston and Wolfgang Sternefeld (Berlin: Mouton de Gruyter, 2007), p. 25.

151. Julia Kristeva, "Prolegomena to the Concept of 'Text,'" in *Literary Debate. Texts and Contexts*, ed. Dennis Hollier and Jeffrey Melhman (New York: The New Press, 1999), p. 304.

152. As cited by Rodney Needham, who explicates it as a guide to his own anthropological findings in Rodney Needham, *Exemplars* (Berkeley: University of California Press, 1985), p. 163.

153. Richard Biernacki, "After Quantitative Cultural Sociology," in Alexander and Reed, *Meaning and Method*, pp. 148–151.

154. Chandler, *Hollywood Highbrow*, p. 117.

155. Raymond Chandler, "Oscar Night in Hollywood," *The Atlantic*, March 1948. Note: Baumann quotes Chandler as writing only he "has a hard time not sounding a little ludicrous" praising film as art.

156. See notes 7, 8, 9, 11, 12, 13, 14, 15, 16, 21, 22, 24, 25, 26, and 29 in chapter 3 of Karen Cerulo, *Deciphering Violence. The Cognitive Structure of Right and Wrong* (London: Routledge, 1998).

157. Giorgio Agamben, *Homo Sacer: Sovereign Power and Bare Life* (Stanford: Stanford University Press, 1998); *State of Exception* (Chicago: University of Chicago, 1995).

158. The initially unattributed quotes all appear at Giorgio Agamben, *The Signature of All Things* (New York: Zone Books, 2009), p. 31.

159. Gérard Genette, *The Architext* (Berkeley: University of California Press, 1992), p. 71.

160. Goffman, *Frame Analysis*, pp. 435–436. At his sentencing in 1970, Abbie Hoffman advised the presiding judge to try LSD via a dealer in Florida (February 20, 1970, trial transcript, "http:/law2.umkc.edu/faculty/projects/trials/Chicago7/Sentencing.html").

161. Angus McDougall, "Reckless CDS Will Contribute to Marx's Prophecy on Capitalism," *Financial Times*, July 13, 2011, p. 10.

162. Jean-Marie Schaeffer, "Literary Genres and Textual Genericity," in *The Future of Literary Theory*, ed. Ralph Cohen (London: Routledge, 1989), p. 176.

163. Panofsky on the exemplary "sense" of ideal types: "This 'sense' is, therefore, fully capable of being applied, as a control, to the interpretation of a new individual observation

within the same range of phenomena. If, however, this new individual observation definitely refuses to be interpreted according to the 'sense' of the series, and if an error proves to be impossible, the 'sense' of the series will have to be reformulated to include the new individual observation. This circulus methodicus applies, of course, not only to the relationship between the interpretation of motifs and the history of style, but also to the relationship between the interpretation of images, stories and allegories and the history of types, and to the relationship between the interpretation of intrinsic meanings and history of cultural symptoms in general." Irwin Panofsky, *Meaning in the Visual Arts* (New York: Doubleday, 1955), p. 35.

164. Weber, *The Protestant Ethic and the Spirit of Capitalism*, p. 47.

165. Erich Auerbach, *Mimesis. The Representation of Reality in Western Literature* (Princeton University Press, 2003), p. 556.

166. David Lodge, *The Modes of Modern Writing* (Ithaca: Cornell University Press, 1977), p. 25.

167. Austin Quigley, "Wittgenstein's Philosophizing and Literary Theorizing," in *Ordinary Language Criticism*, ed. Kenneth Dauber and Walter Jost (Evanston: Northwestern University Press), pp. 24–25.

168. Weber, *The Protestant Ethic and the Spirit of Capitalism*, pp. 221–225.

169. Weber, *Methodology of the Social Sciences*, p. 93; emphasis in the original.

170. Gallagher and Greenblatt, *Practicing New Historicism*, p. 40.

171. Auerbach, *Mimesis*, p. 11.

172. Charles Muscatine, *Medieval Literature, Style, and Culture* (Columbia, SC: University of South Carolina Press, 1999), pp. 72, 213.

173. Roger Starling, "'Scenes From the Life of One Who is Suited for Nothing': Shakespeare and the Question of Mimesis," and Peter Holland, "Hamlet and Auerbach," in *Refiguring Mimesis. Representation in Early Modern Literature*, ed. Jonathan Holmes and Adrian Streete (University of Hertfordshire Press, 2005), pp. xiv and 23.

174. Erwin Panofsky, *Gothic Architecture and Scholasticism* (New York: Meridian, 1976), pp. 59–60.

175. Pierre Bourdieu, "Erwin Panofsky's *Gothic Architecture and Scholasticism*" appended in Bruce Holsinger, *The Premodern Condition. Medievalism and the Making of Theory* (Chicago: University of Chicago Press, 2005), p. 227.

176. Robert Marichal, "L'écriture latine et la civilisation occidentale," in Centre Internationale de Synthèse, *L'écriture et la psychologie des peuples* (Paris: Armand Colin, 1964), pp. 232–241.

177. See Ernst Gall's criticism of Panofsky's *Gothic Architecture and Scholasticism* in *Kunstchronik* 6 (1953): 42–49.

178. Michael Baxandall, *Patterns of Intention. On the Historical Explanation of Pictures* (New Haven: Yale University Press, 1985), p. 131.

179. Panofsky, *Gothic Architecture and Scholasticism*, pp. 27–28; Richard Biernacki, "The Action Turn? Comparative-Historical Inquiry Beyond the Classical Modes of Conduct," in *Remaking Modernity*, ed. J. Adams, E. S. Clemens, and A. S. Orloff (Durham: Duke University Press, 2005), p. 89.

180. Ilse Grubrich-Simitis, *Back to Freud's Texts* (New Haven: Yale University Press, 1996), pp. 118–125.

181. Lynn Hunt, *The Family Romance of the French Revolution* (Berkeley: University of California Press, 1993).

182. Ibid., pp. 53–64.

183. Amir R. Alexander, *Geometrical Landscapes. The Voyages of Discovery and the Transformation of Mathematical Practices* (Stanford: Stanford University Press, 2002).

184. Oleg Kharkhordin, *The Collective and the Individual in Russia. A Study of Practices* (Berkeley: University of California Press, 1999).

185. Ibid., pp. 117–122.

186. Sherry Ortner, "Patterns of History. Cultural Schemas in the Foundings of Sherpa Religions Institutions," in *Culture through Time*, ed. Emiko Ohnuki-Tierney (Stanford: Stanford University Press, 1990), pp. 57–93.

187. As cited by Moore, *Political Power and Social Theory*, p. 143.

188. Clifford Geertz, *Local Knowledge* (New York: Basic Books, 1985), p. 35.

189. Robert Musil, *Gesammelte Werke* (Hamburg: Rowohlt, 1978), vol. 8, p. 1170; Arne Naess, *Interpretation and Preciseness* (Oslo: Skrivemaskinstua Universitets Studentkontor, 1947), p. 51; Stanley Cavell, *Philosophical Passages* (Cambridge, MA: Blackwell, 1995), p. 81. Bibliography: http://www.biernackireviews.com/.

INDEX